Praise for *Nine Lives*

"Claire Kahane has written a memoir for our times: an account of a life spent in pursuit of lived experience long before it was permissible for women like Kahane to do just that. Rich and lively, vivid and bold, *Nine Lives* is bound to reach a wide and responsive readership."

—Vivian Gornick, essayist, critic, and author of numerous memoirs, including *Fierce Attachments, The Odd Woman and the City,* and *Unfinished Business: Notes of a Chronic Re-reader*

"Claire Kahane's memoir is a riveting account of a life dedicated to self-discovery. The early part of it involved living dangerously, but her later role as professor, mother, and wife grows naturally from those initial experiences. Her story is also a vivid mirror of the times, from the fifties to the present."

—Robert Alter, translator of the Hebrew Bible and author of numerous books and essays on European and American literature from the eighteenth century to the present, as well as literary aspects of the Bible

"Claire Kahane's *Nine Lives* recounts a history of wild wandering and wayward romance en route to self-discovery. A sophisticated scholar of psychoanalysis, Kahane is also a deft writer whose life journey takes her from an immigrant home in the Bronx to motherhood and love, with stops along the way in Mexico, San Francisco, Greenwich Village, Paris, Tangiers, Ibiza—and more. The decades she evokes in her memoir, culminating in the present, come vividly to life as she travels the world."

—Sandra Gilbert, poet-critic and co-author of *The Madwoman in the Attic, No Man's Land,* and *Still Mad*

"The noted feminist critic Claire Kahane looks back on the multiple surprising, often risky life roles she enthusiastically adopted in a restless quest to forge her own identity. The aptly named Clara Katz, Holocaust survivors' kid, finds herself code switching from good-girl Bronx high school student to country-western singer, Greenwich Village bohemian, San Francisco beat, expat nomad, graduate student and college professor, wife and mother, analysand and analyst, and happy late life partner. Each of these stories vividly brings to life the particulars of its own uniquely American subculture, fusing seamlessly into a highly satisfying read: the remarkable personal trajectory of one woman's bumpy but triumphant journey through eighty-plus years of our shared cultural history."

—Victoria Nelson, author of *Neighbor George* and *The Secret Life of Puppets*

NINE LIVES

My Risky Road from Fifties Rebel to Feminist Critic

CLAIRE KAHANE

ISBN (Paperback): 978-1-962416-82-5
ISBN (Hardcover): 978-1-962416-83-2
ISBN (eBook): 978-1-962416-84-9
Library of Congress Control Number: 2024924576

Designed by Sheenah Freitas
Project managed by Robert Pruett

Printed in the United States of America

Published by
Brandylane Publishers, Inc.
5 S. 1st Street
Richmond, Virginia 23219

Brandylane
Publishers, Inc.
Publishing books since 1985

brandylanepublishers.com

For Lukas, Julie, Tilda, and Raina, my lines into the future

And for Robert, here and now

Contents

A cat has nine lives. For three he plays, for three he strays, and for the last three he stays.

Old English Proverb

Prologue

It would be interesting to make the two people,
I now, I then, come out in contrast.

Virginia Woolf

"I am now entering the death decade." So, in 2015, I dramatically announced to family and friends who had gathered around me to celebrate my eightieth birthday. A wave of shock passed over their faces at my unexpected remark, but they could not deny, as I told them, smiling to show that I could face facts, that "not many people live past their eighties." It was an acknowledgment I was also making to myself, for despite the birthday toast just given me, "and many more," there were likely *not* many more ahead.

As for the years behind, I couldn't help but feel a sense of satisfaction at how unusual my life had been for a woman of my time, surprising given my background as the daughter of Jewish immigrants growing up in the Bronx in an era when a woman's place was in the home. Yet few of my intimates celebrating here with me knew anything about my past incarnations or the kind of vagrant and risky life I had led for several decades. Even my son, happily visiting with his own family for my special event, knew little about my life before he was born, before I changed both my bohemian life-style, becoming a feminist professor, and my surname, from Katz to Kahane. Realizing that those stories would disappear with my death, I determined at that moment to write a memoir, not only to memorialize my life's curiously adventurous trajectory, its steps and missteps, but hopefully, in the process, offer my readers an understanding of how a Bronx working-class girl named Clara Katz, born in the Great Depression, became, after the second wave of feminism half a century later, the well-known feminist critic Claire Kahane.

Almost immediately, and perhaps coincidentally since I was entering my ninth decade, a title popped into my head: *Nine Lives*, evoking the theme of risk and survival that linked so many of my past experiences. Growing into adulthood in the fifties, I had ignored the conventions of my time and the ambitions of my parents, and as soon as I could, had gone on the road, determined to know the wider world in all its variety. Like Jack Kerouac, I believed that "there was nowhere to go but everywhere." Yet how different "everywhere" was for a woman of my generation. How precarious were my travels, in this country and abroad, driving or hitchhiking my way into and out of risky escapades and romantic affairs, not knowing where the road would take me. How often did I find myself running breathlessly down a dark lonely road to escape some male predator? These scenes of escape, and there are many in my memoir, are so similar in structure that they play out like a recurrent nightmare that was the inevitable underside of my youthful dream: to pursue experience in its various guises, seeking, as Walt Whitman had urged all men, to extend my sense of self into the world—without knowing either myself or the world.

I see now that much of my experience involved a kind of play—a performance of sorts. Playing at being a country music singer in Queens. Playing at being a beatnik in San Francisco. Playing at being a flaneur in Paris. Playing at being down and out in Casablanca. Playing at being a graduate student in Berkeley. But like all play, these experiences offered me rich possibilities for imagining, learning about, and understanding others as well as myself.

Playing, also, as in "playing with fire"—risky, especially for a woman straying off the well-worn path.

When, in midlife, I changed my patronymic from Katz to Kahane, it signified a sea change in consciousness and in story. From a wayward woman addicted to the pleasures of marginality, I became a reputable feminist professor as well as a mother and wife, open to a different kind of future. But that too would change. In the pages that follow, I describe each stage of my errant development—from the primal conflicts of childhood, to the surge of erotic desire in adolescence, to the excitement of illicit activities and serial affairs in adulthood, to the illuminations of feminism and psychoanalysis that helped me, late in the game, to heed Freud's purported advice for the good life: to work and to love.

Inevitably, my personal journey has embodied and reflected the historical eras I lived through: from the thirties' Depression to the devastation of the European Jews in the forties, from the straitlaced postwar fifties to the breakout drug-inflected sixties, from the cultural realignments spurred on by an advancing feminism in the seventies and eighties to a new millennium dominated by a technological revolution imposing new ways of being in the world.

Now, toward the end of my ninth decade, I find that the diverse identities I inhabited throughout the years, with all their competing tensions, have been melded into a relatively stable sense of self—relatively, for all that lives changes. But the mobile energy that had pushed me forward and outbound for so long has turned inward. Although I am still driven to reinvent myself, I do it now in writing, surfing the past for what Virginia Woolf called those "moments of being" that still shimmer in the cotton wool of memory, hoping those moments will have meaning for a younger generation of women facing their own traumatic encounters and self-transformations in an increasingly threat-filled world where the struggle continues.

1

A Bronx Tale:
Growing Up and Out
(1935–1951)

*We live with those retrievals from childhood that
coalesce and echo throughout our lives . . .*

Michael Ondaatje

C *ats go for your throat when you're sleeping.*
Who was it that had told me, well before I was five years old,
that old country superstition? My mother, no doubt, who often whispered
magical forewarnings into my defenseless young ears, terrifying me as a
child with her secret knowledge before I reached my age of reason. *Cats go
for your throat!* A piece of folklore never forgotten, it was no idle threat in
my timorous young mind, for there *was* such a creature that might go for
my throat—a striped, gray tabby, with cold green eyes, always slinking, tail
up, head down, lurking, peering around the corners of the dilapidated gray
clapboard house my mother and I often visited. With its warped wooden
steps, paint-chipped porch, and peculiar odor of decay—a yellowish smell,
tinged with brown—the house itself seemed menacing, especially since
inside, I knew, lived Tante, the keeper of the cat.

An ancient and forbidding figure Tante seemed to me then, with her
pointy nose and her steel-gray hair pulled into a bun at the back of her head.

I can still see her standing in the big, dimly lit basement room, her long full black skirt almost touching the floor, her worn gray slippers peeking out from under the hem, her eyes crinkling, her almost toothless grin deepening the lines in her already withered face. Adding to her formidable aspect, Tante, unlike my mother and father, had a whole house to herself.

But Tante wasn't completely alone in that malodorous old place. There were often one or two old men sitting at a long wooden table in the basement, drinking tea from glasses. Later, when I was old enough to ask questions, I learned that Tante ran a kind of in-house basement cafe and served tea to elderly Jews who lived in the neighborhood. But at three, four, even five years of age, I was puzzled by the sight of those grizzled beings hunched over their steaming tea, alien figures in a mysterious underground world to which Tante belonged.

I had gone often with my mother to visit Tante, but there was one visit that remains sharply etched in memory: I was sitting at the wooden table in her basement watching an old man opposite me sip his tea noisily, his hand wrapped around his glass, while Mama—belly swollen, a shopping bag at her feet—sat next to me chatting in Yiddish with Tante, who was washing glasses at the sink. I didn't warm to Tante. I didn't like sitting there. Nor did I like looking at her lined face. When she smiled, her thin lips revealed dark spaces where there should have been teeth.

After a while, moving heavily, Mama stood up, picked up the shopping bag, and turned to me.

"Clara, you know you're gonna stay here a few days. Like I told you, I have to go to the hospital to have the baby and Daddy has to work. Tante is taking care of you until I get back home. So listen to her; be a good girl."

A moment of blankness, then dread, as I took in the words that had made me uneasy this morning, now immediate and frighteningly real. Alone with Tante in that big house. And the old men in the basement. And the cat.

"So now let's go upstairs, and you'll see where you're sleeping."

My mother took my hand, and we followed Tante up the narrow staircase.

And there, at the top of the stair, stood the cat, tail twitching, eyes narrowed, watching, waiting. A scream tore from my throat. I pulled on my mother's arm, crying "no, no," while my mother and Tante tried to calm me. Or at least I suppose that's what happened, for all I can recall now are flashes of staircase, of cat, of my mother's fierce brow, of Tante with her full black skirt and her pointy nose, intermingled with pictures from my library book of fairy tales— "Hansel and Gretel," "Sleeping Beauty," and always, the witch—bits and pieces of terror all coming together, embodied in the cat at the top of the stairs, waiting to go for my throat.

Did I sleep that night? Not likely. But clearly, I survived the narrow cot, with chairs placed at its side to prevent me from rolling off, and the smell and the dark shadows and the cat. Eventually—how long the hours must have seemed, I can't imagine—my father came and, laughing at my fears, rescued me, took me home, and introduced me to a frail and delicate creature with big black eyes and tiny hands who lay swaddled in my mother's arms: my new baby brother.

I must have been excited, I who was already five and loved to play with baby dolls whose eyes opened and closed. Here was a real baby to play with! But the pleasure was short-lived, for already this infant had usurped my pride of place. He was the beloved son who would bring *naches* (pride) to the family. And now, all these years later, I remember a story about my own birth that my mother had once laughingly told me: "When you were born, your father told the doctor to take you back and bring him a boy."

Words, noxious messages taking insidious root.

The Bris

Soon after my brother Albert was born, my parents held a bris, a ritual circumcision to celebrate the arrival of the male child. I trace my first hangover to that event. From a very early age, I had delighted my father, who often drank a shot of whiskey before dinner, by imitating him, downing a bit of whiskey from a shot glass myself. My father would sit back in his chair beaming at my imitation, especially pleased to show off my performance to his friends when they came to dinner. And how proudly I would drink down the liquor and their adulation: "*Oy, vas far a kind, und a maidel nokh!*" What a child, and a girl even!

And so, when I found myself at my brother's bris in Bronx Hospital in a room crowded with family friends and relatives, all busily talking to each other, no one paying attention to me, and I spotted the honey cake and the little cups of dark red wine on a nearby table, I squeezed through the clustering adults and helped myself to one of the cups. It was delicious, sweet and thick on the tongue, and it slid down my throat so easily. I took another. A few moments later the mohel (the figure who performed these ritual circumcisions) arrived and everyone moved away from the table toward the glass window at the other end of the room. I helped myself to another little cup, and this time to a piece of the sweet honey cake, and made my way carefully through the crowd and stood on my toes peering through the window.

My baby brother lay naked on a table. The mohel hovered over him with something in his hand. Everyone watched, a few gasped, someone clapped. I didn't feel so good, so I went back to the table and took another little cup, tasted again the lovely sweet thickness as it slid down my throat. But then, the room began slowly to spin. Something sour inside me hurtled upward toward my mouth, and, on the verge of expelling it, I ran out of the room, mouth tightly shut, and down the hospital-green hallway to the nearby exit opening to the street. At the sidewalk's edge, I bent over and vomited honey cake, wine, and ceremony. A short time later, one of the adults found me sitting on the curb, disoriented, sweating, and scared, and brought me back inside. Did I know then that I too would feel "circumcised" by my brother's arrival? *Bring me a boy…*

Family Snapshots

They were a tumultuous pair, my father and mother. Both were dark-eyed and sensuous-looking, but antipodes apart in temperament. My father was clearly the dominant one; his word was Law. As if to underscore his authority, his Hebrew name—the name used by his *landsleit* (his old-country friends) was Meilech—the King. A fiercely proud man, he refused to work for anyone else, even though he belonged to the Workmen's Circle, a Jewish mutual benefit society that he joined when he first had arrived in New York and become a "worker" in a shoe factory. Having initially emigrated from Poland to Cuba when he was fourteen (where he was known by the Spanish name Manuel), he would tell me in a voice deep with prideful nostalgia, "In Havana, I had my own shoe factory."

Eight years later, he met my mother, Dina Rubinstein. In a matchmaking ritual common among the immigrant Jewish network in New York, she had traveled to Cuba on a vacation carrying an introduction to him from her social network. Both must have seen what they liked in each other. A year later, after making the necessary legal arrangements, my mother returned to Cuba, they married in Panama—an American outpost at the time—and two weeks later, filled with dreams of life in America, Manuel Katz from Cuba emigrated to New York with his new wife and became Max Katz.

In their wedding photographs, my mother sits in a flowered print dress, her dark hair flowing over her shoulders, her eyes shining with pleasure at the camera, while my father stands erect behind her, white suit, hands comfortably on her shoulders. They are both smiling. They have not yet lived together.

My parents' wedding photo: 1932

But what a disappointment the actuality of New York must have been to Meilech once he became Max and settled into his new circumstances! How humiliating for one so proud, so invested in the image of material success, to find himself in a strange land, lacking the language of his new home, and no longer enjoying the privilege he had earned for himself in

Cuba. The owner of a shoe factory in Havana became a worker in a shoe factory in New York.

Not for long, though. Meilech himself had to be "the boss." And indeed he found a way to feel in charge again, buying a small kiosk-like candy stand where I, at the age of four and five, occasionally stood behind the counter and sold penny candies and single cigarettes, each with its own wooden match. I loved being behind the counter, loved being teased by the customers for my precociousness. "A penny a piece," I cried. Everyone wanted cigarettes.

Max at his candy store counter circa 1940

After the war, Max became the owner of an actual "corner candy store," a unique New York institution later immortalized on *Sesame Street* as Mr. Hooper's candy store—though Max was no Mr. Hooper. Newspapers, magazines, comic books, cigarettes, unwrapped penny candies (or nickel ones already wrapped) ice cream, and sodas at the fountain—this was the realm over which Max Katz ruled, from four in the morning, when the newspapers were delivered and had to be brought inside, until two in the morning, with a midday break for a few hours of rest at home when Dina, my mother, took over.

It was a family business especially suited to his needs and personality: he enjoyed giving his opinion on the news to men who stopped to buy a newspaper on their way to work in the early morning; he had a warm smile for mothers who stopped by later in the day with their children to buy them a sweet or themselves a magazine. But although he appreciated the business of teenagers coming home from school in the afternoon who wanted malted milks and comic books, with them he was brusque. "This is no library," he would say harshly, shooing them out if they loitered to browse a magazine or comic book, while I cringed, turning my face away.

Since it was a family business, the entire family was pressed into service. When I was seven, eight, nine, it was no hardship. I liked making egg creams, serving two-cent plains, liked especially watching my father hold his customers captive with stories and jokes, his face lit up by a broad grin. And he did the same at home. He had a knack for storytelling and clearly enjoyed his own anecdotes, laughing heartily and easily as he told a tale usually about someone doing something stupid: "*Vie naarish is die Welt! Haben zy gehert die geschicte von meine shtetl? Ein man hat s'clapt dy ferd biz er'yz gestorben! Vus far a naar!* What a stupid!" he declaimed as he finished one of his favorites about a man in the old country who, wanting his horse to do more than it could, whipped it, and ended up inadvertently beating it to death. But if he was quick to laugh at the foolishness of the world, he was just as quick to anger when the world thwarted him, in the home as well as in the store. Then his face would darken, and his voice thunder with the force of a god cracking the universe.

My mother had an altogether different nature. An emotionally volatile and impulsive woman, hot-tempered yet empathic, she yielded more readily than my father to the desires and feelings of others. Yet she was also courageous. Orphaned in Russia when her mother was killed by a marauding Russian soldier looking for food, she had traveled by herself at the age of fourteen, sponsored by Tante and aided by HIAS (Hebrew Immigrant Aid Society), from Minsk to Hamburg and emigrated on a ship carrying refugees to New York.

My mother's HIAS sponsored immigration photo, age 14

Somehow, she quickly found work as a milliner in one of the many shops that dotted the Lower East Side. Before long, she became part of a vibrant group of young Jewish women like herself, making their way in the new world.

But she was ineluctably old-world. Superstitious my mother was: she pulled the window shades down in the bedroom at night because the moonlight gave sleepers nightmares; "If you sing before breakfast, you'll cry before supper," she warned if I was humming while getting dressed; "Don't open an umbrella inside the apartment," she would cry out when I checked to see if my umbrella worked. Sentimental my mother was: once,

I caught a tiny fish at Coney Island and took it home in a jar that I filled daily with fresh tap water, ignorant of its need for saltwater to survive. Each day, I watched and worried as the fish became increasingly limp, until one day it floated to the surface and my mother said: "It's sick. Let's take it back to the ocean where it can maybe get better." And so, with the fish in the jar, we two took the subway from the Bronx to Coney Island, a two-hour ride, and, hotfooting my way down the sandy beach to the water's edge, I threw the fish into the foamy waves while my mother watched, her face mirroring my anxious hope that it would live.

We had no better luck with the stray dog she brought home one night, a dirty white poodle that followed her home from the candy store and that she lovingly washed and presented to my brother and me the next morning as a gift. Thrilled to have a pet, I named him Prince, but clearly a prince could not long abide our crowded apartment. Despite our loving attentions, Prince ran away so often, returning mud-covered and wounded from his less-than-royal street fights, that finally my mother, without telling anyone, took him to the SPCA, and then cried for days afterward, certain that Prince would be killed.

Often, she would enter into conversations with strangers on the subway, and if they told her their troubles, her eyes would dim with their pain. At home, she sang songs from the Old World in a minor key—though never before breakfast. She had a lovely lilting soprano voice which would float across the room as she sat at the Singer treadle sewing machine, pedaling away in a dark corner of the apartment: "Just Molly and me, and baby makes three, in my blue heaven. . . ." "*Ochi chyornye, ochi zhguchie, ochi strastnye i prekrasnye. . . .*" Words and songs in Russian, English, Yiddish, from the old country and the new—lyrics that I heard without fully understanding them, though I understood the feelings that filled her voice, exuding a sweet sadness, like a huge tear, brimming over, enveloping us both.

But my mother had a temper too and often lost it, violently. On those occasions, she went straight for whatever object was at hand—a glass, a toy—flinging it at the source of her exasperation, most often me. A jar of milk! Because one afternoon I didn't want to drink my milk—a daily ritual of nurturance that she imposed—she threw the jar in my face with such force that it broke my front tooth.

Nurturance so often unbound. My mother's hand, holding a spoon, trying to force it into my mouth, which remained clamped shut. First came the blandishments, then the threats: "You can have a jelly candy if you eat this first.... I'll give you a sweet.... I'll give you a pudding." Melodious offerings, my mother's voice singing to me while the spoon, held by her hand, remained rigidly in front of my mouth, waiting for an opening. And if the sweet talk didn't work? "Listen, if you don't open up, I'll send you to the home for orphans!" Listen, she said. I listened.

A dream from early childhood: I am in my baby carriage and my mother is pushing the carriage toward the end of the block on which we live, which is at the top of a big hill. When she gets to the corner, she pushes the carriage with great force so that it hurtles down the hill. I huddle inside, terrified.

Love in a Time of Choleria

Love was especially tough between my parents. Each seemed always under siege by the other, the two of them shouting in the bedroom in Yiddish, one on each side of the big bed that took up most of the room, my father throwing out a torrent of curses at my mother, she throwing them back. What fierce storms they generated, thunder and lightning crashing around the room as they hurled invectives at each other while I, at age two, three, or four, cowered under the bed, trying to keep a safe distance. "You *choleria*, you ..."—the fiercest insult, hurled back and forth. "Choleria." Pestilence. Was I safe from this pestilence? Would we all survive it?

As if in answer, memory breaks open the door to another stormy argument between them that suddenly stopped when my mother shouted, "Enough. I'm not staying with such a choleria!" Rushing to the bedroom, she pulled a suitcase from the closet, tore open the bureau drawers, and wild with frustration, threw clothes into the open case, slammed it shut, grabbed my hand, and dragged me out the front door of our second-floor apartment and down the stairs.

"No, no, no, I don't want to go," I screamed, sputtering—*nonono*—choking on my own spittle, the storm now in my head, tears blurring my vision, until one flight down, my mother finally turned to look at me, and as if afraid of what she saw, she stopped, hugged me to her breast, saying, "All right, all right, we'll go back." With a surge of relief, my four-year-old heart still pounding, I stumbled back up the stairs holding my mother's hand, back to the apartment, back to my father, back to my world. A world that somehow I had saved.

A victory?

I knew even then it was the power of my frenzy, an involuntary performance to keep the Katz family from falling apart, that saved me. It was the magical power of the performer that I would call upon in later life, with more mixed results.

The Katz Meow

In first grade I played Mother Cat in a classroom drama, *The Three Little Kittens*; it was I who got to point an admonitory finger at the naughty kittens:

The three little kittens have lost their mittens
And don't know where to find them.
What! Lost your mittens, you naughty kittens?
Then you shall have no pie.
Mee-ow, mee-ow, mee-ow.
No, you shall have no pie.

I enjoyed being the powerful mother cat scolding my charges, my long black tail, sewn onto my cat costume by my mother, dragging behind me. At home, I wagged my finger at my baby brother Albert, bedazzling him with my five-year advantage. *Mee-ow, mee-ow. You naughty kitten!* Although my mother would regularly intone "why can't you be more like your brother," it was my brother, the "good kid," who took his cues, and often his orders, from me. A frail, thin, shy toddler, he followed me around as if I were his minder, his big dark brown eyes always looking tentative, quizzical, apprehensive.

Although I too was shy, being the commanding older sister gave me a certain measure of self-confidence that would serve me well over the years. No longer afraid of cats by the time I was seven, on the contrary, I imagined I had a special relationship with them, for didn't my surname, Katz, announce it? My favorite fairy tale was "Puss in Boots." I warmed to the image of the cat wearing the blue knee-high boots, striding seven leagues at a step across the countryside though I had no sense of what a league was—his gait made possible by the magical boots, and reaping the rewards of such mobility through his canny intelligence. Oh, to have such boots and go so far!

But such travels could be dangerous. One day, having wandered away from my neighborhood on an imaginary expedition in Crotona Park, I was scanning the grass for *schav* (the Yiddish word for sorrel), a tasty sour green used for soup that my mother had discovered growing there, when suddenly, an older boy appeared blocking my way along the path. He held a large gray rock in his hand. Towering over me imperiously, he asked, "Are you a Jew?" I cowered, looking up at him, at the rock: "No, no, not me. I'm Russian." A tremor of shame passed through me as I spoke those words; they seemed a betrayal. Yet I knew I had to say "no, not me" to save myself, even if that meant denying my Jewish identity. *No, not me.* Clara Katz was a survivor.

Cats were survivors. Cats had nine lives. Nine was a miraculous number, it seemed. And so, when, in my second-grade classroom contest involving numbers, I called out the number nine and received from the teacher the sweet smile of success, nine became my magical link to Lady Luck, who, I hoped, would stand me, her devoted daughter, in good stead. My mother had her superstitions; I had mine.

Magic: the word itself intimated a realm of pure possibility, a future that I might, like Aladdin with his lamp, even control. So, sitting on the front steps of my apartment house one sunny afternoon and playing jacks, I announced to my two playmates that I had a special power called "My Magic," as if "My Magic" were the proper name of my personal genie. "You'd better do what I say, or I'll sic My Magic on you," I warned them in a deep whisper as I swept up the jacks victoriously, infusing my voice with mystery. I knew I claimed a power I didn't have, and yet I half-believed I did. More importantly, so did my friends, who were wary whenever I reminded them of it.

Mobile Accommodations

Until I was five, my parents moved regularly from one apartment to another. From the apartment on Washington Avenue where I was born, with its long dark hallway leading to the room where my uncle and aunt slept, all of us living in crowded family disharmony—to our own smaller brighter apartment on Fulton Avenue bordering Crotona Park, where the exterminator sprinkled a luminescent blue powder under the linoleum in the bathroom that I was forbidden to touch—to a railroad flat on Bathgate Avenue, a legendary street of open-air food stalls, where vociferous bargains were struck among a volatile immigrant population and where, one afternoon, my mother found me squatting in the building's courtyard showing my genitals to the neighbor boy—to Belmont Avenue, where stickballs came flying through our second floor bedroom window, causing my mother to furiously berate the boys on the street while I cringed beneath the window sill, embarrassed by her accented anger—and finally, to the three-room apartment on the corner of 175th Street and Crotona Avenue, our first apartment with actual hot running water. I still remember my mother turning on the spigots and marveling: "Look, the water's hot!" Although this apartment would be our home until I was a teenager, the rhythm of movement from place to place during those formative years laid down tracks for my later attraction to an "auto-mobility" I held dear for many years.

Our sleeping arrangements were characterized by mobility. At first, Albert, the baby, slept in a crib in the bedroom with my parents while I slept on a convertible couch in the living room. But as we grew older, Albert and I moved into the bedroom while our parents slept in the living room. Between the bedroom and the living room was a small bathroom, the only room with a door that closed—my refuge when I was being pursued by my mother in one of her rages. Then, pushing against the closed door with all my might, I would pray to whatever god might listen: *Don't let her get in.* Eventually her rage would subside, and I could step out safely. For the moment.

Near the front door of the apartment was a small kitchen with a white enamel-topped table and three wooden chairs squeezed around it. Here, Albert and I did our homework. Or ate the unappetizing meals that our mother prepared. Always the steak was too hard and the carrots too soft. At mealtime Albert and I were coconspirators; we waited until our mother left the room and then, liberated from her watchful eye, we gleefully threw the overcooked, unpeeled carrots, brown threads of carrot skin still clinging to them, out the kitchen window. Fortunately, the kitchen overlooked an empty lot three stories below where trash—old chairs, broken sinks, jars and bottles, even carrots—mysteriously accumulated. The lot was also my playground until I broke my toe on a broken sink lying there.

No doubt that ever-mounting detritus was why we had to deal with rats, one of the more repugnant memories of my childhood. My mother set out large wooden traps in the apartment, and when she caught one, she put the dead rat in a brown paper bag and gave it to me to take down to the cellar, where the garbage was stored. The foul odor as I walked down three flights, holding the bag as far from my nose as I could, was unforgettable. To this day, I know intimately the smell of a rat.

Apartment buildings in the Bronx were like small villages, each floor its own small neighborhood. Ours, a five-story walk-up, was multiethnic: Polish, Italian, Jewish, and Irish. Our third-floor apartment, 3A, was directly across from 3D; the front doors of both were usually open, a radio blaring the news from at least one. Coming home from P.S. 64, my elementary school a few blocks away, I would find my mother standing in our apartment doorway in her housedress chatting with Jean, the shrewd American-born woman who lived across the hall. What did they talk about? How the war was going? Their admiration for Roosevelt, whom they all loved? How to deal with ration coupons? Big-hearted Jean, with full bright red lips and a cigarette dangling from ringed fingers, knew the score and was always willing to tell my mother what it was. Prompted by apartment house proximity, this unlikely pair were intimates. And I was proud of that connection, for it meant my uneducated immigrant mother was acceptable to real Americans. I didn't have to be ashamed of her thick Yiddish accent or her habit of always wearing a shapeless housedress. But most of the time, I was, anyhow.

I had two close friends in the building: Patsy and Sheila. Patsy O'Brian, the super's daughter, was two years younger than me and lived on the first floor. Every Saturday, I accompanied Patsy to St. Joseph's Church for confession, and always, as I entered its dark interior, a space stretching upward toward the light filtering through the stained glass windows, I felt awed by its mystery. Once I even followed Patsy down the aisle and, like her, knelt down to kiss the cross held by the priest, expecting at any moment to be struck down for this sacrilege. But nothing happened. And once, we peeked into a side room off the entryway and saw a dead man stretched out on a marble table. I stared at the waxy skin of the rigid body lying on its stone pallet. So this was death.

Patsy wanted to be a nun, but she was scandalously and deliciously criminal. Regularly, she would raid her mother's purse and share the benefits of the loot with me—a banana split at the ice cream parlor on Tremont Avenue, a ride on the subway, our noses pressed against the window of the first car, staring into the darkness of the tunnel, breathlessly watching the tracks speeding toward us. Just as regularly, we would go to Fischer's barbershop around the corner, where Patsy would offer to sweep the floor or mind the shop. When Fischer wasn't looking, she would steal coins from the till—a just reward, we felt, because Fischer was a lecher. How often would his eyes greedily light up when he saw Patsy. He would bend over, spittle forming at the corner of his mouth, and pinch her cheeks while I looked on, envious of her greater appeal but also relieved not to have attracted his grotesque attentions.

More shocking to me were the times that Patsy would surreptitiously rummage through her parents' bureau drawers while I looked over her shoulder. Once, she discovered strange photographs tucked among her father's underwear, "dirty pictures," Patsy called them, and we puzzled over these images of naked men and women in peculiar positions, some merely bodies without heads, all part of the secret world of grown-ups.

Patsy's family, observant Catholics, fascinated me by their difference from my own. I couldn't abide my mother's accent, but I loved listening to the accent of Patsy's mother Brydie, a thick, lilting Irish brogue that sounded like music. Brydie sang a different kind of song from my mother's, a joyous one: "Shake hands with yer Uncle Mike, m'boy, shake hands with yer sister Kate, and here's the girl ye useta swing down by the garden gate...." But there were other times when Brydie terrified me: she would take Patsy into the bedroom and swing a leather strap on Patsy's behind while I waited in the living room, listening to Patsy scream. Somehow, my own mother's explosive rages at my misdeeds never seemed as appalling as this coldly deliberate wielding of the strap. At those moments, I was glad I wasn't Brydie's daughter.

Patsy's father, Mickey, "tall, dark, and handsome," as I thought him, was of an easier temperament. He was never Patsy's punisher; he let my brother and me sit on his big motorcycle parked in front of the building and took photos of us.

Albert and me on Mickey's motorcycle circa 1942

But he always teased me. Sitting at his kitchen table having a beer, he would lift me up in his muscular arms—the first I'd ever seen tattooed—put me on his lap, and bounce me up and down crooning "fatty, fatty." It made me uneasy to sit on his lap; it confused me, though I didn't know why. "Mick, stop misbehavin'," Brydie would say.

Fat. A heroine of a story is not supposed to be fat. But there I was, at the age of seven, eight, nine, not only chubby, but nearsighted, with thick round-framed glasses and braids, a bright but shy girl who waddled down the street flat-footed, my body a source of almost constant misery. In the winter, with the raw wind blowing up my skirt as I walked to school, I would feel the fat inside of one thigh rub raw against the other and wish I could wear long pants like the boys. In the spring, I imagined my eyeglasses, glinting in the sunlight, a defensive surface holding the outside world at a distance. Instead, they drew taunts from the boys in the schoolyard—"four eyes, four eyes"—that made me feel freakish. As did the clothes I had to wear, dresses and coats my mother had sewn by hand. How I hated the velvet hat trimmed with squirrel fur—"dopey hats" they were called because their tops came to a point—and the matching velvet coat with the fur collar and giant buttons; they shouted my difference from the kids that wore store-bought clothes. But I forced myself to smile when my mother took my picture wearing the dopey hat.

Feeling dopey in my Dopey hat

The End of the War

During my childhood, the war in Europe was a distant yet constant presence, not only in the newsreels that I saw every week at the De Luxe theater across the street from my father's store, but also in various tasks I was given, both in school, where we knitted woolen squares for quilts for the troops, and at home, where we saved fat and crushed tin cans that we tied into bundles, which I proudly took to the collection center down the street, imagining my bundles transformed into weapons of war. "A slip of the lip will sink a ship" warned the posters in the store windows. I believed them.

When the war ended, my parents tried to get news about their families in Europe, writing to relatives and hoping for some reply. It came for my father one day, in the form of a letter on a sheet of the thin blue airmail paper. I watched him unfold it carefully, read it in a language I couldn't understand, and then, with a sobbing intake of breath, drop the letter, his body crumpling into the kitchen chair. I had never seen my father cry. Something awful had happened but I was too frightened to ask what it was. Later, my mother explained: The letter was from the postmaster of Pruzhany, my father's hometown in Poland, telling him that his family—mother, father, sister—were all dead. The Nazis had locked them in their house and set it afire. His private Holocaust. From that time forward, my father became God's angry man, shaking his fist at religion and literally bringing home the bacon for breakfast every weekend—out of spite.

"It was nice of the postmaster to answer his letter," my mother said to me afterward, her voice trailing off into her own private wasteland. She would never learn what had happened to her remaining family—brothers, cousins, all disappeared.

Learning the Body's Secrets

My body, always an uncomfortable fit, became a mystery as I approached puberty. Watching my mother undress, I was fascinated by the complicated corset that restrained her flowing flesh, the bra that held her pendulous breasts, the big white bloomers that I could see were stained. When my mother drew me close in an embrace, pressing my face against her ample bosom, I smelled the sweat from her unwashed body and wriggled away from her. When she mysteriously bled, stopping the flow with rags, I knew intuitively that the source of that internal wound would someday stain me too. The female body had its awful secrets, I sensed, not yet knowing what they were. My mother was not one to enlighten me.

"What's Kotex, Ma?" I asked one day, coming home from my sixth-grade class after the word had been hurled at me by some boys in the schoolyard. "Don't ask such dirty questions," my mother responded, embarrassed by the word, waving it away with her arm like a curse dispelled. That mystifying word and the bodily functions it signified remained imaginatively alive in me until my own blood flowed, and I understood the "curse" would be mine. "Be careful. Men don't want damaged goods," my mother warned me years later when she found me, at age eighteen, trying to use a douche after my period. Damaged goods? Those words resonated for years, perversely challenging me to prove her wrong.

But that was years later. At age eleven, twelve, thirteen, sex was still a guilty adventure behind closed doors. Despite my aversion toward my mother's female body, there were strange, sensuous stirrings in my own, urging me to touch myself furtively, assuming a prohibition not fully understood. Even more daring were the times my school friend Dorothy and I would curl up in her bedroom, each of us playing at being the man, being the woman, practicing for an unknown future we knew depended upon the pleasure of touching, massaging each other's genitals. Someday I would do this with a real man, I hoped. Until then, it was all play, and like all play, a learning experience as well as a thrill.

Some forms of teenage play last beyond adolescence. Nicknames, for example, offer us iconic identities we can inhabit. What's in a name? Because my last name was Katz, I became Kitty, a name that sounded sexy, seductive, and slightly disreputable to my ears. It was a name I was pleased to answer to for many years. But if "Kitty" sounded seductive, "Kitty Katz" sounded like a comic book character. Was she real? Among my friends I was Kitty, and indeed often felt kittenish: frisky yet coy. In school, I was the shyer and more serious Claire, a name apparently written on my birth certificate by the attending physician, his translation of the Hebrew name my mother had actually given me, Chaia, "Life." Or so I was told. At home I was "Clara," the name I wanted most to shed. "Clara" sounded foreign to my ears, especially as pronounced by my mother when she called me from the third-floor window as I played in the street. *Claarrah . . . Claarrah . . . Come dhrink your milk.*

Besides, the only other Clara I knew of was a cow in a storybook.

Neighborhood Seductions

In the late spring, when the weather warmed, women in their cotton print housedresses dragged folding chairs out to the sidewalk and turned it into a pavilion. The jelly apple man pushed his cart down the street, selling apples on a stick that he dipped into a hot sweetened red syrup. The Italian ice man waited at the corner for passersby to buy lemon ices that he scooped into a small white paper cup. Stickball players assumed their diamond positions in the middle of the street, grumbling when they had to stop for the rare car that pushed its way through. The block came alive.

My block: 175th Street, between Crotona and Clinton Avenues. Five-story walk-ups with graffiti scrawled on the bricks by a kid announcing his presence: Kilroy was here! On my street corner: a group of Irish boys hanging out, leaning toward one another in heavy laughter over some victory, or scowling over some defeat. To walk to school and back, I had to pass them, ignoring the stares that always made my body tighten up, my heart beat faster. Still, I was learning to be street-smart. At twelve, I practiced how to stroll past the corner boys without seeming intimidated, past Eddie with his freckles and flaming red hair and mocking look, past Jimmy, who was always leaning on a motorcycle, propped up by its wheels. Just as disconcerting were the hard-faced girls who strutted their stuff down the block, sweaters drawn tightly across their newly burgeoning chests. I walked straight past them all, not looking at anyone, hoping they didn't look at me.

But a few blocks away, on another corner, was a group whose eyes I wanted on me: the sexy Italian boys in pea jackets and navy wool caps, their tough eyes crinkling up warm when they smiled. At thirteen, I snapped them with my Brownie camera and put their photos in my album, writing a line in white ink beneath each picture on the black page: "We're all pals together." Louie Provenzano, who had seemed so unapproachable when I was twelve, smiled at me when I turned thirteen. I took his picture too.

The corner boys with inscription, "We're all pals," in my photo album

Further east on 175th street, the buildings were posher—six-story, yellow brick, with elevators and casement windows that opened in and out rather than up and down. There sat the old Biograph Studio, where they had made movies years ago. Abandoned in the late thirties, the Biograph was still a neighborhood landmark. Across its mustard-colored concrete walls, chalked in dirty white, were the names of the older guys on that block—Heshie, Bernie, Stan—guys who were cool in their sporty wide-legged trousers and suede shoes. No longer an ugly duckling at thirteen, I imagined each boy as the hero of a romantic movie with me the costar.

When, at the beginning of my fourteenth summer, Ike Sedaca, a dark-eyed, curly-haired junior high school dropout, asked me to be his girl, I was thrilled. I was finally entering into a romance. For all of six weeks, I proudly sauntered hand in hand with Ike through the neighborhood, his swagger a mark of my own standing. In the evenings, we would walk to Crotona Park, where, amid the cool scent of grass, in a corner of the handball courts now illuminated by lamplight, the older men squatted in a circle at their nightly crapshoots. Occasionally, Ike would play while I watched, puffed up like a peahen, glorying in *his* knowingness. When one of the men asked me to blow on the dice for luck, I felt myself confirmed. Lady Luck herself!

But the idyll didn't last beyond that summer. One afternoon, Ike asked me to go with him downtown to a new jazz club in Manhattan. We would have to pretend we were eighteen, Ike said, but he had done that before; it wouldn't be a problem; I looked older; I could pass. Downtown! I already had just the right dress—orange, brown, and black paisley that left one shoulder bare, a popular style that summer. But when I told my mother I was going downtown to a club with Ike, she not only forbade me to go but demanded that I stop seeing "that *trumbernick*. He's no good! You'll get into trouble with him. I'm warning you. I'm telling you. Break it off!"

That night I tossed and turned in bed, wanting desperately to go downtown yet somehow reluctant to defy my mother. Still tormented the next morning, as if in a trance, I automatically put on the paisley dress with one shoulder bared without having made a decision. In the late afternoon, still in a trance, I left the apartment to meet Ike. There he was, waiting eagerly for me near the subway entrance, so good-looking, spruced up in a dark blue suit, his curly black hair brushed back, gleaming, and going up to him, I heard myself say, "I'm sorry, Ike, but I can't go . . . and I can't see you anymore. My mother won't let me."

My mother won't let me? Amazed at these words that signaled my capitulation, I returned home, brooding. From that experience, I learned not to tell my mother anything about my plans—at least, not until after the fact. My father never asked.

Downtown

Although I had yielded to my mother's demand, I hadn't given up the dream of the high life—downtown. Vague scenes culled from the movies swam before my eyes: penthouse apartments overlooking the city, night-clubs where torch singers sang sultry songs to adoring audiences. And then, one evening, I heard a siren call in the form of Ted Mack's *Amateur Hour*, a radio program that prided itself on welcoming talent of all ages. I had never formally studied voice but could easily carry a tune and loved to sing. Without telling anyone, I called the station, set up an audition, and spent weeks practicing a song popular that year, despite its vocally demanding high note in the bridge: *Longing to tell you but afraid and shy, I'd let my golden chances pass me by. . . .* I wasn't going to let *my* golden chances pass me by.

As the day approached for the audition, my self-confidence sagged. I needed a secret sharer for this venture, and so after considering my options, I enlisted my nine-year-old brother Al as my confederate. On the appointed Saturday morning, with Al in tow and my sense of self magnified in his eyes, I took the subway downtown to Rockefeller Center. We emerged from its depths right in front of the RCA Building. I looked up; it stretched dizzyingly toward the sky. Holding tight to Al's hand as a ballast, I pushed the huge revolving door and entered.

I had no trouble finding the Ted Mack studio, and, after announcing myself to the receptionist, was told to sit in the waiting room. Al sat next to me, bemused.

"Kitty Katz?"

I rose quickly to the sound of my name and followed the receptionist into another room. A balding man in shirtsleeves sat at a baby grand piano; next to it stood a microphone. "What key?" he asked, running his fingers along the keyboard. Key? I had no idea what key I sang in and could only answer: "You choose one." As the pianist began to play, my dream turned into a nightmare. He was playing in too high a key! Too embarrassed by my ignorance to say anything, I began to sing, moving determinedly through the familiar lyrics toward the dreaded high note in the bridge: *pass me byy.* . . . At *byy,* I emitted an awful squeak and felt my face flush with the heat of humiliation. Mumbling, "I'm sorry, wrong key," I rushed out of the audition room, and silent before my brother's quizzical stare, I took his hand and left the building. "It was the wrong key," I explained calmly once we were on the train.

Still, I hadn't given up my desire to perform. About to enter high school in the fall and already reluctant to attend my neighborhood school—on the edge of the Bronx's tough Little Italy, Roosevelt High was said to have a maternity ward on the fifth floor—I applied to the School of Performing Arts in Manhattan. I was still hoping to train for a career in musical theater. With the help of my English teacher, I prepared the required monologue for an audition, practicing it for weeks. The monologue itself went well, but why had no one told me I would be asked to perform a "mime" piece? What was "mime" anyhow? "Just peel a banana and eat it," the test instructor said when I asked. Not surprisingly, I slipped on that banana and failed the entrance exam. The neighborhood high school it would be, then, fifth floor maternity ward and all.

Happily, there was no fifth floor in the building, nor was the school dominated by street gangs. Instead, there were "social clubs," each with its own special jacket or sweater that identified the wearer as "belonging." Mortified by not having been asked to join any of them, I gathered several of the brainier girls in my class who, like me, were too smart to be popular, and formed my own club: the Vixens—a word I declared to be our identity after looking it up in *Webster's Dictionary*—"a female fox"; also, "a sexually attractive woman."

Club Vixens

But despite the name, there was only one true vixen among us: Phyllis Birnbaum, an orphan from Pittsburgh who had been sent to live with her aunt in our neighborhood. Phyllis knew how to be a vixen: in class, she instinctively assumed a seductive position, standing with one hand limply on hip, her sweater stretched tightly across breasts that pointed provocatively outward in a challenge hard to ignore. How I admired Phyllis when, late for English class one day, she goaded Miss White, the gray-haired teacher with thin lips and cold blue eyes, whom we all ridiculed as a "spinster" (I curl into shame writing that word now!), into a moment of vindictive attack. "Remember, Phyllis, boys don't make passes at girls who wear glasses," Miss White smugly proclaimed, inviting the class to enjoy her barb. Slipping blithely into her seat, "Oh but you're wrong, Miss White," Phyllis responded archly. "They do." How the class loved Phyllis! How the Vixens needed her!

But if the yellow sweaters with their blazing black cursive title—*Vixens*—that I had ordered for us were meant to assert a sexual attractiveness that I felt essential to my self-confidence, I also prided myself on my quick intelligence. I was doing very well in my classes, and didn't intend to yield the field of academic excellence to my rival, the sharp-eyed, sharp-nosed

Rita Bernstein, who flaunted her high grades arrogantly before her class-mates. Nevertheless, I lost by a nose: Rita became class valedictorian when we graduated, while I, second in grade rank, wore the lesser honor of salutatorian. Still, I was proud to have been singled out, and as I welcomed the audience into the auditorium for the ceremony, I felt anything was possible.

A Premature Automobility

At a relatively early stage in my adolescence, automobiles became a passion of mine. I yearned for the freedom that cars offered, the sensation of sheer movement, of going somewhere—it didn't really matter where. Occasionally I went for a ride after school with Bobby Gans, a boy who had access to his father's convertible. Riding with the top down along the Bronx River Parkway, indifferent to the cold wind messing up my hair, I would show off my expertise by naming the different makes and models of cars that we passed. I loved cars, and wanted others to know. It marked my difference from other girls.

One afternoon, Bobby made a revolutionary suggestion.

"If you want, I can help you buy a car. I know a salesman who doesn't ask too many questions."

Buy a car? Could I really do that? I felt a quickening.

"I can teach you to drive," Bobby continued, as if answering my unspo-ken question. "We can practice on this car when my pop's at work."

I knew it wasn't quite legal—I was only fifteen and couldn't get a learner's permit yet—but the temptation was too great. I already had saved money from my part-time job at Barricini's Chocolates. I'd be sixteen soon.

For the next few months, I met Bobby for lessons, practicing until I felt confident enough to drive on my own. Finally, one chilly afternoon in early spring, with learner's permit in hand, Bobby and I took the subway to a used-car lot in Yonkers. As previously arranged, I handed over my

150 dollars to a friendly used-car salesman and, with Bobby sitting beside me, drove my new car, an old black, four-door Dodge sedan, off the used-car lot and back to the Bronx.

"Ma, I bought a car today," I casually remarked a few hours later to my mother as I sat at the kitchen table drinking a cola while she made dinner.

"*Vus?*"

"It's parked downstairs. Want to see it?"

For a moment a puzzled look crossed her face, and then it contorted with disbelief as she took in my remark. "Are you crazy? How could you buy a car! You're not old enough!"

"I'm sixteen!"

Disbelief turned into fury. "*Vus far* a *mensche* sells you a car?" Without any pause, she grabbed my arm. "Let me see."

And out the door and down the three flights we went.

"There," I said, somewhat nervously, pointing across the street to the black sedan, aware of her growing anger.

Holding her hands to her head, she stared a few moments with furrowed brow at the offending object. Then she turned to me.

"What's wrong with you? What is WRONG with you! We are taking this back right away! Now!"

And so, that very afternoon, my mother made me drive her, and the car, back to the car lot, where to my great embarrassment, she heatedly admonished the salesman.

"You sold this to a young girl underage? Shame on you! Take the car and give her the money back or I'll go now to the police."

Looking sheepish, he made the exchange, and Ma and I took the train back to the Bronx.

Catskill Criminality

Like many other working-class Jewish families, every year, my family ritu-ally went for a two-week vacation to the Catskills, to one of its many modest hotels. In that last year of these family vacations, I befriended Randy, the handsome, coffee-colored bellhop at our hotel. He and I would often sit on the porch in the late afternoon and lazily chat together—that is, when he wasn't carrying suitcases up or down the stairs or running errands in the hotel limousine. But the errands he ran weren't always for the hotel, as I discovered one afternoon when he invited me to ride with him while he made some "deliveries." Although, at first, I didn't quite understand the true nature of our jaunt, after Randy had made several quick stops at a number of hotels, I began to suspect something illicit was being deliv-ered. Excited rather than disturbed by that probability, I confronted him. Smiling breezily, his dark eyes twinkling, he admitted he was delivering "grass"—marijuana—to various musicians working the Catskills. "They need it to play well," he explained.

To further educate me, when we returned to our hotel, Randy invited me to his room and showed me how to smoke marijuana using a brown paper bag: "You take a long drag, inhale the smoke, put the paper bag over your head, hold your breath, and then let it out slowly." I did as I was told, feeling ridiculous as I put the bag over my head, and smelled that peculiar odor for the first time. After a few tokes, nothing had happened, at least nothing noticeable. Really, I wondered, why all the fuss about smoking "grass"?

On my last day at the hotel, Randy made me an offer: in January, when I would start attending City College of New York, he would get me an apartment on Central Park West and pay the rent, if I allowed him to store packages there. I didn't have to know what was in them, he said. I was the perfect foil; no one would suspect a young college girl like me of wrong-doing. And only he would know about the arrangement, so there was no danger of anyone snitching and my getting into trouble.

An apartment of my own on Central Park West! "I'll think about it," I said. "I'll let you know at the end of the summer." We made a date to meet at three o'clock on the southwest corner of 125th Street and Lenox Avenue the day after Labor Day when I would give him my answer.

I got very little sleep those last weeks of summer, turning around in my mind the risks of a criminal involvement with Randy, but also imagining its reward: an apartment in Manhattan. Risky, but maybe worth it? I rationalized: at worst, I could get arrested for complicity in a drug scheme, but given my background and age, I wouldn't get a harsh sentence—at most a year or two. I wanted to live on my own; Central Park West was such an attractive location, and it would be so easy to get to CCNY from there. I would do it!

Finally, the day for our meeting arrived. I took the subway to Harlem and arrived at 125th Street and Lenox Avenue a bit early. I stood on that well-known Harlem corner waiting, the only White girl in the vicinity, more than a bit apprehensive about this adventure I had chosen to embark upon. It was a sunny day; people were briskly walking past me as I stood there, but a chill in the air foretold the coming season. And then it was past three o'clock, and Randy was nowhere in sight. Thirty minutes later, I realized he was not coming. The decision had been made for me.

"The Bronx? No Thonx." —Ogden Nash

That same fall, I discovered a safer way of gaining entry into the promise of Manhattan: jazz dancing at Central Plaza (CP to its patrons), a jazz club on lower Second Avenue. Dancing was a self-induced intoxication, the body finding pleasure through rhythmic movement. But it was also a passion, as necessary to life, I thought, as breathing. Florence, my best friend, was equally ardent about it. "Can you imagine marrying a guy that couldn't dance!" one of us would say, cackling as we wandered across the Bronx to Washington Heights on one of our walks, imagining possible futures, unable to draw fine lines between what we needed and what we wanted. Dancing, we were sure, was what we needed.

At fifteen, we had danced in one of the improvised basement social clubs that dotted the East Bronx, swaying together with heavy-lidded boys, bodies leaning into one another, arms encircling necks, intoxicated by the slow grind that the music demanded. Vic Damone, Johnny Mathis, Frank Sinatra—those smooth-voiced crooners emboldened us with their seductive lyrics. In high school, such basement dancing, two by two, was a sensual pleasure beyond thinking and beyond prohibition.

But a year later, downtown at Central Plaza, it was the Charleston, the body singular, that made us high: mad frenzy of legs kicked up in front, kicked back behind, the sheer impulsion of rhythm generating an ecstasy of motion. *Whoo, daddy, look at me!* Wild Bill Davison, Muggsy Spanier, Sidney Bechet, Hot Lips Page—the names alone sounded erotic and wild. And so, every Friday night, eager and expectant, Florence and I took the subway downtown to the Lower East Side, first weighing ourselves on the penny scales that stood as monitors on the train platforms. (On the way back, we checked to see how much weight we had lost in sheer sweat-pounds and gloried in the loss.) Once at the club's front door, we straightened our shoulders, and, pretending to be the legal age of eighteen, sauntered past the doorman nonchalantly and into the center of the club's explosive energy.

The musicians played on a bandstand off to one side of a small, crowded dance floor where couples formed and re-formed, shifting partners as they hopped to the rhythm of "Muskrat Ramble" or sang the lyrics of "When the Saints Go Marching In." Surrounding this floor space were round wooden tables, each seating about six or eight people. In the center of each table stood a pitcher of beer, bought by someone from the bar along the wall. Florence and I would choose a table with two free chairs, and when the band started up, we would leave our seats and throw ourselves onto the dance floor, dancing into the center of attention for hours. We were good, we were young, and we were inexhaustible.

Except for the musicians, the crowd was White and mixed in age. Only the music was Black, and how I loved it, loved feeling the syncopated rhythms enter me and push my overheated body onto the dance floor. One night, as the club was closing, Willie Moses, one of the musicians, asked us if we'd like to come up to his apartment and see a movie he'd just brought back from France. Thrilled to have been noticed by a worldly musician, we accepted the invitation and when the club closed, rode up with him by cab to his Sugar Hill apartment in Harlem. How were we to know that his "French movie" was a euphemism we had not yet encountered? After watching the first few frames—a maid in scant costume opens the door to an unknown salesman—and recognizing the genre, we nervously elbowed each other, and bidding Willie an uneasy good night, hastily retreated, taking the subway back to the safe and familiar comforts of home.

But if that night's experience of sophistication sent us running back uptown, there was another downtown invitation at CP that we accepted with far different consequences. The band had been especially hot that night. With the sweat pouring off us as we danced, and only half-aware of other bodies on the floor, Florence and I became part of a sea that surged and heaved and throbbed along with the music. Then, as if a biblical Moses had stretched out his hand, the crowd parted, and we found ourselves alone on the floor, surrounded by couples who had stopped dancing to watch us and were clapping rhythmically, driving us on.

When the set was over, a woman stepped out of the crowd and invited us to sit at her table. Anna—she quickly introduced herself—and her husband Paul were middle-aged, better dressed than most at CP, obviously tourists, I concluded, but tourists with class. Talking with that special kind of intimacy reserved for strangers, Anna introduced us to the two young men—Yale college students—already seated at the table. We all chatted awkwardly for a few moments, but when the band started up again, Florence and I bounced up from our seats, returning to the table only during the brief intermissions. When, an hour or so later, the club manager announced the formal "good night," and the band played its last licks,

37

Anna turned to the four of us and said, "Why don't you all come up to our apartment for a nightcap?" A nightcap? No one I knew had ever used the word though it was familiar enough from the movies. Florence and I looked at each other and nodded.

It was raining when we walked outside into the night. I could smell Second Avenue—beer-smell mingled with sausage-smell and the stench of rotting vegetables from storefront garbage cans. But the streetlights glimmered in the rain puddles as Anna hailed one cab and Paul another, and we were ferried up to Sixty-Fifth Street and Fifth Avenue.

Once again, I barely nodded to a doorman in passing and, following the others into a dark-walled elevator, was lifted to the fourteenth floor. To my amazement, the elevator door opened directly into an apartment, and I stepped into a space of deep yet muted colors that I can still recall: purple and gold and brown and maroon. Warm golden low light suffusing a spacious living room. A small bar in the corner. Plush, silvery-gray velour chairs facing a long, curved couch. A coffee table with magazines casually strewn across its glass surface.

I sat down gingerly on one end of the couch, my knees folded tightly together. Florence sat next to me. Paul brought the drinks. Anna lounged against the sofa cushion at the other end and asked us questions—I no longer remember exactly what they were. What I do remember is how readily Bill and Jim, the Yale students, laughed, how easily they four conversed while Florence and I sat in gawky silence. Occasionally, one of us would tentatively interject a remark, but it only broke the natural flow of their conversation.

But memory does hold on to a particular anchor to that night: Winston Churchill. Paul mentioned an article in the *New York Times Magazine* about Churchill's paintings, and Jim and Bill entered into a conversation with Anna and Paul about the kind of artist Churchill was, about his limitations, about the nature of watercolor in contrast to oils. I listened to them closemouthed, uncomfortable, excluded by my ignorance. Was this artist the same Churchill who led England during the war? Was he also a painter?

I observed Anna, who sat on the couch, her arms open in a posture of cool grace while Bill pronounced Churchill a Sunday painter; Paul agreed, but Anna, leaning forward to make her point, insisted that Churchill had produced some very fine watercolors.

But how did anyone determine how fine a painter he was? I felt lost.

So, sipping my Scotch and water, trying not to make a slurping sound, I felt the ecstasies of the night turn to ash. Yet as I sat there with the occasional smiles of Anna and Paul passing in my direction as if to reassure me, I felt, mingled with my humiliation, a hunger I had not known before. I wanted and wanted. And what I wanted took the shape of the room in which I sat. There and then, I vowed to educate myself, to make myself worthy enough to sit in such a room someday, conversing about Churchill's paintings with the cool confidence of those born into it. The Charleston would have to play second fiddle in my future.

2

Transgressions: An Education in Social Boundaries (1952–1957)

Growing up is losing some illusions in order to acquire others.

Virginia Woolf

The City College of New York in 1952 was not the ivy-covered college I had dreamed of, but it was what my family could afford: it was free. Open only to the high performers of the city public school system, it sat imperiously on Sugar Hill, a residential citadel in the midst of Harlem. Although the surrounding neighborhood seemed relatively safe, its stately apartment houses looking much more reputable than my own, that first year I felt apprehensive about going to school in the middle of a "Negro" ghetto, as we called it then. Of course, *I* wasn't prejudiced, I assured myself. Hadn't I invited Colette, the only colored girl in my high school class, into the Vixens when I formed the club? Didn't I wholeheartedly support racial equality? Impatient with the ignorant prejudice of my parents who worried about the *schwarzes* moving into the neighborhood, hadn't I determined to do my part to fight for racial integration?

Yet the reality was that each time I got off the subway at 145th Street and walked past the group of Black men hanging out in front of the barbershop near the corner, I held my breath. Turning the corner at the top of the hill, onto Convent Avenue, I relaxed as I walked six more blocks, past Sugar Ray Robinson's pink Cadillac, a familiar neighborhood icon always parked on the same block, toward the wrought iron arch that signaled the entrance to the school grounds of this mostly White university. It was not exactly a gated community, but it might as well have been. In the early fifties, even at progressive CCNY, the line between White and Black seemed clearly drawn.

And what would I choose to study in that gated community? English literature, of course. Like many other children of uneducated Jewish immigrants, I had excelled in English in high school—perhaps because English was *not* the language spoken in my home. Or perhaps it had something to do with Roosevelt's eloquent speeches to which my parents listened in awe, or Churchill's stirring wartime orations that poured from England into our apartment over the Philco radio. For whatever reason, I had been drawn early to the distinctive cadence of the English language— its rhythms, its sensual vowels, its rhetorical power—had even won the English Department Award at my high school graduation: a copy of Louis Untermeyer's *A Treasury of Great Poems*. And so, still under the spell of an idealized Fifth Avenue gentility, I set my sights on learning to talk about literature and the arts with a degree of rhetorical sophistication sufficient to catapult me upward and outward, from the East Bronx into the brighter world of cosmopolitan Manhattan, or even beyond.

Luckily, the mandatory courses for a BA at CCNY fit my plans. Students were required not only to study the liberal arts and sciences, but also to take a speech course to rid themselves of their outer-borough accents, those dentalized t's and d's and sibilant s's that indicated their Bronx or Brooklyn provincialism. "Learn to curl your tongue and reach the roof of your mouth," we were told, to which I added, *if you want to get out of the Bronx. Or get the Bronx out of you.* In a class called Techniques of Prose, we had to imitate the styles of the great nineteenth-century masters of English prose: Macauley, Hazlitt, De Quincey, Arnold—all men, although unremarked at the time. "Not a having and a resting, but a growing and a becoming is the character of perfection as culture conceives it," Matthew Arnold had written, and I immediately agreed. Yes, a growing and a becoming. And so I gladly learned the rhythms of each master in order to overwrite my own.

Given my desire for the touted social amenities of college life, I was relieved to see that CCNY did have a traditional quad despite its urban location—a large green square surrounded by neo-Gothic buildings where students gathered to relax or cavort between classes. And the college soon proved to have other appealing features to a teenager looking to expand her world. Florence's older sister Mae, already a student there, introduced us to House Plan, a more diverse version of a Greek Life social organization housed in a brownstone on Convent Avenue and open to everyone. Although I dropped in regularly to socialize, my inner eye was still fixed on Churchill's paintings and that room with a view, and so I joined the only Greek sorority that had managed to gain a foothold at CCNY: Sigma Tau Delta. Belonging to a sorority, I strategized, could put me in touch with the affluent world I yearned to enter, and perhaps even lead me to a rich husband. I would never marry *just* for money—I had no such crass desire! But as I told myself repeatedly: "You can fall in love with a rich man just as well as a poor one." The sentiment was far from original, but I made it mine. Pledging my fealty to the sorority that first week by wearing a costume on campus, without recognizing the sad irony, I chose to dress as an American Indian—perhaps the most impoverished minority group in the country.

Pledging Sigma Tau Delta at CCNY

But after a year of sorority cocktail parties where I drank too much, and Harvard weekends with fraternity boys who bored me with their chatter or clumsily put the make on me—one evening, at Harvard, in an involuntary drunken gesture, I had even vomited all over the shirtfront of a Sigma Chi just as he was about to embrace me—I found myself gravitating toward the folk singing crowd who regularly met in the CCNY cafeteria. They were an impassioned group, strumming their banjos and guitars, singing songs about the miners in East Virginia and the banks made of marble and the brothels in New Orleans—songs ringing clarion calls for social justice. But they also sang Renaissance madrigals with poignant melodies that catered to my desire for romance. By the end of the first year, I no longer wanted to talk about Churchill's paintings. These conversations were far more compelling.

At City, the student body was almost entirely progressive. In the pre–civil rights days of the early fifties and long before the second wave of feminism, McCarthyism and the Red Scare; socialist versus communist critiques of capitalism; and the US investment in the Korean war were the hot issues being fervently debated in the school cafeteria, CCNY's virtual Roman Forum. And debates there were! The left had its own discordant splits, identified by acronyms I couldn't keep track of: LYL, YCL, YSL. There were the serious radical politicos like Al Sirota of the Labor Youth League. Short, tough, and muscular, his black eyes flashing as he argued for the need to organize the proletariat, he was already primed for the job he declared he would take after graduation: working in a steel plant in Pennsylvania. There were the student journalists like Selwyn Raab and Joan Snyder, both of whom wrote for the more progressive of the two student newspapers, *Observation Post*. Rabb would become an investigative reporter for the *New York Times* and Snyder, who was the first female student reporter to the *New York Times* on campus, would become one of the first women news producers at CBS TV.

The rival paper, *The Campus*, attracted the more conservative, even cynical, student journalists, who found the leftist politics of their classmates material for public parody. In my first year at City, the Young Progressives of America (YPA) were being baited by an editor of *The Campus*, Sheldon Podolsky, who had derisively founded an alternative YPA: The Young Pidookies of America. Naming himself the "Prime Pidookie," Podolsky ranted almost daily from the base of a lamppost on the quad, a self-mocking Don Quixote shaking his fist at the political windmills in parodic battle. And then there were those like me who remained in a political borderland, drawn to the idealistic goals of the left but unable or unwilling to make an active commitment to either socialism or communism. We were "the pinkos," pale shadows of the reds. Beyond the pale were the true conservatives, a small minority found mainly among the apolitical engineering students, whose strongest extracurricular commitment was to the wrestling team.

It was during my second year in college that I met Valerie, another pinko, who would become my dearest friend despite the differences in our dispositions—or probably because of them. We met in the Catskills while working as waitresses, jobs we both took every summer during our college years for the quick money—we made enough in two months to cover our expenses for the next year. That first summer, we bonded over our common enemy, Mrs. Pitts, the hotel owner, who regularly stirred the sour cream vat with her fleshy arms dripping with sweat. This woman, who looked so grandmotherly, would regularly go fishing for food in the kitchen garbage pail and serve the throwaways to the staff for dinner. When several of us came together to protest, we were not only fired on the spot but forced by the local police, who had been called in by Mrs. Pitts, to pack our things quickly and leave.

"Off the grounds now or you'll be arrested!"

Valerie and I had skulked around the corners of the hotel looking for the guests we had served during the week, trying to collect our tips, the only real payment for our work since our actual salary was a mere three dollars a day. It was just the sort of injustice to cement our attachment.

Yet we both quickly realized we were in so many ways opposite in temperament. Valerie was more articulate, eloquent in her sharp critique of the world we were coming to know, while I, lacking her verbal skills and moral certainties, leaned toward those sensual pleasures that required no language. As we often admitted to one another, she was my conscience, and I was her wild side. Together, we formed such a visible friendship that our Catskill Mountain busboy took to calling us "Heckle and Jeckle," two birds of a feather in the comic strips of that time. Crows, I had thought then, not knowing much about birds. As I later learned, they were magpies, considered one of the most intelligent animals in the world because they can recognize themselves in a mirror. That was us. Mirror images.

Heckle and Jeckle

Kitty and Barney: The Rhythm Rangers in Border Territory

Like most young women during the fifties, I wanted to meet "Mr. Right," a sexy romantic partner who would share my political views, my engagement with literature, my love of dance: in short, a male mirror. How, then, in the Jewish urban leftist milieu of CCNY, did I fall for such an improbable figure as Barney McCaffrey? An ardent Catholic and a Republican, he strode into the student cafeteria one day wearing a buckskin jacket and carrying an artist's folio under one arm, a guitar slung over the other. Buckskin Barney, as my friends affectionately nicknamed him, was running for president of the Student Council. With a roguish smile that traveled from his eyes to his mouth, he asked for my vote. He had it. I was immediately smitten.

He must have felt some similar stirring, for after we'd met in the cafeteria several times, he offered to accompany me home on the subway one night, a hardship, I knew, since he lived in Queens, miles and hours away. An hour or so later, hovering at the shadowed entrance to my apartment building, with the streetlight throwing a yellow glow over our animated faces, we both couldn't stop talking, challenging one another's politics. Barney defended the radically conservative position of Joe McCarthy, while I, incredulous that anyone at City College could think McCarthy a hero, fiercely attacked his position until we found ourselves at two in the morning, still arguing. Passionately.

The debates continued for months, each of us increasingly committed to converting the other. But now it wasn't just politics that fired our passions; it was also religion. He gave me Thomas Merton's *The Seven Storey Mountain* to read, hoping it would lead me toward the Catholic Church. I gave him Paul Blanshard's anti-Catholic *American Freedom and Catholic Power*, a Marxist diatribe that essentially damned the Church as well as Barney's convictions. Of course, what could have been more erotically provocative than such fierce conversations between a young man and woman whose pheromones were already madly whirring about?

But it must have been more than hormones that drew me to Barney. Was it his vivid difference from the familiar in my life? His very "otherness"? Was it the charismatic charm of the performer that he exuded as he sang and played that very American music called "country western," songs about love, loss, and hard drinking? Or was it his uncanny resemblance to that fair-skinned, handsome, sandy-haired youth suffering on the cross in that painting hanging in Patsy O'Brian's bedroom? Perhaps it was just that Barney had a space between his two front teeth, a seductive detail that always caught my eye. The gat-toothed man. Whatever the reasons, as D. H. Lawrence, whose novels I was now hungrily devouring in my English literature class, would have put it, "my blood was roused." Whether pressed against Barney's lean body on a street corner near the subway trilling "good night," or kissing for deliciously illicit moments in a campus nook between classes, I longed—and expected—to lose my virginity to the intensity of this first love.

Happily, Barney shared my ardor, and that first semester of our relationship stretched out in a warm haze of first love. But as my desire grew more heated, it confronted a wall. Sex was sinful outside of marriage according to his faith, and faithful he had become—even more since knowing me, he said, much to my chagrin. And he was true to his word: the more I plotted—and plot I did, increasingly obsessed with the idea of seducing him—the more devout he became. Even when we rented an apartment together for a month in one of Columbia University's resident apartment buildings to see how well we could live together—I told my parents I was staying with a female classmate in order to study for important exams—and we were actually sleeping together in the same bed, he adamantly refused "to go all the way." Instead of having sex, he painted my portrait and told me how much he loved the contours of my body as I reclined nude on the couch.

Barney's portrait of me

Perversely challenged by his resolute abstinence, I plotted an extreme course of action: I would get him drunk on New Year's Eve when he was playing a gig at a club, and seduce him when we returned to the apartment. I knew it was an unscrupulous strategy, but I was desperate, and the time was ripe. New Year's Eve was traditionally the occasion for new resolutions. Mine was to change the sexual status quo. We danced that evening between his sets, and I can still recall the sweetness of melting into his slim body, of looking up at him dreamily and saying, "You're so different from the other boys I've known." I savored the moment as he tenderly returned my gaze. Then he spoke: "That's because I believe in God." My spirits sank. I said nothing, but my resolve hardened: Tonight! I would seduce him tonight! But it was four in the morning when we finally returned to the apartment and fell into bed, and almost immediately, Barney fell asleep. And although I intended to try my wiles again in the morning, I awoke to an empty bed: he had already sneaked off to church. *Because he loved me!*

Defeated, I gave up my crusade and let myself enjoy what we had. Our intimacies took more indirect routes. Mainly, we coupled through country music and its rough-and-tumble lyrics. He taught me to play guitar accompaniment to his accordion, and it wasn't long before I too found myself with a guitar case slung over my shoulder, playing alongside him in the school cafeteria and giving myself over to a music-world quite different from that of the folksingers I had been drawn to earlier—a hillbilly culture whose features belied my own. Gone from my mind was not only the elegant Fifth Avenue room with its conversation about Churchill's paintings but the political protest songs as well. In their place were the lyrics of popular country music, songs like "A Satisfied Mind," which dealt with social inequality by offering comforting clichés about how money didn't bring happiness.

On weekends, I accompanied Barney to country music clubs where he played with a trio while I sat at a table in a corner, an adoring fan drinking him in. How many nights did I spend in New Jersey honky-tonks crowded with farm workers and truckers from nearby rural towns, all gathered to hear songs made famous by Hank Williams and Hank Snow, Ernest Tubb and Ferlin Husky, Faron Young and, my own favorite, Kitty Wells. They came to listen, to drink, and inevitably, to brawl.

"Play louder," I would hear Barney say to his band when a fight erupted, the music covering the sounds of men shouting and chairs overturning as I pressed myself into a corner until the set, or the brawl, was over. Rattled by the violence, I was nevertheless fascinated by the frontier atmosphere of these barroom scenes and especially by the sight of Barney, so self-confident, so talented—a showman in the midst of it all. And so, when he asked if I wanted to play with him regularly at the Crazy Horse Café in Queens on his band's night off, I was elated. I would become the figure I had been watching from the sidelines—finally, the performer. Even more gratifying, we would be a duo—Kitty and Barney: The Rhythm Rangers.

The Rhythm Rangers

Making Believe: A Western Wear Store On Forty-Second Street

Kitty: I want a buckskin jacket with fringes along the arms. A Western shirt with mother-of-pearl snaps. Western boots.

Salesman: You got it, little lady. C'mon right over here, and we'll get you outfitted for who you want to be.

Making Believe: The Crazy Horse Café

A smoke-filled room. The bar, shaped like a flattened oval donut with a hole in the center. In the middle of the hole, a raised platform with a piano and microphone. A small number of tables scattered around the room. Mostly men in uniform, some standing, smoking, drinking, some sitting at the bar, elbows crowding one another. A few women sitting with men at tables. All waiting for the entertainment. Eyes on me, on Barney, as we make our way through the crowd to one end of the bar, lift the bar top at its hinge, and go up the few wooden steps to the platform. The accordion on his back, the guitar on mine, we both position ourselves in the center of the platform and place our instruments in front of our bodies. Barney takes the mic.

"I'm Barney, this is Kitty, and we are The Rhythm Rangers—from New York City!" He laughs with the audience, such an easy laugh, at the ironic contradiction, and after a few squeezes of the accordion, begins to sing:

"*I had a friend named Ramblin' Bob,*" he rocks back and forth, his voice belting out the song; he squeezes, I strum. "*He's in the jailhouse now. . . .*"

"Yeah!" The crowd is with him.

"Whoow-ey. . . . Go for it. . . ."

"Hey, boy, where'd you learn to sing like that?"

He finishes to applause. Now it's my turn: I strum, he squeezes, both of us playing with different chords, deciding on the song.

"Hey, little lady, sing some Kitty Wells." Good. I know her songs well. I choose "Makin' Believe." I do that a lot. The words come out easily. For a few hours, one night a week, I enter a place where I am not known, even to myself—where I am Kitty, the strong and sexy saloon proprietress whose very presence grounds Matt Dillon as he fights the bad guys on *Gunsmoke*. In this saloon, however, when the brawl erupts, as it usually does, and Barney stage-whispers, "Play louder," I get nervous. But after a few moments I drink in his confidence. Here, up on the platform, I am out of harm's way, the performer, protected from the fray. I can smile comfortably at those soldiers who continue to listen raptly while I sing and strum until the few rowdy others settle down, and bar-scene order is restored.

When we finish the set, Barney and I separate, each of us accepting the inevitable invitation from a soldier to sit at a table and have a drink. Keeping the customers happy is part of the job.

"So where are you from, soldier?" I ask, sitting down at the table of a soldier who has lifted his glass and motioned toward me. I know that this sentence works, that it elicits a nostalgia that will start us talking, as with this boy tonight, who, scarcely a man, is wearing a uniform that asserts his patriotic role as my protector and defender.

"Tulsa, ma'am, and boy do I miss it. Not that I'm complainin', mind you, but I sure wouldn't say no to a weekend pass, even if it took most of that to get there. . . . What will y'all have to drink?"

"A beer, thank you kindly," I say in turn, falling into the rhythm of his speech, as I do with others every Monday night.

I enjoy playing *Gunsmoke*'s Kitty, the independent woman in a tough surround. But what I love more is being Kitty of The Rhythm Rangers, and when it's time for the next set, I feel my heart almost bursting with the fullness of being here, now, believing in the emotional truth of the songs I sing as I step up to the platform. I pick up my guitar, change the position of the fret—I'm getting more musically sophisticated—choose my bone pick, and looking lovingly at Barney. I catch his eye as I belt it out:

"As long as I live if it be one hour
Or if it be one hundred years
I'll keep rememberin' forever and ever
I'll love you dear, as long as I live."

I'm nineteen years old. What do I know of forever?

At the break, a Black soldier standing at the bar as I walk by invites me for a drink. He's from Birmingham, he tells me; I listen to him talk about his love of country music; I tell him how although I'm from New York, I love country songs too.

"What's your favorite?" I ask, hoping I know it and can play it in the next set. "Almost anything by Hank Williams. . . . You know he learned the guitar from a colored street musician called Tee Tot. Yeah, Rufus Tee Tot Payne. Everybody in Alabama knows he gave Williams guitar lessons in exchange for meals. Taught him to play."

"Wow. I didn't know that. We'll do Hank Williams next," I promise.

When I get back on stage with Barney, we start with "Lovesick Blues." Barney sings it; I haven't yet mastered the yodel it requires.

"I got a feelin' called the blueoo oo oo es oh Lawd
Since my baby said goodbye. . . ."

Then, too soon, our night's play is over; it's almost closing time; the bar is emptying out; we are putting away our instruments. Jimmy, the owner, always so jolly, comes over, but now his face is set hard.

"I want to talk to you in the back."

He's speaking specifically to me, not to Barney, and I wonder what he has in mind. We walk silently to a back storage area; he closes the door, and turns to me, his face suddenly twisted with contempt and anger.

"Listen, you a nigger-lover or something? What d'ye think you're doin'? I blink, startled.

"We don' wan' nigger-lovers here. No drinkin' with niggers, understand?"

I'm shocked, frightened, confused, and then outraged as understanding follows confusion. I want this job, singing and performing alongside Barney, but faced with this ugly assault, this unjust fury, this racism, I must answer it. But how? What to say? I want to scream loudly, "I quit, you racist bastard!" But instead, I nod mutely, too scared to say anything to this man with the twisted, angry face.

On our way back to the car, I tell Barney what has just happened, and now, at last, I let out my own anger and disappointment.

"What a disgusting racist! How can you play there?"

"That's just the way it is there, and in a lot of places," Barney answers softly. "But country is what I do."

"Anyway, I quit!" I announce angrily, unable to do otherwise. But even as I say the words, I feel the loss, and the shame at not having said it to Jimmy.

Catskill Foreboding

It was summer, my time for making quick money as a waitress. Barney came up from the city to the Catskill hotel to be with me for a few hours. He waited for me in his car until I finished serving the dinner hours, six to nine, and cleaned up—carrying pails of silverware to the cleaning station, putting out the new breakfast settings for the morning: waitress work. Finally, around ten o'clock, I joined him outside and we went for a drive. It had been a long and tiring workday; I relaxed into the front cushion while he drove to a nearby bar and restaurant and parked the car. He'd brought me a gift, an ankle bracelet that he fastened around my ankle; we kissed and I leaned back, happy, satisfied. In the shadowed light, he began a familiar conversation about our future, but I was really tired; he was saying something I knew was important, something about. . . . And though I tried to resist, I felt myself slowly drifting off, sinking into the descending darkness. As from a distance, I heard his voice asking a question. About love? About marriage?

"Prune juice or orange juice?" I replied from elsewhere.

"What?" His querulous voice abruptly brought me back to the two of us sitting in the car, in the darkness, talking of serious matters.

"I must have dozed off and been dreaming, I'm so sorry. . . ."

We both laughed at this bizarre consequence of my exhaustion, and he took me back to the hotel. But I could see his disappointment. Not what he had expected from the evening, this interaction at cross-purposes.

Star-Crossed

Barney and I decided that even though the hurdles were enormous, we would marry. I had especially agonized over this decision. For while I'd refused to convert, under the pressure of Barney's religious passion, I'd agreed to raise our children—we'll have nine of them, we joked, a baseball team—as Catholics. But before we could move forward, we needed to meet each other's parents, to forge some kind of connection between his Irish/Polish/Catholic family and my Russian/Polish/Jewish one. Although our families shared Poland as a country of origin, I was aware of how different the Catholic Poland of Barney's mother was from the Poland my father fled and detested for its antisemitic pogroms. But I didn't have to go that far for family enmity: for my parents, the goyim were all potential persecutors who could never be trusted. "Someday," my mother had warned often enough, "no matter how good a friend you think someone is, they say, 'Dirty Jew.'" I'd fought that familiar Jewish paranoia all my life, but I still wondered: how would Barney's parents respond to me as a potential daughter-in-law? I couldn't forget how Gloria Falconetti, a childhood friend who lived in my apartment building, ran down the street after me one day, tauntingly shouting: "Christ-killer, Christ-killer."

"Ma," I had asked later, "Ma, did the Jews kill Christ?"

"No, the Romans did, and blamed the Jews." Her easy answer had calmed me then. I knew Barney didn't blame the Jews. But his parents? And the Church?

Girding myself for the encounter with each of our families, I took the first step: I invited Barney to dinner at my house. Mercifully, my father always worked through the dinner hour and wouldn't be there. *A Polack!* I dreaded to hear the angry contempt in his voice; I had heard it directed against me only last week, and the memory still stung. . . . I had been sitting in the candy store chatting with my father, when through the window, I noticed a man making his unsteady way across the street stumble and fall. Without thinking, I rushed out, helped him get up, and led him to a safe spot on the sidewalk. But when I returned to the store, my father, who had watched the entire scene through the store window, shouted at me: "What's your business! Who are you to get involved helping a drunken bum!" I felt the pain of his unjust fury cut into me. How unfair! *Mind your own business.* The command inscribed into his soul by Jewish history. The way to survive there, perhaps, but not here. Silent as always before his fury, I swallowed my own righteous anger, a pattern I would shamefully repeat before angry men, bullies all, for many years.

My mother, more empathic than my father, was usually more open to the pain of others. Eager to meet my new boyfriend, she was cooking a special dinner.

"Is he Jewish?" she had asked.

"Of course, Ma."

We had had this short dialogue often over the years; my answer to her inevitable question about whomever I dated, whatever his background, was always the same: "Of, course, Ma." Luckily for me, the Italian boys I usually dated in high school could pass. Barney? Clearly not.

That evening, as planned, Barney appeared. I was relieved to see that he wasn't wearing his buckskin. Still, my mother took in his goyish looks, and raising an eyebrow, seemed wary. Barney sat down at the kitchen table and my mother, looking at him out of the corner of her eye, quickly put out bowls, spoons, and forks. She had made a beet borscht as the first course, to be eaten with dollops of the sour cream she had already put on the table. She ladled a serving, thick with sliced red beets, into a bowl and set it before him. He picked up his *fork*, and said delightedly: "Oh, red beets! My favorite!"

My mother paused, turned her head toward me, her eyes narrowed, and then indicated, with a small gesture of her chin, that I should follow her into the living room.

"Red beets!" she echoed with a stricken look. "He's not Jewish!"

Quickly and unthinkingly, I responded: "Well, Ma, he's part Jewish. His grandmother was Jewish, so that makes him Jewish, right?" She gave me a disgusted look that said "you're lying." But she remained silent, and we returned to the kitchen.

"How do you like the borscht?" I asked, picking up my spoon and adding the sour cream. Barney took my cue and picked up his spoon.

Later that evening I had to justify myself; lying once again, I invented and elaborated on the story of his "Jewish" side: his Jewish grandmother, his attraction to Jewish culture, his Jewish friends at CCNY. Much to my surprise, my mother didn't argue the point. She just sat at the table, lips clenched.

Next, it was my turn to be inspected. Barney invited me to his house in Queens—alien territory. Queens in the fifties was where you lived to get away from the Jewish immigrants in Brooklyn and the Bronx—from people like my parents. Barney greeted me at the door of a small, two-story red brick house on a street with many such houses, and we entered the parlor. There in a rocking chair, looking like Whistler's mother, was Mrs. McCaffrey, her brown hair braided across the top of her head like a crown. Speaking softly, she invited me to sit down; her eyes were cool, appraising. She and I made small talk, Barney covering the awkward gaps as we three waited for Barney's father to get home from work. Some twenty minutes later he arrived, a short stocky man, balding and red-faced, with a churlish expression that immediately put me on my guard.

"Who's this?" he asked, pointing his chin in my direction as he stumbled toward his wife.

Barney, smiling to cover up his father's rudeness, introduced me: "This is Kitty, Pop. I've told you about Kitty."

His father asked Barney for the name again, the full name, and then repeated it as if it were a puzzle: "Kitty Katz? Kitty Katz?" I smiled, hoping he would find the name amusing, as so many people did, but instead, his face darkened.

"What's she doing here?" he bellowed after a few tense moments. "A Jew-girl. Get her out of here."

Barney told me to go into the next room, and I quickly left the scene, my heart hammering in my body. From behind the closed, curtained French doors, I heard Barney's father loudly ranting against the "dirty Jews," cursing his son for bringing one into the house, heard Barney and his mother trying to calm this storm I had raised, heard that very diatribe my mother had prophesied. There was no question of staying for dinner; I allowed Barney to walk with me to the subway station. But all the way home, I replayed the scene in my mind. Dirty Jew. His father. My father. No way.

Carnival: Beyond the Pale

Two years later, Barney and I met again in New Orleans to play in the Mardi Gras celebration. So much had happened in the interval. Ironically, it was not the fathers but the mothers who had successfully separated us. That saintly-looking Polish-American woman with the soft voice and cool eyes had phoned the hot-headed Jewish-Russian immigrant woman, and both had conspired to abort this ill-conceived romance between their offspring. Barney's mother had come up with a plan: she would persuade Barney to join the navy after graduation, convince him that he needed some time and distance for "mature consideration" before he married out of his faith. And it had worked. Although I visited Barney at the naval base in Oklahoma during that first year of our separation, and again in Maryland, where we spent his weekend pass in a nudist camp—he had become a naturist and had persuaded me to join him—inevitably time, distance, and our youth did their work.

During the past year, I had moved on to other life experiences: traveling around Mexico for several months after graduation, waitressing and playing music in Los Angeles, living the beatnik life in San Francisco's North Beach, where I had crossed lines with the police, and now, in February of 1957, on my way back from California to New York, was stopping to meet up with Barney in New Orleans for Mardi Gras. But the romance was over. I had lost my virginity during my last stint waitressing in the Catskills. Lost? No, rather finally found my sexuality, though in a manner that stripped away its romantic aura. For just as Barney had been adamant with his no, Richard—the blonde, curly-haired, blue-eyed butcher at the hotel where I was working—was adamant with his yes. Privileged because he was the son of the Polish chef, he courted me, not like Barney with an ankle bracelet, but with steaks that he brought to the back door of our staff quarters. I accepted the steaks, his attentions, and ultimately, the sex, at long last initiated into its mysteries. But without being "in love." Without Barney.

And Barney? More committed to Catholic service than ever, he was now following in the path of Dorothy Day and the Catholic Worker rather than Joe McCarthy. He had written me of his plans to travel to Peru with Emmaus, a Catholic missionary organization that helps indigenous people climb out of their impoverished circumstances. And he'd met someone, a Catholic girl he was going to marry; they were planning to go on this mission together.

I felt a pang of regret as I realized how far each of us had moved from our dream of a life together. Yet here we were, together again, The Rhythm Rangers, accordion and guitar, making music as we marched in the Mardi Gras parade behind women in colored gowns and feathered headdresses, cowboys in the Hopalong Cassidy contingent, children blowing whistles and fifes and holding balloons. Everyone stepping out of their ordinary lives, playing out their dreams.

We passed a small house decorated with colorful beads, which hung from its wrought iron balcony, and a woman in a bright orange dress, bracelets tinkling, came out with a platter and invited us in to share some Creole food and beer. We paused, joked, ate, and drank with her, and then laughingly took our leave. This was Carnival, anything could happen, and as we continued along the streets, walking and singing and strumming and squeezing, my delight in being here grew. Again and again, we were stopped and invited to share food and drink along the way. Intoxicated as much by the atmosphere of abandon in the street as the drinks, I felt the old magic of performance well up as the crowds on the sidewalk waved and cheered us on in this fabled city of music and friendship and fun. It was Carnival.

We stopped at the curbside for a few moments to watch the floats pass by. Fire-breathing dragons pulled a float on which red and yellow costumed devils cavorted with little pink angels wearing white masks. Anything could happen, I thought again, recalling the ardor of our past attachment, looking at Barney as he smiled that sweet gat-toothed smile, and at the same time knowing that it was gone, the old passion, now feeling the loss grow inside me, a flattened oval shape surrounding an emptiness. And we never even went all the way! Cheated. The mothers had done their work too well.

A float carrying a masked jazz band passed by slowly beating out its rhythms. Moved by an impulse, I tore away from Barney and scrambled up onto the jazz float, as if I could ride it back into some former life, wanting what I no longer had. Almost immediately, I was dragged off it by two White men, who glared at me as I tried to recover my balance. "That's not a float for you," one said. "That's the float for the niggers. This is their part of the parade." "Nigger lover," said the other, "Watch out!" And they walked away.

Race. Religion. The lines of difference that had dogged me through the fifties were still starkly drawn, the borders kept intact. In 1957 New Orleans, there were limits even to Carnival. But I had already crossed other borders, elsewhere, and would continue to do so for some time.

3

Underground Attractions: San Francisco Beat (1956–1957)

I am a social climber climbing downward.
And the descent is difficult.

Lawrence Ferlinghetti

It took a few seconds for me to realize that the police siren was screaming at me. I had just dropped Richie off at the Swiss American after he, Mal, and I had breakfasted together at New Joe's. Now with sunlight breaking through the fog, I was on my way out of San Francisco, once again on the road as I had been since graduating from college, this time driving down Columbus Avenue, heading for LA, my first stop on a cross-country journey back to the East Coast, with a break for Mardi Gras in New Orleans. Mal was sitting beside me, smiling at the prospect of the drive. He had offered to accompany me as far as Half Moon Bay. He felt like getting away for a few days, he had said, and I was grateful for the company.

I really liked Mal, Malcolm Braly by full name. "You'll be one of the few people who will know how to pronounce my name correctly," he told me when we first met last year at a literary café in North Beach. *Brah-ly.* I had already been tooling around the Beach for a week or so, exploring the neighborhood attractions and had walked into the Co-Existence Bagel

63

Shop on Grant Street for a poetry reading. He was sitting in a corner, and as I was looking around for a seat, he pointed to the space next to him on the bench. He was, he told me later that evening, a writer, though he made his living painting signs. Soft-spoken, hunched over as he talked, he had a gentle expression on his long thin face that was disconcertingly at odds with his crystalline blue eyes, which sparkled even in the dim light of the Bagel Shop. And there was that unruly forelock tinged with just a bit of gray touching his forehead. I had liked him immediately.

The police car appeared on my left and swerved in front of me. I braked, and the car squealed to a stop in the middle of Columbus Avenue. Through the rearview mirror, I could see another police car pulling up behind me. Two policemen jumped out of the car in front and rushed toward me. I rolled down the window, but before I could ask what was going on, they were on each side of the car, shouting, "Police! Outta the car." I opened the door, and as I was getting out, a cop grabbed my arm and told me to put my hands on the hood. I could see that Mal was getting the same rough treatment from the other cop. What the hell was going on?

"Take off your jacket and roll up your sleeves," the cop demanded after patting me down. I did as he asked, scared, not knowing why this was happening. He examined my arms, then stood back.

"Driver's license?"

"What's going on?" I asked. "Why did you stop us? I wasn't driving fast."

"We'll let you know when we're ready," he snapped back. "License!"

I reached inside the car for my bag, fumbled for the license, and showed it. He looked at it, at me.

"Where are you heading?"

"I'm driving down the coast to LA."

"Who is the man with you?"

"He's a friend of mine. He's going with me as far as Half Moon Bay,"

"Where have you just been?"

"We just had breakfast with a friend of ours. I just dropped him off at the Swiss American." I could hear my voice tremble. "Why are you asking these questions?"

"Just relax, young lady," he said, in a more conciliatory tone. "We're just going to do a background check." He walked over to his car with my license in hand. My heart was pounding in my chest; the ground beneath me seemed to shift. I took a few deep breaths. Standing close to my car door while traffic went around us, I tried not to shake visibly.

One of the other policemen sauntered over to confer with the one who had my license. I looked back: Mal was being pushed into the back seat of the other car. Then the policeman who had my ID approached. "You can go now. Here's your license."

"But what about my friend?" I asked, taking back my ID. "I can't just leave without him."

"He comes with us."

"Where are you taking him?" My panic rose as I saw the other police car take off with Mal in it.

"Down to the precinct station. . . . Why don't you just be on your way now," he added, dismissing me. "Enjoy your trip."

That was it. He turned and walked back to his police car, leaving me standing alone in the street.

I forced myself to calm down and took stock of my options. I couldn't just abandon Mal, but I had no idea what to do. Why had they stopped us? Why had they taken him? The adventure of being a girl on the road ratcheted up a few notches. This was another level of real. My mind quickly raced ahead: I knew where the precinct station was; I would have to go there.

Fifteen minutes later, I found myself in the drab entrance hall of the station, facing a uniformed clerk behind the front desk. He was flanked by two flags, the only color in the hall. One was the American flag. I assumed the other was the California one, though the grizzly and some words were partially hidden in the folds. Both seemed to declare an official indifference to my needs.

"I want to know what's happened to Malcolm Braly," I said as assertively as I could. "He was just brought in."

"How do you spell the name?"

I spelled it and he browsed the open page of the large book in front of him.

"You'll have to wait here until I can contact the arresting officer, miss. Take a seat."

Arresting officer? Still shaking inwardly, I sat down on a bench, rested my head against the wall, and planted my feet on the polished marble floor as if to assure myself by these hard surfaces that this was real. Yet I still didn't quite believe it. What had happened? Was it only six months ago that I had driven up from LA to take a look at the burgeoning literary scene of North Beach? What was I now doing in a San Francisco police station? How did I end up here today? Looking for answers, I began to recount to myself the events of the last year.

Turns and U-Turns

It had all started with the Mexico trip in my new car, which had allowed me a getaway—from my family, from the Bronx, even from my friends. Or maybe it started before then: hitchhiking, even before I graduated from CCNY—to Quebec; Washington, DC; Cape Cod—delighting in the adventure of being a girl on the road able to handle the few edgy situations I had occasionally encountered. After graduating from college, with money earned waitressing I went even farther from home, driving with three college friends—Sandy, Edie, and Valerie, all from the Bronx—to Mexico in my shiny new red Plymouth, a surprise graduation gift from my parents. How odd that my parents, who felt a girl should live at home until she married, should have contributed so dramatically to my *automobility*. I made immediate use of it.

Oddly enough, that trip to Mexico had also been interrupted by the police. Midway in our journey, I had made a U-turn on some deserted Main Street in a small Missouri town when a police car appeared, lights flashing, and stopped us. Looking at my license plate, the cop had sneered, "Just because you're young and good-looking and from New York, don't think you can get away with anything." And demonstrating that his word was law, he ordered us to follow him to the police station to pay a fine. But when he disappeared into an interior office, leaving us sitting in the waiting room, Edie stood up and whispered, "Let's scram." And we did, proving to ourselves at age twenty-one that we could get away with at least some things. Good girls wanting to break the rules—that was us.

In Mexico, we were again confronted by police; they appeared just after we'd all been nearly killed in an auto accident. Sandy had been at the wheel; we were all energetically singing "La Cucaracha," when the driver of the truck in front of us stuck out his left hand from the open window and waved as if signaling us to move ahead. Sandy pulled out quickly to pass but suddenly, the truck was turning left, and we were heading straight for it. The hand not waving us on, but signaling "left turn." About to hit it broadside and certain I would be killed, from some unknown depth of need, I cried out "Maa!" as the car crashed into the truck and rolled into a ditch on the right-hand side of the road.

Maa? Calling for my mother? What a surprise! But I had no time to reflect on it, for as we four clambered dizzily out of the car, bruised but amazingly unhurt, villagers appeared on the barren horizon and straggled toward us. Moments later, a police car pulled up, and two policemen got out. Relieved to see them, we quickly discovered that instead of rescue, they had profit in mind, threatening us with arrest for hitting the truck unless we paid up. And so, with this stark introduction to Mexican authority, and with the villagers around us watching closely, we each dipped into our travel money, gave the two cops two hundred dollars, and with our sensibilities more bruised than our bodies, were towed to a garage in Mexico City.

The repair took three months. Sandy, the prettiest and most brazen of us, agreed to stay with me after the others left. With Sandy taking the lead, we made the most of my misfortune, opening ourselves to chance encounters wherever we were. We city-surfed the streets of Mexico City first, and then went farther afield, hitchhiking around the country. In lush and gorgeous Acapulco, we breathlessly watched the pearl divers diving from a high cliff into the turbulent waters below and flirted with wealthy older men who took us to elegant dinners in classy beach hotels. Cuernavaca's hot and dusty stone streets, in contrast, were surprisingly barren and unwelcoming, and we left quickly. Veracruz was more industrial-looking than I had expected, its black sand beaches no match for the soft white sands of Acapulco. *Vaya, vaya*, then, back to Acapulco where, fed seafood tacos by the friendly beach-combers hawking tourist goods, we freely floated between sea and shore, waterskiing with the instructors in the late afternoon, sleeping on the beach at night, luxuriating in our sense of having left the Bronx far behind.

And yet, almost weekly, I sent a picture postcard to my parents, assuring them I was safe and learning a lot from my travels. A screen protecting them, I hoped. A tether, protecting me?

Quite amazing, how it had all turned out. With the car finally repaired and my new Mexican guitar lying in the trunk, Sandy and I had headed back to the US, our destination, California. But we stopped in San Miguel Allende, a village with a small art colony, and that evening, sitting around a fire in the village pub, I fell into an intense tête-à-tête with one of the locals, an expat alcoholic artist, Jack Wise. Soft-edged and dreamlike, the next few days passed horseback riding with him in the hills, bathing in a natural hot spring in the woods, drinking at the pub in the evening, high on my sense of living out a romantic adventure. And so, when Jack asked me to help him dry out, how could I not be the rescuing heroine to this talented artist? I spent forty-eight hours nursing him in a motel room—cool wet towels for his sweats and his nausea—until he recovered. Our bond strengthened by those dysphoric nights, he promised to meet me in LA as soon as he could free himself from his ongoing obligation to a wealthy widow—his San Miguel patron, as he called her. I didn't question their relationship; I could guess what it was; it satisfied my sense of story.

On the road again heading west with Sandy, my car ran out of gas near Las Vegas. We literally rolled downhill until the car stopped, luckily, near an outlying motel. We checked in and immediately fell asleep. To our surprise, when we awakened, two days had passed. We had slept through forty-eight hours! But as we soon discovered, time didn't matter in Las Vegas. Inside the casinos there was neither day nor night, only the glitter of lights—neon, fluorescent, incandescent—lights of every variety barely masking the visible darkness of the surrounding desert.

Vegas: corrupt in its very genesis. Yet perversely, its illicit ambiance excited us both. That first week, we haunted the top floor at The Sands Casino, where the high rollers played. Sandy, fly-fishing with her body, caught some man almost immediately to stake us at the crap table and buy us drinks. While Sandy flirted, I became addicted to rolling the dice on the crap tables as I had seen men do on the Bronx sidewalks of my childhood. How sophisticated I had felt—like Barbara Stanwyck in *The Lady Gambles* or Ann Dvorak in *Flame of the Barbary Coast*, women who knew how to play the system and come out ahead. Staked for luck by high rollers for nights on end, we won enough money to stay in Vegas—for how long, we had no idea. A gray-haired croupier we met put us up at his place and taught me a system for winning at craps, which I practiced daily. (Months later, living in LA, I returned to Vegas to try it and lost all my savings in thirty minutes.) But our luck didn't last; our playing funds dried up; we resorted to shilling for the Golden Nugget, keeping whatever change we won, but it didn't feel good. The Vegas glitter had faded into sleaze. Time to leave.

We headed west again. Sandy had a friend in Hollywood, "Peanuts" Cohen, who managed a folk music club, the Unicorn. A short, dark-haired Bronx boy, he put us up and let us spend evenings at his club. We tooled around Hollywood, visiting the famous sites and studios during the day; our evenings were spent at the Unicorn listening to music, relishing our insider status. But my real pleasure began after hours, when I could "sit in" with some of the musicians who dropped by, strumming my new Mexican guitar, and singing. When Sandy left LA, I moved in with some friends from my CCNY days, found a job waitressing at Piece O'Pizza on La Cienega, and waited for the anticipated arrival of my expatriate artist from San Miguel. When Jack finally appeared—he had a sister in LA with whom he was staying—we renewed our interrupted relationship. But the blossoming romance of San Miguel quickly withered in Hollywood. Somehow, he didn't seem as attractive as he had in Mexico. In the ambient light of LA, he looked weaker, and without thinking about it, I became deliberately provocative toward him. Shameful, now, thinking about it. Having actively encouraged him to leave Mexico and join me in LA, I provoked him to leave LA by stealing a bottle of Chianti from Piece O' Pizza—it had become a habit of mine—and gayly waving it before his eyes after he had specifically asked me not to steal. He left LA a few days later.

Relieved to see him go, I continued to revel in my after-hours life at the Unicorn—playing my guitar, singing folk songs, enjoying the club performance camaraderie. Yet when one of the up-and-coming folk singers, Billy Faier, a talented five-string banjo player, suggested I form a professional duo with him, despite being tempted—Billy was such a good musician; this was a chance for a real career as a folk singer—I said, "Sorry, I can't. I'm leaving town."

Why did I refuse? Afraid I wasn't good enough? Or because it would have been a commitment, a stop sign on the road, and I hadn't yet seen the Golden Gate? And what about that new literary scene I'd heard about in San Francisco's North Beach? Clearly, I didn't know myself, nor did I question my actions. Whatever the underlying reason, life was a passing spectacle. I was not ready to stop in LA. And so I took off for the Bay Area in my once shiny red car—the Mexican paint job on the new hood had begun to fade to a mottled unpleasant pink—driving up the breathtaking coast-road, its twists and turns periodically opening to menacing rocky gorges and views of giant crested waves crashing onto rocks below—a sublime landscape as far from the Bronx as I could get.

* * *

Now, ironically, I was sitting in a police station, far from the Bronx, waiting.

The wall behind my head felt uncomfortably hard, forcing me back to the present, and I leaned forward, stretching my neck. How long had I been sitting here? The policeman at the desk was bent over his record book. Other than the slight scratching of his pen, no sound was audible. Nothing was happening. No movement. I was in limbo, waiting. I sank back into recollection, continuing to trace the path that had led me here, to the precincts of the law.

* * *

In San Francisco, I'd headed first for City Lights, Lawrence Ferlinghetti's bookstore, already known as a center for new poetry and soon to become famous for publishing Allen Ginsberg's "Howl." (An obscenity trial the next year would bring the City Lights Bookstore to international attention.) Parking my dusty red Plymouth in the small alley beside City Lights, I had entered the bookshop, and there, sitting behind the counter looking like a samurai with his black ponytail and black T-shirt, was Shig, its genial manager. Smiling broadly, he told me about the cheap rooms at the Swiss American, a small hotel just around the corner that catered to transients, and Vesuvio's, a bohemian bar just across the alley from the bookstore.

I went first to Vesuvio's and was pleasantly surprised by its unconventional yet cozy interior, its dark walls, tiled floor, and stained glass lamps. There were only two men standing at the bar conversing. I ordered an Irish coffee, and one of them, beer glass in hand, turned toward me.

"I haven't seen you here before."

"I just drove in," I answered, glad to be noticed. "I'm new to the Bay Area."

"Welcome to the Beach. I'm Whitey," he said. "This here's Trent."

Tall and brawny, Whitey was a seaman, named no doubt for the pale albino hair that framed his ruddy face. His buddy Trent, a longshoreman, appeared even more massive, a veritable colossus. I marveled at the bulk of each of them as they stood at the bar, towering over me, while I told my story of living in Mexico for the past three months, then driving across the Southwest to Los Angeles, and finally up to the Bay area. I was crashing at the apartment of an old school friend in Berkeley, I said, but "Berkeley is such a straitlaced place; my Berkeley friend was put out by my being there for more than a few days! I plan to get a room at the Swiss American—Shig told me about it—and then a job."

Trent and Whitey had listened to my rush of words and offered to help me move into the "Swiss A." Trent lifted my two heavy suitcases out of my car as if they were grocery bags and carried them to the hotel. By the end of the afternoon, I was installed in a small room, costing eight dollars a week, with a daybed, a small desk and a chair, and bay windows facing Broadway, right in the commercial heart of North Beach.

Looking out the bay window that first night at the blue neon signs blinking greetings across the street and the lights of the cars passing below, I felt very pleased with myself. Here I was, in North Beach, center of bohemian life in San Francisco. By the end of the week, I had a temp job as a dance instructor at Arthur Murray's and was already on a fast track to the local in-spots of the Beach. Whitey had taken me to the International Settlement, a one-block stretch of Pacific Avenue marked by an iron arch over the street, that was "free territory"—that is, off-limits to the police. Barhopping along the street, we ended up at the notorious Black Cat. As I stood at the bar trying to figure out the crowd without seeming unsettled by the heavy drinking and rough male camaraderie, I felt clearly out of my league. A brawny guy next to me boisterously encircled the waist of his male companion while raucous laughter rang out. I was not ready for that.

International Settlement

My comfort zone was the less exuberant North Beach of painters and writers: 12 Adler, The Co-Existence Bagel Shop, The Coffee Gallery, City Lights, and visible across the street from my room, the Jazz Cellar, where California poets read weekly to a jazz accompaniment. On my first Wednesday night at the Cellar, Ferlinghetti read a poem about a dog urinating on a fire hydrant while the jazz trumpet played comic interludes to its beat. *How cool!* I thought, as I sat at a table with my Scotch, neat, exhilarated by being in the midst of this avant-garde scene. I loved feeling on the edge.

That was the week I met Mal, a sympathetic soul who quickly became a friend. And now he had been arrested? Why? I remembered the night he and Richie had asked me to drive them around to pharmacies and buy Vicks inhalers for them. I knew they were after some kind of high, but that was okay with me. I drove from one pharmacy to another, buying an inhaler at each one while Richie and Mal waited in the car. Fascinated, I watched as they broke open the inhalers to get at the drug-infused soft cottony material inside, then cut it up and ate it. A cheap high, maybe not legal, but no big deal. I myself preferred Dexamyl, an amphetamine usually prescribed for dieting that I had started using in college because it sped up and clarified thinking. Not hard to get under the table, it had become my regular mental support, giving me the self-confidence I felt I needed in anxiety-producing situations. And here I was in the midst of one: Mal's arrest.

Mal had real talent; of that I was sure. He had shown me a short story he was writing about a visit to a smug psychotherapist that subtly pilloried the profession. That was after I had told him I was thinking about going to graduate school to get a degree in social work. "You don't want to do that," he had advised, shaking his head. "What a waste that would be. If you're going to graduate school, study literature, not that Good-Samaritan hogwash you'll get in the school of social work."

He's right, I thought, and promised to apply to the Berkeley English Department when I was ready. After all, it was a better fit. I had chosen to spend my time in North Beach among writers and rebels, not social workers. At Vesuvio's, my favorite spot on the Beach, seamen mingled with poets, painters mingled with jazz musicians, and I, a good decade younger than most, felt myself granted the special privilege of being accepted as one of their company. Only Marco, a handsome rakish regular at Vesuvio's, had ever hit on me, but then, I had so wanted his attention that he finally paid it, and I ended up in his bed—alas, only for one night. But generally, Vesuvio's felt like a comradely space, and I earned my place merely by being an attractive twenty-one-year-old girl eager to meet the world in all its variety. Almost all.

I had my Vesuvio's ritual: I would take a seat at the bar with great aplomb and order a drink, putting my money on the counter like a pro. If there was no one there that I knew, I would assume a melancholy demeanor and stare into my coffee royal in a pose that suggested sad thoughts too profound to utter. That it was a pose, I vaguely knew, meant as a lure to attract the attention of a potential rescuer. Yet somewhere in the back of my mind was the sense that the pose was real, that I was actually death-haunted, governed by a melancholy apprehension that life was short, that I needed to experience as much as I could before it was all over. And there was so much out there to take in. Eventually, someone at the bar would break into my ruminations and bring me back to the pleasures of conversing with strangers.

Behind the bar was the taciturn Henri Lenoir, the owner, always wearing his signature Parisian beret. Smiling at his patrons enigmatically, he would on occasion tell us about his previous life in Paris, when he was Silvio Velleman. Coming to America, he had "disappeared" in southern California for lack of a visa, and then resurfaced in San Francisco as Henri Lenoir. Above the bar, there was usually a slide show of antique postcards projected onto a screen on the wall: Henri's signature card was of a woman in a turn-of-the century costume with the caption: "We are itching to get away from Portland Oregon."

Henri Lenoir in Vesuvio's

I knew the sentiment. It was my story too.

Riffs and Raffs

The desk cop got up noisily from his chair. He looked at me apologetically and turned away, walking quickly down the corridor. My plan to leave North Beach today had gotten totally screwed up, and I still had no idea why we were we stopped. Sitting here instead of on my way to LA, where I was supposed to say goodbye to my CCNY buddies, and then on to a one-day reunion with Barney in New Orleans—a farewell reunion, it was meant to be, before I headed back to New York and he to his naval base. So many goodbyes for a girl traveling light. I thought of those on the Beach I was leaving, aside from Mal, those others with whom I'd formed a sentimental bond: Whitey, Ken, Richie. But the saddest of all was Bob Kaufman, a poet who was continually blowing his mind apart with drugs and alcohol, yet still able to play words like musical notes: *San Fran, hipster land, / Jazz sounds, wig sounds....*

How touched I was the other night at Vesuvio's when I told Kaufman I was going to New Orleans. His slack face had become concentrated, and struggling to compose himself, he took my hand and led me outside to the public telephone booth. Dialing long distance collect, he called his sister in New Orleans—his hometown—and I heard him ask her to put up "my special friend Kitty, and you know... show her around." But even as he spoke, his sentences became halting phrases, then words barely mumbled: "Here, talk to my sister." Blinking heavily, he handed me the phone, defeated by the task of practical communication. Ah, Kaufman, how your words owned the blues, sweet and hard and sad.

* * *

"This way, miss."

The voice of the policeman who had checked my ID on the street inter-rupted my musings. I followed him down the hall and into a small spare room. He seated himself behind the desk; I took the seat opposite him, and catching my breath, I asked once again, "What's happened to Malcolm Braly? Why are you holding him?"

"He's under arrest . . . for breaking parole."

The words broke like shock waves into my consciousness. I tried to make sense of what he was now telling me. Mal had been on parole? Had been in San Quentin for armed robbery? Hadn't seen his parole officer when he was supposed to? Was now arrested for breaking parole? And Richie whom we had just dropped off, under surveillance for drug dealing? That's why we were stopped?

"Young lady, you shouldn't be hanging around these people. You don't belong in their world. You seem like a nice girl. If you know what's good for you, you'll just leave town and forget him." He stood up from his chair, gave me a long avuncular look that spoke both judgment and concern, and led me out of the room.

It took a few moments for me to figure out what I was feeling. The person I was closest to in my North Beach circle of acquaintances, the aspiring writer with the poetic sensibility had been in San Quentin for armed robbery! And he hadn't told me—*that* felt like a personal betrayal. And Richie, who always had a warm smile for me when he told me stories of his boyhood in LA that wrenched my gut, a known drug dealer! Who were these people I had spent the last six months with? Now I could see that I had been on the *outside* of the Beach's real life—a life that I had flirted with, but didn't really know. I felt my innocence like an accusation—and an insult.

Still, when the full impact of these revelations subsided, I found I was on the side of the Beach against the police. I couldn't abandon Mal and just leave town! But I needed to find someone who knew him and would know what to do in this situation. Leaving the police station, I headed back to North Beach and almost by instinct went directly to City Lights. Sitting at the checkout counter was Ferlinghetti himself, browsing a magazine. He knew the Beach and its habits; he could advise me.

"I need your help," I broke in, "or rather my friend Malcolm Braly does." Ferlinghetti looked up and listened—seriously, I was relieved to note. I told him what had happened as best I could, concluding with the question that overshadowed all else for the moment: "What should I do?"

He pointed to a rack of books. "The best thing you can do, the only thing, in fact, is bring him a stack of books. Help yourself to any of the paperbacks on that rack: not the other—they're fussy down at the station, they censor the reading materials, but any of those books they'll allow in. And don't worry about paying: they're on me."

Carrying eight paperbacks in a brown paper bag, I returned to the police station, where the presiding officer inspected the bag and then allowed me inside the gates to give it to Mal, in person.

"Don't worry about me," Mal said when we met, that familiar melancholy smile passing across his face. "I can handle this. Go on with your trip, Kitty. Go on with your life. Not anything anyone can do now. But thanks for the books."

As I got back into my car, I was struck by the irony. The avuncular cop and my buddy Malcolm were both were part of a shared world of cops and robbers, and both gave me similar advice: "You don't belong here." Where did I belong? That was still an open question.

San Franers, falling down. / Canneries closing. / Sardines splitting / For Mexico. / Me too. Me too, Kaufman. What was this beat, this compulsion to keep moving on? Off to LA, staying with my displaced CCNY-mates again, this time leaving a friend in prison: Malcolm Braly, Armed Robber. Yet in some perverse way, I felt proud of my criminal connection, almost as if it were a badge that confirmed my own worth. I didn't ask myself why I was drawn to society at its most marginal, befriending its most alienated figures. They seemed to offer their outsider friendship generously to me. I couldn't, I wouldn't refuse it. So much intense living there, such a depth of experiential knowledge.

As if fate were commenting on the value of experiential knowledge, a half hour down the coastal road to LA, my car sounded that recognizable thump indicating a flat tire. I pulled over to the side of the road, opened the trunk for the spare and the jack, and jacked up the car. Getting down on my knees, I removed the bolted-on nuts with the wrench and put on the spare. As I got in the car again, I could feel mixed in with my frustration at this unexpected task the pleasure of knowing I could change a tire if I had to. I'd be fine down the road.

* * *

Five years later, a graduate student of literature at Berkeley, I was sitting in my kitchen one morning and listening to an NPR interview with a former San Quentin inmate who had written a novel, *Felony Tank*, that had been nominated for an award as the best suspense novel of the year. I recognized the voice almost immediately—even before the author's name was mispronounced. *Not Brae-ly, Brah-ly*, I thought, silently correcting the interviewer. Years later, in 2002, I would read about the publication of another novel, *On the Yard*, which the *New York Review of Books* called "a book of penetrating psychological realism . . . arguably the finest work of literature ever to emerge from a US prison." And again, I would feel my value somehow confirmed in having been his friend.

4

Automobility: Breathless in the Old World (1958)

To be running breathlessly, but not yet arrived, is itself delightful, a suspended moment of living hope.

Anne Carson

einz and Gerhardt are driving Valerie and me from Heidelberg to Paris in Heinz's ancient wreck of a car, no headlights, Val and I in the backseat, taking turns holding a flashlight out the window, searching for the center line as the treacherously dark road flashes by.

Heinz checking his car en route.

A bit crazy, a bit dangerous, but we laugh through the night. Having weathered a tumultuous Atlantic crossing on the *Cristoforo Columbo*—sister ship of the ill-fated *Andrea Doria* (which famously sunk in a collision in the Atlantic)—and then hitchhiking through Italy, Austria, and Germany these last three months, are we not sufficiently experienced to make light of the hazards of travel by now? Or so I feel, with the self-satisfaction of a twenty-three-year-old on a roll. There were, of course, a few precarious moments along the way, but as if on a magic carpet, in each country, we managed to fly over them unscathed.

Italy in January: Disembarking in Naples, Mario, our Neapolitan ship-mate, invited us to his family home for dinner. Proudly anticipating giving his parents his earnings from America, he cautioned us to be on guard against pickpockets on the bus—"Hold on tight to your pocketbooks!" But it was *he* who had his wallet stolen on the bus—the irony too great for us not to smirk even as we sympathized with poor Mario, thankful for still having our own caches safely pocketed in that notorious city. Then, a week of wet gray days, hunched over uncomfortably on the large iron-frame bed in a cold, high-ceilinged room in our pensione. I passed the time reading Simone de Beauvoir's roman à clef, *The Mandarins*, a weighty tome I had dragged with me from home, intending to prepare myself for our visit to existentialist Paris later in the season. Camus, Sartre, Beauvoir—my holy trinity, each preached a freedom of action that mocked us as Val and I huddled together for comfort.

But then, escape from the chill, by boat across the bay to Sorrento, and farther south, to glorious Positano, a sun-warmed fishing village along the vertiginous Amalfi coast. The hillside was blanketed with orange trees, heavy with fruit and fragrance; on the beach below fishermen mended nets—fresh catch for dinner. For company, an upper-class, decadent British couple living on the hilltop, with whom we had cocktails that first week, an austere Belgian artist who came to see us every afternoon from neighboring Priano, and Giorgio, a local boy who took a fancy to me as a liberated American girl: "Take me to America," he crooned in my ear.

Ah, Giorgio, who taught me to drive his Vespa along the treacherous road that ran between Sorrento and Salerno, an adventure in itself. But when I lost control and crashed his scooter into the mountainside in a strategic maneuver to avoid going over the cliff, his ardor cooled.

On the road again: hitchhiking to Rome, where we roamed the city one night into the early morning hours with Shel Silverstein and Ramblin' Jack Elliott; Trieste, where we searched for signs of James Joyce; Florence, surprised when the affable man who drove us to Florence, going out of his way to show us the view from Fiesole, told us he was a fascist. Italy's political history suddenly made itself felt in my consciousness, briefly piercing my naivete. (I put my discomfort aside: we were in Florence for its beauty, its art, and its cookery). Valerie and I gorging ourselves on apple fritters on the Florentine streets and Renaissance painters in the galleries and churches, Florence yielding its sweet delights to mouth and eye.

Despite these pleasures, Valerie declared that Italy's focus on the past doomed it to irrelevance and decadence. She was ready to move on: "New York has energy; Italy with its face to the past, has nostalgia." True, perhaps. But I was into decadence, especially when it assumed aesthetic form. I stood entranced for hours before Michaelangelo's *David*; its muscular grace seemed the epitome of male beauty. And the Berninis at the Borghese! *Apollo and Daphne*, its curved lines intertwining so sensuously, such a contrast to *The Rape of Persephone*, with its bruising detail—Persephone's desperate yet futile struggle, her marble tears, her agonizing resistance as Pluto's brutal fingers dig into her body. Rape: the word means abduction, I know, but the Bernini sculpture unveiled the true meaning of abduction when a woman is its victim. Rape: always shadowing my travels, always feared, always resented. Still, I never felt threatened in Italy, Italian men more like boys, playing at being lotharios, always flirting. And why not? I'm good-looking, Valerie too—we could have been Italian!

But Germany! Italy was child's play for a hitchhiker; Germany seemed, at least initially, to offer a more sinister playing field. From the moment we hitched a ride across the border from Austria into Germany, I was anxious.

I had already had a disorienting experience skiing in Innsbruck when I heard someone scream "Achtung!"—the word itself awakening old nightmares motivated by World War II films—so that I froze on the slope, only to learn from another skier that Achtung means "pay attention, be careful." A friendly admonition, not a despotic command. Still, that momentary misrecognition had brought to mind my father's bitter prohibition: "Don' go to Germany, don' buy German, *Daitsche besterds!*" German: the very language *erschreckend*, deeply verboten. And yet there I was, radically defying my father by hitchhiking into Germany.

The driver who picked us up was friendly at first, but after we crossed the border, his attitude changed. Pointing to a barbed wire fence that ran alongside an abandoned military base on one side of the road, he sneered, "A gift of the Americans!" Taken aback by his tone, Valerie asked him to explain what he meant. As if now unleashed, he began to rant about how the countryside was pockmarked with American army bases. And then he said it: "Hitler made only one mistake. He lost!" As I took in his words, I heard again my father's commanding prohibition and felt a wave of apprehension. How many other Germans sympathized with Hitler's aims and bemoaned his defeat? Was the driver intentionally trying to provoke us? We rode the rest of the way in silence, Valerie and I occasionally exchanging nervous glances. An hour or so later, we entered Munich to the unexpected sight of bombed-out buildings. Block after block after block, gray skeletal structures stretched out before us like some vast urban cemetery, monumental remnants of the war Hitler had "mistakenly" lost. And though I knew it was wrong, I felt gratified.

But I found that our several weeks in Germany blurred my focus on its appalling history. Although I certainly didn't forget its responsibility for the brutal massacre of European Jews, including my own never-to-be-known grandparents, aunts, uncles, cousins, that horrendous past seemed somehow irrelevant as Val and I explored Munich's Schwabing, a bohemian neighborhood filled with "caves," clubs below street level carved out of bedrock where people like us, too young to accuse of war crimes, gathered for music, beer, and conversation. If I still shuddered involuntarily whenever I heard German being spoken, Munich offered an easy sociability as these young people welcomed us to their tables in English. Happily, without any trace of resentment, they told us about the existence of a US Army base nearby. It was welcome news.

In Italy, US Army bases had been our source of American cigarettes; we'd find a soldier who would buy us cartons at the PX. Expecting to raid the Munich base in the same way, the next day we found our way to the army base and the PX, but were short-circuited when a military policeman noticed us lurking and pulled us aside. When we identified ourselves as Americans wanting cigarettes, he sternly warned us we were breaking military law and asked us to prove we were Americans.

"Describe the difference between windows in the United States and windows in Europe," he said, crossing his arms and waiting for a response. Val and I couldn't imagine the "right" answer.

"The windows in the US go up and down; the windows in Europe go in and out," he said smugly unfolding his arms, and warning us not to return, he let us go. Giggling over such inanity but sorry to have lost our chance to buy cigarettes, we were about to leave when two soldiers, who had apparently witnessed our exchange, offered to buy them for us. Mission accomplished. And an evening date in Munich promised.

We met them again that evening as arranged: Special Services musician Don Ellis (famous decades later for his avant-garde jazz) and his buddy Ira Serkes. Most evenings, I went with Don to a jazz cave where I sat at a table with a few of his army buddies, listening to his mellow trumpet, while colored pills were passed around, and no one, least of all me, asked what they were before we swallowed them. I was totally into the experience, at one with the jazz mood. Valerie was not with me on those jaunts. She would have asked. She would not have approved.

A week or so later, after hugs and promises to write, Val and I set off for Heidelberg, both of us eagerly anticipating our visit to that historic city. To our surprise, Heidelberg seemed untouched by the war; its castle was still perched high on a slope overlooking the Neckar River; its eighteenth-century Old Bridge was still intact. We headed first for the university, making our way through the city's labyrinthine network of medieval buildings to the cafeteria, where we hoped to get a cheap meal and meet some English-speaking students. And there at the counter was Heinz. Tall, lanky, dark-eyed Heinz, with the longest, thickest eyelashes I had ever seen. Heinz, whispering German poetry in my ear the following evening as we walked along the romantic Philosophenweg, the river streaming moonlight below us. Heinz, speaking not the harsh guttural Prussian *"Achtung!"* that had assaulted me in Innsbruck, but whispering the soft *"Liebling"* and *"süßer Schatzi"* of Southern Germany as we lay on the narrow cot in his small attic apartment. Heinz, whose velvety *Ich* and *Du* lulled me into imagining myself a romantic heroine like Goethe's Charlotte, fated to leave him heartbroken.

But I was not a nineteenth-century German heroine. I was a twentieth-century Jewish New Yorker, and I couldn't deny feeling titillated as I listened to his German terms of endearment. Valerie, always more politically engaged than I, preferred arguing with his friend Gerhardt, a radical political activist, red-haired and red-faced, who hated America from the left rather than the right. Poetry and politics: Valerie and I each had had our own bittersweet dalliance with postwar Germany, and now we were leaving with warm feelings toward these boys who were driving us in their clunker of a car through the dark night to the city of light. Auf Wiedersehen!

An American in Paris

April 8, 1958

Dear folks,
I've settled myself in Paris, so you can write to me c/o American Express.
Valerie's gone to London to find work there. We're going to meet later
in the summer. I've got a nice little room in the student area, and an
office job as a clerk with the New York Herald Tribune. *Don't worry.*
All is well!

Love, Claire

Journal Entries

April 8: April in Paris. How lucky to have found a cheap room in the perfect neighborhood, near St. Germain as well as the Sorbonne. It's in a no-name residence hotel known only by the address, 9 Rue Git-le-Cœur. A concierge in the lobby, a bathtub on the first floor (reservations needed!), spiral staircase up to the second floor with a French toilet halfway up—two foot-placements in the floor, one on either side of a smelly hole—wash sink in my room, bed, table (I've bought an alcohol stove for heating water and simple cooking), one window overlooking the rooftops of Paris. And Allen Ginsberg and Gregory Corso next door!

I last saw Ginsberg in San Francisco last year. A group of us were sitting in a circle on the floor of an apartment in North Beach, with Ginsberg practicing a kind of extemporaneous poetry, a sort of vocal automatic writing while the rest of us passed around a joint and listened. Now I hear not Ginsberg's voice but his typewriter echoing down the hall. *Click, click, click, click.* Song of the typewriter. It thrills me to be living so close to the act of writing.

April 10: This morning Corso knocked on my door to borrow the proverbial cup of sugar. Good-looking, impish, but clearly a hustler with a thuggish demeanor, I think he's just checking me out as a potential sweetener.

"Where're you from?" he asked, leaning on the doorframe.

"New York," I answered, feeling a bit intimidated. He gave me an appraising look and then peered past my shoulder into the room, holding out a little metal cup. I took the cup, filled it from the canister on my table, and gave it back. "I'm working for the *New York Herald Tribune*," I offered, along with the sugar.

Lifting the cup as if toasting me, he told me that he and Ginsberg were going to give a reading Sunday at Le Mistral, the English-language bookstore facing Notre Dame just a few blocks away. "Come by," he said. I intend to.

Le Mistral is a gem, a sort of freewheeling literary salon, its labyrinth of rooms filled with books from floor to ceiling and funky couches to sprawl out on and read. Every Sunday, George Whitman, the tall, thin, bearded, and eccentric American expatriate owner of the store, holds literary events in the back room. A supporter of young writers, he has beef stew cooking on his stove upstairs most nights for those whom he especially likes. He even allows some of them to sleep in the store in return for working a few hours, sweeping the floors or tending the cash box. "Tumbleweeds," he calls us. I love the ambiance of this place, its gathering of readers and writers. I already know it will be a comfort to me when I feel lonely.

April 13: Today, it seemed as if all the Americans in Paris had heard about the reading by Ginsberg and Corso. I could see the crowd spilling out onto the esplanade even before I got there. I managed to squeeze and elbow my way into a spot in the middle from where I could—barely—see Ginsberg and Corso cavorting naked on a table at the far end of the room. Ginsberg was intoning a verse, then Corso began his own chant, both of them dancing in the buff, engaged in a poetic intercourse. When they finished their performance, George served fruit punch and cookies to the crowd as if this were a church social.

Afterward, I walked along the Seine, browsing among the used-book kiosks that line the street, frustrated by my meager ability to read the books sold there—even after studying French for four years. I found a copy of Baudelaire's *Les Fleurs du Mal*—side-by-side translations in French and English—and happily bought it.

April 15: Hurrah! I've changed jobs; from sitting inside the *Tribune* office while outside Paris burns incandescent, to being a hawker, selling newspapers *en plein air*. Forty papers to sell, fifty percent commission, and the pleasure of walking the streets of Paris. What a glorious job to have in this city. My route changes weekly. This week: the neighborhood near Notre Dame. "*New York Herald Tribune*," I shout at the top of my voice as I wander around seeking English-speaking readers. After work, the Odéon café, where I sit, have a Calvados, meet new English-speaking acquaintances, and feel myself a citizen of the world.

April 16: I'm learning about the multifarious life of the city, including the shadow side of urban life that has always attracted me. Selling papers, I meet the grifters who also work the streets. Yesterday, in front of the main entrance to Notre Dame, I met *un type*—a street-smart character who sells pornographic postcards. He told me the cathedral entrance is a particularly good spot for his trade, as it is for mine. He was there again today, and did a brisk business. *Merde alors!*

April 18: Today I had a brush with authority that threw me off balance. It was raining, so I ducked into the entrance of the Louvre and found myself among a crowd of frustrated tourists standing in the vestibule. Although I wasn't hawking, someone asked to buy a paper, then a few more people did the same, and suddenly, there was a uniformed guard in front of me, hand on hip, looking stern: "*C'est illégal de vendre des journaux ici.*" Before I could explain the situation in my broken French, he took my arm authoritatively and insisted I go with him to the director's office. So off we went down the hall. I didn't know what would happen, but I knew I had done something prohibited, perhaps even punishable. The guard pushed me into a thickly carpeted posh office, and there, at the far end of the room, sat the buttoned-up *directeur*. He fixed me with a cold stare and an accusation: "*Vous avez violé nos règles.*" I apologized nervously—"*je m'excuse*"—indicating as best I could that I had just stepped in from the rain—"*la pluie*"—for a few minutes and had been deluged—"*inondée*"— with eager customers. Without changing his expression, the *directeur* warned me never—"*jamais!*"— to come in again with newspapers. And then, he dismissed me.

Outside the Louvre, a fine mist drifted through the air. I took a deep breath, relieved not to have been arrested or fined. Hunching down to protect my papers against the light drizzle, I walked toward the corner, and my old sense of wounded innocence kicked in. It wasn't really my fault. I was unjustly accused. Yet a little voice inside my head whispered, "You knew you shouldn't have been selling papers in the Louvre. How pleased you were to do business there!"

April 20: *Quelle surprise!* I was selling papers in St. Germain when I ran into John Miller and his young Moroccan friend Larbi. "Come have some coffee with us," John said, and when I answered, "I can't. I have to sell my papers," he bought them all. Flattered by his gesture, I accepted his invitation.

I met John only yesterday at a "welcome" reception George gave for him at the bookstore. An American expatriate, he's just returned to Paris with Larbi—the name an anglophonic condensation of "El Arabi"—who seems to be Boy Friday to John's Crusoe. A curious pair. And so we three sat down at the café and talked. Or rather John talked, telling about his recent travels, punctuating his remarks by flicking ash off his cigarette. He and an Australian mathematician had owned a beryllium mine in Northern Rhodesia, sold it last year, and had been traveling for the past year on the profits. But the system they had worked out broke down in

Monte Carlo, something to do with a change in the roulette wheel; they lost everything.

I listened, taking as much pleasure in looking at him as listening. Fine sandy hair; deeply tanned and long, thin face; clear blue eyes; aquiline nose—very Anglo. With an exotic medallion around his neck, he looked very much the professional adventurer that he was.

John the adventurer

April 22: I met John and Larbi again, this time at the Odéon for a drink. John exudes a sense of adventure. Having spent ten years in the Middle East and North Africa, he speaks Arabic fluently and even has a diploma from an Egyptian college. In Tangier, he was part of an expatriate crowd that included William Burroughs, Brion Gysin, and Paul Bowles. A gay crowd, I know, and I wonder: is John also gay? He met Larbi, who claims to be the king of Morocco's nephew—or is it cousin?—in Casablanca last year. Are they lovers? Not an uncommon thing among young Arab boys and older Americans. No doubt that's why Burroughs and Bowles and

Ginsberg and the rest of that crew went to Morocco. Yet I can sense John's attracted to me. He seems so much more worldly than anyone I've known before. Anyway, we've agreed to meet again tomorrow at the Odéon, and I already feel a rush of anxious anticipation.

April 26: Last night John and I went to Le Mistral for one of George Whitman's "dinners" in his private quarters upstairs. George cooked a huge beef stew and about ten of us sat around on pillows on the floor eating and telling stories. George's story was the funniest: he has trained his dog to go around to the various butcher shops begging for bones, which the dog brings back for George to throw into his regular evening stews.

Afterward, John came up to my room, and we made love for the first time. He's very energetic and at the same time very tender. Afterward, we washed each other, standing next to the silly little sink that hangs from my wall. But this morning, as we were leaving the building, the concierge, Madame Rachou, scolded me: "*Vous devez dessineer les nuances dans votre chambre si vous êtes intime!*" Apparently, we had been visible through the window. But do I care? How uninhibited I am with John. How different this relationship is from any I've had before. Am I falling in love? I certainly feel myself opening to a more audacious freedom in his presence.

May 8: A bright and beautiful May day, and *la fête de la victoire*, V-E Day. Feeling my own *jour de la liberation* on my day off, I gathered up my *Les Fleurs du Mal*, bought a baguette, some cheese, and a bottle of wine at the grocer's, and with my little string bag holding my lunch, went to Île de la Cité. It was crowded with holiday flaneurs and families, but I found the perfect spot for picnicking on a concrete ledge overhanging the Seine. With the sun warming my face, I tore a piece of bread from the baguette, pulled out the cork from my wine bottle, took a long swig, and felt a glorious sense of well-being spread through me. The sunlight glimmered brightly on the Seine. An occasional excursion boat drifted by, disappearing under a bridge downstream. This was what I was after in Paris, the sense of living fully in the present moment, all my senses fine-tuned, on a perfect afternoon. I opened my *Fleurs* and began to read the French page, and there was a passage that I recognized as somehow belonging to me.

Mais les vrais voyageurs sont ceux-là seuls qui partent
Pour partir; coeurs légers, semblables aux ballons,
De leur fatalité jamais ils ne s'écartent,
Et, sans savoir pourquoi, disent toujours: Allons!

Without looking at the English language page I translated:

But the true travelers are only those who leave
Just to leave; hearts as light as balloons,
From their destiny they never deviate,
And, without knowing why, always say: Let's go.

I too had been saying *allons* without asking why, enjoying the sheer experience of moving from one place to another. But this afternoon was different. I was feeling—*comment dire?*—*une plenitude d'être*. And this fullness of being seemed an answer to the question of "why?" Such an ecstatic sense of harmony with my surroundings, as though I were flowing into what I was seeing—becoming part of the river, the sun, the bread and wine, without the tension that marks a division. Perfection. No need to go anywhere else.

May 10: Life in Paris has taken on a new shape. After work, John and I meet to drink mint tea on the rue de la Huchette, beer on Boul'Mich', or Calvados at the Odéon. I'm learning his habits, rolling my own cigarettes, and becoming familiar with the inexpensive bistros and bars in the Algerian *quartier* (though John is assured of economic survival—he gets a small veteran's disability pension for having been bayoneted when he was seventeen in the

Battle of the Bulge). Yesterday, we went to the public baths together. I greedily watched the huge tub filling with hot water, steam rising in our little cubicle, and then we stepped in and sank down together. Afterward, we returned to Git-le-Cœur and made love. As we were lying next to each other, I pleasurably exhausted, John reached for his Gauloises on the side table, lay back again, and after a few moments said, *"Post coitum omne animalium triste est."*

"What's that mean?"

"After sex, every animal is sad."

I thought about it for a moment. In a way it was true. How can one not experience a sad moment of separation, of something missing after such an intense union? But then an unwelcome thought: *Was* something missing? Was John unsatisfied with me as a woman? Was I an inadequate lover? Or did he want a man?

"I'm not sad," I said, uncertain of my own feelings now.

John turned to look at me and, as if tuning into my thoughts, confirmed what I'd once suspected: "You know, I've been gay . . . ever since high school. You're only the second woman I've had sex with." He gave me a searching look. I smiled in answer, surprised myself at my pleasure in now knowing for certain that he'd been homosexual.

"I'm glad you told me. . . . Actually, I don't mind your past at all."

And it was true. He assured me that his relationship with Larbi, who follows him around like an eager puppy, is not sexual, but I'll bet at some point it was. Still, thinking of John as bisexual feels liberating. I'm crossing boundaries into new terrain, where my former notions of sex don't apply.

"I've always been afraid of women," he said this morning, washing himself at the sink while I lay back in bed looking at his slim, hairless body, more boyish than mannish, though he's thirty-six years old. "I always connected with men more easily than with women. I never had sex with a woman . . . until this year. But then I met Zora—a Bulgarian princess—in Monte Carlo, and we ended up in bed. And I really enjoyed sex with her!" He shook his head as if amazed himself at having discovered heterosexual pleasure. "I wish I had known earlier how great women are!"

"Well, I'm pleased to know that I'm only the *second* woman you've had sex with."

And indeed, such exclusivity made me feel special. But then, my mother's voice popped into my head: *Men don't want damaged goods.* Was my own pride of place in his heterosexual life a reverse reflection of that crude proposition? Some primitive ownership instinct in women too? Zora was the first, and clearly still excites his imagination. Questioning my feelings, I discovered I was not jealous. I was grateful. This phantom lover had released him to me. And after all, she's a figure in his past.

"*J'ai faim. Mangeons,*" I said, and turned to reach for my own clothing.

May 12: A day that has really shaken me; I have to record it fully. After work, I met John at the Algerian café next to his hotel; we had an aperitif and then went up to his room. We were making love on the huge, creaky old iron-frame bed that takes up most of the room's space when there was a heavy-fisted knock on the door, and a deep voice demanding: "*Laissez-moi dedans.*" It was Hakim, the stocky Algerian whom I had met with John a few days ago. What was he doing here now? The knocking became louder and the voice more insistent. Alarmed by the vehemence of the knocks, I grabbed my clothes that were scattered on the floor while John got out of bed nervously and went to the door.

"Don't let him in," I whispered in a panic as I dressed hurriedly. The knocking grew louder.

"*Allez-vous en. Je vous verrai plus tard,*" John said, speaking to Hakim through the closed door. But the knocking grew still louder. "*Laissez-moi dedans, je sais ce que vous faites dedans là!*" The voice was gruff and adamant. "I'll get rid of him," John whispered and opened the door a crack, but before he could say another word, Hakim pushed his way in, lurched over to me, and grabbed my shoulders roughly, just as I was fastening the clasps on my sandals.

"*Attends, Hakim!*" John shouted in his ear, pulling at his arm, catching his attention long enough for me to wriggle free from his grip. I ran out the door and down the stairs with Hakim lumbering noisily behind me in clumsy pursuit, and John running behind him, calling out for him to stop.

In retrospect, it seems a bizarre scene from a silent comedy. There I was, running down the rue de la Huchette, pursued by a fat bear of a man, and behind him, my lover waving his arms. To cap it all, one of my sandals had fallen off. Not daring to stop, I ran with one shoe on my foot and one in my hand. And for one absurdist moment, Satchel Paige's famous remark came to mind: "Don't look back. Something might be gaining on you." When I finally did stop to look back, there was no one in sight—not Hakim, not John. Catching my breath, I tried to assimilate what had just happened: I had almost been raped by John's buddy.

Later, John came by Git-le-Cœur and apologized; he had finally caught up with Hakim and explained that I was his girlfriend, that I was not for sale or trade as Hakim had assumed. That scene wouldn't be repeated, John assured me. Just a misunderstanding. Not to worry. But I do. I don't understand the ground rules of this community I've entered. Or at least its Arabic component. How do I fit in? I've leapt blindly into a relationship without really knowing fully my part in it. Why had Hakim assumed he could intrude so readily into John's love life? Once again, I felt my innocence as an accusation.

May 13: The politics of Paris is changing. And the headlines on my newspapers today tell it all: "Pflimlin Wins."

Selling New York Herald Tribunes in Montparnasse

Nominated for prime minister, with rioting rampant in Algiers, Pflimlin has just won approval to fight the Algerian nationalists. But the French military are not satisfied; they want de Gaulle as president and they have local support: "Vive de Gaulle" is the new graffiti being scrawled on walls around Paris.

In the Algerian quarter, Arab men pass me on the streets, their faces set grimly. I feel their hostility directed toward me; I fear them now. Tensions are particularly high around Boul'Mich'.

"I got stopped today for my ID papers," Larbi said irritably when I met him and John after work at the Algerian café.

"Any Arab is a target for them," John said, flicking an ash from his cigarette. "Fucking gendarmes."

I nodded. My political sympathies are with the Arabs, but it's more complicated now. "Women too," I added. "I feel hassled just walking around here.... And not by the police, but by Arab men." Larbi shrugged his shoulders looking unconvinced, or was it unconcerned? He is, after all, an Arab man.

"No really, just coming here now, walking alone through this neighborhood," I continued, my outrage stoked. "I was afraid. You should have seen the angry looks I got from some of the Algerians I passed. A few weeks ago, there was nothing like that. But now, because I'm a Caucasian woman ..."

"You don't have to worry about the Arabs," John said, his voice tinged with a bitter irony. "The quartier is crawling with gendarmes now. Just try not to step on one." He flicked his ash again.

But it's not safe for me here now; and it's not just me who's at risk; all non-Arabic women are becoming targets in the quartier, subject at the very least to verbal assaults and, at most, as *Le Monde* reported yesterday, rape. Women's bodies have become the scapegoats for men's wounded pride.

May 26: A unity march against de Gaulle is planned for May 28; I probably will go, but I'm nervous. The gendarmes have a reputation for bashing heads with their truncheons, no holds barred. The gendarmes! Today, on the metro, in a rush-hour car packed with commuters, I felt someone touching my ass from behind. Forming the French words in my mind to say "stop or I'll call a policeman," I turned around and found myself *face en face* with a gendarme! Outrage swallowed. In a face-to-face confrontation with male authority, I seem unable to voice a protest. I'm afraid of their anger. *Lâche.*

May 29: Yesterday, the protest march—thousands taking to the street in an exhilarating show of unity, and no major violence. But to no effect. Today, the headlines show the result: the French President René Coty appealed to de Gaulle, whom he called the "most illustrious of Frenchmen," to become prime minister of the Fourth Republic. There's an element of Shakespeare's *Richard III* in the politics of this drama: "Please rule us or the ignorant masses will take over, and the nation will be destroyed!"

This afternoon, John, Larbi, and I sat at the Algerian café, drinking mint tea, enervated. Everyone around us looked glum. Rumor has it that if de Gaulle does not accept Coty's proposal, the army will seize power. The people I know, mostly expats, are depressed, and talking about leaving France.

John rolled two cigarettes and gave me one, his lips pursed in thought. "With de Gaulle taking over, we're in for a military dictatorship," he announced, lighting up first his, then mine. "More power to France and less to the Algerian people. Another chapter in colonial history."

Larbi sipped his tea and nodded in agreement, his forehead wrinkling with worry. "I bet it's not gonna be so easy to travel from Morocco anymore."

I took a deep drag of my cigarette and thought of my own disappointments. The political tensions sweeping through every corner of Paris are creating bitter conflicts among the intellectuals I admire. Sartre is badmouthing Camus because of his reluctance to fight against the colons—those of European ancestry who had settled in Algeria, among them Camus's own family. Camus wants some kind of political compromise. Sartre attacks him in the press for refusing to acknowledge the need for a violent revolution and calls him a coward. But Camus's public position against killing is the more profoundly moral one. I'm reading *The Rebel,* his long protest, in the name of a moral humanism, against the excesses of revolutionary fervor. "Every act of rebellion expresses a nostalgia for innocence and an appeal to the essence of being. But one day nostalgia takes up arms and assumes the responsibility of total guilt; in other words, adopts murder and violence." Prophetic and wise: the nostalgia for an impossible innocence inevitably leads to its violent antithesis. Camus is my moral mentor now.

June 25: I've quit the *Tribune,* Larbi's off to Morocco soon, and John says he has to go to Yugoslavia to say goodbye to Zora, the Bulgarian princess, who has sent for him by American Express. He's clearly eager to see her, and I can read between the lines of his hemming and hawing when I ask about his plans. Knowing he will sleep with Zora doesn't bother me much—or rather, I won't let it. John is not the sort of man who makes a virtue of monogamous relations, and if I'm honest with myself, I know that's part of what attracts me. His rejection of conventional social mores, his laid-back sexuality, his adventurous spirit—those qualities drew me into his orbit. When I'm with him he gives me the feeling that anything can happen. Anyway, he and Larbi and I are going to the World's Fair in Brussels for the Independence Day celebration before we three split up. Celebrating independence: an appropriate climax before everything changes.

Brussels, July 4, 1958

Dear Mom and Dad,

Having a wonderful time at the World's Fair in Brussels. I'm here with some friends, and we're camping out. The exposition is really fantastic. It's the world of the future seen today. I'm so lucky to have this educational experience. Tomorrow we return to Paris. Don't worry. I'm fine.

Love, Claire

Larbi and I camping outside of the 1958 Brussels World's Fair

July 6: John's gone. We plan to meet in Barcelona later in the summer. This break will be kind of a vacation for both of us. In the meantime, Valerie is coming to Paris, and we're off with friends to Pamplona for the running of the bulls, something I've wanted to do ever since I read *The Sun Also Rises*. For Hemingway, the bullfight was a ritual confrontation with death that tested the courage of men. Yet women often confront mortal danger in their daily lives without the ritualized acknowledgment of their heroism. In childbirth, for example, or in the ubiquitous threat of rape. But in such confrontations women are not seen as heroic, just long-suffering. To actively seek out and formalize that mortal encounter, like matadors do, in a ceremonial ritual is a powerful experience for the spectator as well. Barbaric, perhaps, but powerful and heroizing.

July 7: George asked me to mind the bookstore this afternoon. It was a hot and muggy day; there were only a few browsers in the store, but no sales. The cigar box where the money was kept had only some small change in it. When George returned and looked in the box, his face knotted up with anger. "Where's the money?" he asked sharply. "Nobody bought any books while you were gone," I explained, surprised at his question. Then he accused me of stealing money from the till! Where did that accusation come from? How could he think I was a thief? My insecurities flared up in a wave of hurt and anger, and I stormed out. Clearly, it was time to move on from my Paris episode.

An American in Spain

The Barcelona address that John had given me turned out to be a hotel of a certain sort in an old nineteenth-century building, located right off the main street—Las Ramblas—and not far from the waterfront. Checking in had been a sketch in itself:

"*Quiero alquilar un cuarto*, but *mi marido* may already be *aqui*," I told the desk clerk in broken Spanish. "*Hay* John Miller *registrado?*"

"*No* John Miller.... *Un cuarto por el día o rápidamente por hora?*" A room by the day or by the hour? Puzzled by this option, I looked around hesitatingly, and as if to clarify the situation, a heavily made-up woman sidled by in a tight leopard-print dress, followed by a short balding man, who kept close tabs on the leopard.

"*Por el día*," I answered and was given a key.

The room was actually quite comfortable though bizarrely outfitted. A huge bed dominated the space; on the ceiling above it was an ornate light fixture operated by a wall switch that had settings for different colored lights. The ceiling fixture was so strategically positioned that I imagined it a peeping device for someone on the floor above to have a view of the bed. On the wall alongside the bed was a horizontal mirror running the bed's full length. The most surprising feature of the room was the shower: near the center of the room, it had a circular floor drain under the showerhead. I had to search for the faucets to turn it on, but when I found them—hot water! That first night, alone in Barcelona, I took a shower, swallowed an amphetamine pill, and played with the colored lights. Red, yellow, blue, purple. The room was as yet still mine alone.

The past month had been filled with incident. After travelling with Valerie from Paris to Pamplona, where I had tried to run with the bulls but was pulled out of the street—*prohibido para una mujer!*—she and I hitch-hiked around northeastern Spain, Franco's rule evident in the frequent police checkpoints on rural roads. Ironically, we two anti-fascists hitched a ride with a unit of Franco's *Guardia Civil*.

Val and me in a Guardia jeep

But the high point of our wanderings in Spain was seeing Hemingway's beloved matador Antonio Ordóñez win two ears and a tail at a local bull-fight. In a crowded arena, bull and man engaged each other in a deadly dance, the bull, repeatedly provoked, heavily rushing the man, the man gracefully eluding him with his cape, until finally, they charged each other in a climax from which only the man emerged whole. With crowds shouting *Olé*, Ordóñez walked around the arena washed in their adoration, exhibiting his trophies, the ears and tail.

Val and I ended our Spanish adventures together on a train, crowded with people and caged chickens, that took us to the Costa Brava, Spain's low-cost Riviera for a few days' respite. With Valerie gone back to the States, I was now on my own again, waiting in Barcelona to meet up with John.

I wandered aimlessly around the city for the first few days. Unlike

Paris, a city familiar to me from literature even before I settled into its bohemian quartier, Barcelona was an unknown quantity. I had no access to its cultural life, no way of making the kind of personal connection I had found so easy in Paris. My spirits were lifted somewhat after I came upon a bar near the waterfront with a *simpatico* clientele of Anglophones. But the weight of my solitude bore down on me each day.

A week after my arrival, a card arrived at the Barcelona American Express office from John telling me he wouldn't get to Barcelona for another two weeks. Another two weeks! Trying not to imagine what John and Zora were doing or where they were, I determined that being alone in Barcelona could also be an adventure if I made better use of the time. So, even though I wasn't really in the mood for touring, I bought a guidebook and spent much of the next week visiting Barcelona's architectural gems: Gaudí's unfinished church, La Sagrada Família—like a sand castle shaped from mud-drippings yet cavernously awesome; its secular counterparts, the Casa Mila and the Casa Batlló, Gaudí's apartment houses; and other architectural structures whose curves, arches, and bizarre embellishments suggested residences more fabulist than real. I walked down to the harbor at the foot of Las Ramblas, relishing its open-air food stalls with their succulent fruits—melons, figs, wild strawberries, apricots—and displays of exotic fish and shellfish. Behind the stalls I could see ships slipping in and out of the busy port on their way to unknown places. All in all, a delight to the senses and the imagination. In the evenings, the Anglo-bar was nearby for company.

On one of those dazzling Mediterranean days, the sky flecked with an occasional cloud, the sun warming my bare arms, I stopped at a fruit stall to buy some luscious-looking purple cherries when a crown of throbbing neon lights appeared before my eyes, blotting out parts of my vision. Before I could question this sudden iridescence, I sank into blackness. When the light returned, I found myself lying on the ground near the fruit stall surrounded by worried-looking bystanders, a stranger patting my face with a wet cloth. I struggled to get up, and assuring everyone in my primitive

Spanish that I was fine, "*estoy bien, gracias, estoy bien*," I tottered away in a state of confusion to my hotel.

What had caused me to faint? And why was I here alone, still waiting for John? I felt a surge of anger; anger led to determination. The following day, I went to the Barcelona maritime office and checked out the various boat passages being offered. The Balearic Islands, reputedly so beautiful, were close by, just across the water. Mallorca was apparently the most popular island, the ticket agent said, Ibiza less so. And so, I bought a ticket to Ibiza. *Allons.*

On the boat to Ibiza, one of the sailors, an affable young man named Alejo, started a conversation with me, and by the time we reached the island, I had accepted his offer to stay at his mother's house for a night or two. He would sleep on the boat, he assured me, but his family would welcome me as a guest. With the sun beating down on my bare head and my rucksack on my back, I followed him from the harbor up a winding narrow stone street, its whitewashed houses stretching from the beachfront upward toward the sky. The higher we climbed, the poorer the houses became.

Alejo's home at the top of Ibiza

At the very top, Alejo paused before one of a small group of earthen huts overlooking the sea. "Here is my home," he said, and disappeared through a doorway. I followed and entered a one-room structure, furnished sparely with two wooden chairs; a small table, on which stood a pitcher and some cups; and, stacked in a corner on a small bench, some plates and a basin. On the hard-packed dirt floor was a large mattress covered with a colorful spread.

Although no one was there as we entered, almost immediately, a small, heavyset woman—Alejo's mother, apparently—came in with a load of wash, followed by Alejo's grandfather and younger sister. All three lived in this one bare room! I had never experienced this measure of poverty, yet to my surprise, no one seemed downcast. Instead, smiling at me, each warmly welcomed me as a guest. His *abuelo*, a wizened old man with a sparse gray beard and bright blue eyes, pulled over a wooden chair for me to sit on and offered me some water. When Alejo told them I would be staying for a night or two, Abuelo insisted that I sleep on the mattress while they slept on the dirt floor; despite my protest, they would have it no other way.

Filled with guilt for the trouble I was causing and for the hypocrisy of my position—I wasn't poor, just out for an adventure—I tried to back out of their invitation. But "they would take it as an insult," Alejo said when I voiced my wish to leave, and so I acquiesced, determined to stay only the one night. After we had all exchanged some broken-sentence, hand-sign pleasantries, Alejo and I walked back down the hill to the beach. For an hour or so, we sat on the sand and chatted under a blazing sun, our conversation punctuated by long pauses. In the late afternoon, I watched him return to the boat.

I sat by myself on the beach for a long while, staring out into the distance until the sky began to spread out duskily, its violet hues tamping down the flames of the Mediterranean sunset across the water. It was the time of day that always hollowed out my spirits. How many late afternoons had I felt a purple melancholy washing over me, making me long for... I knew not what exactly. For some profound intimacy? For comradeship? For the embrace of community? Traveling was exhilarating, meeting the unknown, seeing how other people live. But sitting there on the beach, I felt so adrift, so alone. Perhaps that was the point—to experience the existential isolation of the self as fully as I could and drink it in. Or was the point *to imagine* drinking it in? Sometimes, I felt as if I were the heroine of a fiction written by someone else.

Then, as darkness gathered on the beach, I roused myself, walked over to the nearby outdoor café attached to the small harborside hotel, had an aperitif and a small fish sandwich, and then climbed back up the hill to the little hut. The sun, sand, and climb had exhausted me. After some polite exchanges through gestures and broken Spanish with Alejo's mother and sister—his abuelo was not in sight—I lay down on their mattress and immediately fell asleep.

In the morning, Abuelo brought me a small basin of water to wash up; such generous hospitality embarrassed me. Even as I thanked him, I felt how undeserving I was of his attentions and took my leave as soon as I could. Down at the seaside, I found a spot on some rocks and, quickly putting on my swimsuit, walked into the warm waters of the Mediterranean and took the plunge. Sunning myself afterward on the rocks, my mind emptied of all thought, time passed.

Later that afternoon, I returned to the outdoor café and mingled with several Anglos sitting at a table. A party was being planned for the evening. I went with two of the men to the wine shop down the street and, rummaging through an old wooden barrel in a corner of the shop, found an ancient bottle of absinthe, encrusted with dust and cobwebs. Delighted by my discovery—absinthe was no longer legal in Europe; this was a treasure!—I bought it for a few pesetas, and together with the others returned to the hotel to party. At some point, I must have lost consciousness, for I awoke the next morning in a strange hotel room, fully clothed and apparently intact. I never knew whose room it was. Returning to the marina, I waited for the next boat to Barcelona, hoping that Alejo would not be on it. I needed to clear my head.

Ibiza, July 27, 1958

Dear folks,

Isn't Ibiza a beautiful island! The city is built on a mountain; the streets are not paved and wind in and out, the path occasionally broken by steps that just keep going up. I'm staying at the very top. The sun shines always, and the sea is a clean deep blue. Today I spent the day sunning on the rocks of a lagoon, swimming and talking with some English friends. Don't worry, I'm fine.

Love, Claire

Waiting, waiting, still waiting for John, I decided to buy a Vespa, but not in Spain. I would hitchhike to the factory in Genoa! A reason was not hard to find: by buying it at the factory, I was avoiding the shipping costs. Besides, being alone now, I needed my own transportation. In any case, going to Italy suddenly seemed the order of the day. Excited by the idea of getting back on the road, I hitched a ride as far as Cannes in the sidecar of a motorcycle of an American I had met at my Barcelona bar, and was dropped off at the Riviera.

On the Riviera road

The Riviera! Everything around me shimmered with fierce color, and remembering the fauvist paintings I had seen in Paris, I understood what those "wild beasts" saw here: it was the brilliant quality of the light that made the Riviera a magical place. As if to confirm its magic, when I waved my bent thumb at a car, it immediately stopped. I said thanks to a middle-aged man at the wheel wearing a bathing suit, hauled in my rucksack and guitar, and we took off along the winding coastal road. He was, he told me in perfect English, Dutch and was vacationing with his family in Nice. "I'm from New York . . . going to Genoa to buy a scooter," I told him, and turned to look at the passing landscape: the saturated greens and reds of the foliage, the bright whites of the houses reflecting the sunlight, the differing shades of blue in sea and sky. After a few moments, I caught sight of something in my left peripheral vision, a wriggling movement on the driver's side. I turned my head toward the Dutchman and saw that he was trying to take off his bathing suit while he was driving!

"What do you think you are doing? Stop the car immediately."

Looking abashed, the Dutchman nervously pulled up his waistband and brought the car to a stop on the shoulder of the narrow road. I quickly opened the door and, pulling out my rucksack and guitar in one swell movement, slammed the door shut. Safely standing on the road again, I scolded him in a voice dripping with contempt: "You should be ashamed of yourself!" The car quickly took off. There I was, on the Riviera, but the light had dimmed.

John arrived a few days after I returned to Barcelona from Genoa on my shiny new Vespa, having driven it across the Riviera from Italy to Spain with my gear strapped onto the back of it.

My new Vespa fully loaded

"I barely managed to keep it upright long enough to ride off the factory floor," I told John, pleased to see his admiring look as he walked around the scooter.

"That's great, Kitty.... I'm really glad you bought it. Now we can go where we want without any hassle."

That evening, we were sitting in bed, drinking beer and smoking. The colored lights were on.

"Where did you and Zora go?" I asked, trying to ignore those little jealous pinpricks I was feeling.

"First Athens, and then the monasteries on Mount Athos. It's open only to male visitors, so I had to cut her hair; she wore my clothes." John grinned impishly, obviously pleased with remembering the deception. I was less than pleased.

"We climbed up a rocky cliff to the top of the mountain—really a hard climb, but she managed it. When we got to the top, the monks welcomed us and gave us food and drink. And then they gave us a tour of the ancient manuscripts. . . . They really thought she was a boy! We spent the night there in a place called—listen to this—the 'Garden of the Virgin!'" He laughed, and took a swig from the bottle. He clearly enjoyed the masquerade more than the medieval treasures, and I thought again of his homosexual past. How he loved to play with sex roles!

Shifting our conversation to my own return trip from Genoa, I told him about putting my sleeping bag down near the roadside in the dark that first night, and waking up the next morning to find grapes hanging over my head. I had camped in a vineyard.

"But then, I pulled down a grape and put it in my mouth, and it was sour. Yuck!"

"Must have been grapes for making wine, not for eating," John said.

"I guess so. Big disappointment. Sour grapes." I smiled at my own witty remark, and then continued, now bragging, "But later I picked up a hitchhiker on the road, an English student from Oxford, who turned out to be the nephew of Churchill's doctor. We stopped at his uncle's villa on Cap-d'Ail. His aunt taught me how to put the milk in tea. Put it in first. Never knew that."

John said that was a silly rule that no one followed.

Finishing our beers, we sank back into the bed for our reunion and played with the colored lights. Red. Blue. Yellow. It was good to have him back.

At the end of the week, he said, "Let's go to Morocco."

I said, "Yes, let's go."

Allons.

The Road to Morocco

With John on the back seat of the Vespa directing me, and the warm wind in my face, we headed south *en plein air* toward Algeçiras, passing through dusty villages baked white in the hot southern sun, across a rolling landscape covered by olive trees whose crooked trunks extended into the distance. Occasionally we stopped at a café to refresh ourselves, and I bought a postcard to send home. Urged on by John, I drove the small-wheeled Vespa into the kind of rugged terrain I would never have dared on my own, holding my breath up steep, rock-strewn slopes that I could barely negotiate. I even drove up a cliffside to visit one of the many cave-like homes that had been hewn out of the sides of the rocky hills along our route.

Cave homes in Spain

Driving at night was the most nerve-wracking part of our trip, with me peering into the darkness, praying there was no unseen obstacle ahead. Then one night, going forty miles an hour in the rural darkness, my small Vespa headlight suddenly revealed a truck parked in the middle of the road, invisible until the moment before we smashed into it. Seconds later, I found myself lying on the road with the scooter on top of me, and John nowhere to be seen. "John," I called out several times, terrified that he lay somewhere in the darkness, dying.

A reedy voice answered from the void: "I'm here. . . ." And as I struggled out from under the scooter, a straggling figure slowly emerged from the darkness across the road—John, zigzagging unsteadily toward me. From behind the truck, the driver appeared, wringing his hands while repeatedly apologizing in Spanish for the accident. He offered to take us and the badly dented scooter in his truck to his house where he could fix it. We spent the rest of the night recovering from the trauma while the driver restored the damaged scooter to health.

Did I think twice about stopping this itinerant life as John and I sat up discussing our brush-with-death experience? Not at all. Instead, I felt more alive than ever, enjoying not only the adrenaline rush, but the boost to my ego for not flinching from our close call. The greater the risk, the more powerful I felt for having survived it.

Of course, sometimes the situation got too hairy for both of us—like the evening we stopped in Granada and sought out a small bar in one of the backstreet alleys. At first the men in the bar were welcoming, showing me how to squirt the wine into my mouth from a bota while holding the leather bag up high, everyone laughing as I missed my mouth a few times before mastering the skill. But as the alcohol flowed, they turned surly, whispering among themselves, leering at me, frowning at John. Suspecting that we were now in treacherous territory, John and I nudged each other and turned to leave. Too quickly, one of the men blocked our path to the door, and then real terror swept over me. Luckily, we managed to dodge his arms and run out of the bar. Racing down the dark cobbled backstreets of Granada pursued by our drinking companions, we barely reached the Vespa in time to escape a nasty situation.

So what was I doing? Still proving myself macho? Surely something more complicated than that, for although both John and I had just faced a serious threat, I felt far more vulnerable than John. Rape shadowed *my* road, not his. I thought of Camus's notion of life in overdrive—his belief that living intensely in the moment was a celebration of life, and a tribute to the free spirit. I had taken that credo to heart. Why shouldn't my life also be a tribute to the free spirit? Yet I was learning that, as a woman, I wasn't so free to act. Indeed, although John was always on the backseat as I drove us through southern Spain on the road to Morocco, it was he who directed our journey; I was his agent. And though I didn't connect the dots at the time, I was tethered on a deeper level, by unconscious bonds I thought I had dispensed with. Wherever and whenever I could, I bought picture postcards and sent them home to my parents.

Valencia is beautiful. They make a famous dish here that I tried last night. Don't worry, I'm fine.

Malaga is so interesting, I'm fine. Please don't worry.

Now I'm in Tangiers, Morocco. What an exotic city and right on the sea, with beautiful boulevards. I'm learning a lot and doing fine. Please don't worry.

Love, Claire

Crossing the Straits of Gibraltar

Palm trees lined the wide boulevards of Tangiers. The Mediterranean glittered in the bright sunlight, whitewashed houses spread out in the distance, and framing the central square were the cafés where John and I often sat drinking mint tea and inhaling the atmosphere. The air was soft and fragrant with cardamom and cumin and mint and, not least, *kief*, the local name for marijuana, which we smoked in pipes or ate as hashish candy, wrapped in brown paper and sold on street corners. John introduced me to his young Moroccan friend, Ali, and we three often wandered through the narrow mazelike backstreets and alleyways that formed the medina, the labyrinthine old quarter where animals and pedestrians shared the streets. I gawked at the exotic fare in its markets, and inhaled the acrid smell of leather being cured with camel urine. I bought a large leather bag, not knowing, when I returned to the States a year later to teach, that its distinctive odor would pervade my classroom.

I could never have explored Tangiers so freely on my own. I learned that lesson the first week we were there while waiting for John on a street corner near the medina. He was late, and I was getting impatient, when a policeman came by and, speaking brusquely, said something to me in Arabic. Without understanding, I merely smiled in response. That seemed to arouse his ire, and raising his voice, he threw more words at me while I shrugged my shoulders, trying to indicate my lack of comprehension. Fortunately, John arrived before matters became too heated and clarified the situation: because I was standing on a street corner in Western dress, I was taken for a prostitute and was about to be arrested for not moving along.

I quickly learned that in this culture, except for prostitutes, women were kept, and kept themselves, behind closed doors. Women were absent from public gathering spaces, and to some extent, from their private quarters as well. So I discovered when I was invited to dinner at Ali's home, and found myself sitting on a floor cushion alongside the men in his family, learning to eat with my fingers while Ali's mother and sister served us all a delicious couscous and then stood back and waited, smiling.

"Why aren't the women eating?" I asked.

"They will eat what remains in the kitchen after we finish," Ali explained while the women smiled and nodded. I nodded too, shifting uncomfortably on my cushion, stealing occasional guilty glances at the women's faces as they bent to offer me more food. As an American woman, I was being treated like a man. Women, real women, in the eyes of the Moroccans, served. And then I remembered that my mother too always served meals to my father, brother, and me, but she herself rarely sat down at the kitchen table to eat with us. In fact, there were only three chairs at that table. Closing my eyes, I envisioned a train of women stretching out into the distance, thousands of them, walking up a long unpaved road in Middle Eastern dress, wearing sandals, carrying heavy bundles wrapped in colorful rags, all trailing arduously through the dust smiling.

On another day, goaded by John, Ali gave me a man's djellaba to wear and I, playacting the boy, wandered freely through the network of streets in the medina with both of them, experiencing a new kind of freedom. And I remembered that John had also goaded Zora to playact the boy. As we three posed for a photograph in our Moroccan dress, it seemed as if we were all characters in a play secretly directed by John.

In male Moroccan dress with John and Ali

After a while, we climbed up to the casbah, the ancient fortification that loomed high above the medina. Since I was in disguise, John suggested we all go to a nightclub he knew, secreted among the stone buildings. We entered an arched doorway and passed through a curtain into a dimly lit space crowded with tables arranged in a semicircle; a spotlight lit up a few musicians playing and two young boys belly dancing in the center. Looking around, I saw that the club was filled with fat middle-aged men who were almost salivating, so enthralled were they by the hairless young belly dancers who writhed sensually for their delectation. *Decadent*, I judged silently, but merely asked: "Why are there are no female belly dancers?"

"That's only in Egypt," John informed me. "Here in Morocco, it's young boys who belly dance, not women."

Surprised, I wondered at the implications. Did young men in Morocco seek out pubescent boys for sex because young girls weren't available, and then switch to women when they married? But what of the men in this club who were clearly turned on by the male dancers? Why was there so much gay desire circulating in Morocco? I thought of John's easy midlife switch from men to women. Was it as easy here for Moroccan men? Was bisexual desire more natural than heterosexual? And what, I wondered, did the young unmarried women do with their sexual desire? What was their outlet? I remembered the women I had seen at Ali's, their faces disappearing behind closed doors. What did they really feel about my presence at the table? Were they resentful? Or were they satisfied with their separate sphere? And did gay desire also circulate there?

Terminus

Casablanca, a name conjuring the romance of exile. Tough Humphrey Bogart, an outlier operating on the margins of society, showing his soft side and surrendering his beloved Ingrid Bergman for the greater good. Now that I myself was actually in Casablanca with John, a troubling realism had weakened the exilic fantasy: we had run out of money. John was perfectly calm about this small fact; his disability check was expected any day now; he was accustomed to such setbacks. In the meantime, I learned to accommodate to the tactics of hobo survival: we slept on hard benches in the railroad station; we picked up cigarette butts from the ground, rescued the tobacco, and used it to roll our own cigarettes; we sat in cafés and waited until the diners at a nearby table left, and then discreetly shifted our seats and ate their leftovers.

Admittedly, I found this vagrant life with John no real hardship; indeed, I felt myself playing out a part in a curiously fascinating fiction of survival, one a lot easier than my two-day solo trip on my Vespa from Tangiers to Rabat to meet up with John the previous month. Then, after a day's windy drive along the highway, I had spent a night en route in a shabby roadside bedsit, smashing bedbugs with one of my sandals and watching my own blood spurt out. *That* was hard; *this* was interesting. Yet in both cases, somewhere in the back of my mind was a little finger wagging: *You are only playing at survival; you've got an exit cord that you can use if you need to.* When I allowed myself think about it, I knew that my ability to live under miserable conditions for weeks, even months at a time, came precisely from its being a voluntary fiction with a temporal limit. How long could I play at being a tough heroine? At being Kitty?

In the nick of time, hunger pangs jabbing at us both, John's disability check arrived, and we were restored to relative comfort. As we were celebrating our economic revival at a restaurant, John took my hand and said: "Let's go to the Canary Islands and get married."

Without thinking, I answered: "I can't. I have to go to my cousin's wedding in New York." Words spontaneously erupting from some internal directive. Get married? No, not me. At least not now. Marriage! What would that mean with John ... or anyone? The closing of a door? Or just a different order of experience from what I had been enjoying with John? Marriage was somehow more real, less desired.

Apparently, I was going to my cousin's wedding in order to avoid my own. In any event, it was time to end this journey. It was November, and I was ready to go home to the familiar rather than continue with the exotic, at least for a while. John had no real objections; he said he too was thinking of returning to the States; this was not the end of our relationship. We planned for my departure with some gusto. I had to leave my scooter in Casablanca, but John promised to ship it to me with some surprises in the spare tire. He himself would follow in the spring. But did I want him to? I still didn't know my own mind.

November 2, 1958

Dear Mom and Dad,

Please send three hundred dollars, Western Union, Casablanca, to cover the cost of my return to New York. Hope to be back in time for Rita's wedding. See you soon.

Love, Claire

5

"Go West, Young Woman": In Search of Myself (1959–1963)

The search for meaning, much like the search for pleasure, must be conducted obliquely.

Irvin Yalom

Imagining Max:

How can somebody so smart be such a stupid. What does she know about the world? Sure, she knows books, knows how to read and write better than me. But she doesn't know nothing like what I know. I look at her and see my sister, Chaia. The teacher. She was smart too, and stupid. She wouldn't leave Poland when I went. I said, you should leave too, but she said no. A teacher, some smartie. A stupid! A communist who said she had to stay and teach the children. I sent her a letter—come to America, I wrote, come and be safe. But no, she had to stay in Poland for the sake of the children. Not even her kids. And look what happened. She got let go from her job—fired, and then burned with the rest. The whole family. Burned. Ashes. So, she's lost. And my daughter, also lost. A trumbernick, not married, who knows what she does—a bum. My daughter. How I love her. How she's disappointed me. What will happen to her? I want her to be somebody but not to shame me.

121

Imagining Dina:

I don't understand her. What's wrong with her? She's an educated girl, but she travels around like a trumbernick. Oy, oy, I'm afraid for her. Does she smoke dope? God knows what she does. And she don' care if she's not married. I don' understand. What kind of life is that? Alone. No children. No husband. What is she thinking? I tried to fix her up with the syrup salesman, Sammy, a nice man. She's not getting any younger. My god! She had so many chances. She had such a good boyfriend in high school. Oy, Artie, so handsome, he was going to be a dentist! But she threw him away and went on the wrong track. What does she want? Tochter, tochter. *What will become of you?*

Getting There

I was stopped at a traffic light near the George Washington Bridge, at the beginning of my cross-country trip to Berkeley. I'd lied to my parents about how I was getting there. "Oh, Ma, don't worry, I'm riding with some friends from the West Bronx who are driving to California in a big station wagon. I'm putting the Vespa in the back of their wagon." The words slipped out easily, though I wondered whether my mother believed me, so suspicious was her expression. My father's face was impassive.

The truth was I was taking off on my own on the Vespa to meet John in Cleveland, his hometown. John, the prodigal son, had actually returned to the USA. He had sent my scooter back from Casablanca in the early spring, the spare tire filled with hashish candy and Moroccan silver jewelry, and now had himself returned and was visiting his parents for the first time in ten years. We had spent a very John week together in New York when he first arrived: eating free lunches in sleazy Bowery bars—hard boiled eggs and some kind of chopped fish salad I trustingly put on a cracker and swallowed—and sleeping in a squalid little hotel on Eighth Avenue that was obviously used by prostitutes. (We had to climb up a narrow staircase with a fold-over desk at the top, at which the "manager" sat, blocking entrance to the floor until he was paid.) At week's end, I had agreed to drive my scooter to Cleveland to meet him a month later at the home of his parents. Our plan was to get a driveaway station wagon in Cleveland, put the scooter in the back, and make our way to the West Coast.

But then, as I was leaving the city, who pulled up next to me at the traffic light: Irving, the corner druggist from my neighborhood! Irving, who knew me, knew my parents! He rolled down his car window and, looking at me quizzically, asked, "Where are you going on that scooter?"

"I'm meeting some friends in New Jersey for a cross-country drive to California," I said, quickly composing another lie, but inconsistent with the one I'd told my parents. Acting as if it were the most natural thing to be sitting on my scooter near the entrance to the George Washington Bridge with a knapsack and guitar strapped to the rear seat, I smiled. Irving stared at me curiously, his bushy eyebrows forming two horizontal question marks. The light changed to green.

"Bye, Irving." And I took off, hoping he wouldn't say anything to my parents about seeing me, knowing he probably would.

May 5, 1959

Dear Mom and Dad,

Arrived in Cleveland, an interesting city where my friends have family, so we'll stay here a few days. All is well.

Love, Claire

John answered the door when I arrived. Mrs. Miller stood behind him. A blue-haired, straight-backed member of the Daughters of the American Revolution, her mouth forced into a tight smile, she moved forward to greet me: "So nice to have you here. John's told us a good deal about you."

Her blue eyes were cold as she sized me up, this stranger who had snared her son, but unwilling to antagonize him, her mouth held onto the smile. He'd been away for ten years, and this girl was the reason he was back. Mr. Miller, a gray-haired, mild-mannered midwesterner, appeared from a room off the hallway, book in hand. He greeted me with a tentative smile, and after a brief, polite exchange of pleasantries about my trip, disappeared back into the room he came from, like Mr. Bennett in *Pride and Prejudice*, yielding the fort to his wife. Holding on tightly to my rucksack, I felt it getting heavier as we three remained standing in the hallway.

"Where shall I put my things?" I asked as sweetly as I could. Mother Miller started to point to a room down the hall across from the living room. But John had no taste for her directions: "Kitty and I will sleep in my room upstairs."

Clenching her thin lips, she tried weakly to object.

"Dear, I don't think that's appropriate."

"That's what we're gonna do, Mother," John answered with a look of annoyance, and taking my rucksack from me, closed the question. I was uncomfortable in the role of strumpet, but John insisted. Clearly, he'd fought something like this battle before.

The next day, Mother Miller took me to the local church garden show. As we strolled down the aisles between rows and rows of bright, flowering plants, she gave me a little horticulture lesson: "These are peonies, these coneflowers, and here are the annuals; generally they are much more color-ful than the perennials. . . . I'm especially fond of the pansies—but you do have to plant new ones every year." I listened, mildly amused to find myself at a church garden show. But when we encountered another blue-haired lady, and Mother Miller introduced me as "Kitty, John's little Jewish friend from New York," I was no longer amused. Nevertheless, I smiled.

Two days later, John and I were driving across the United States, scooter stashed in the back of the station wagon we'd contracted to deliver to San Francisco. As the states unfolded their local treasures on billboards—a corn palace in South Dakota, a Western saloon tilting on its foundation in Wyoming, a trading post in Utah, each community trying to capitalize on its resources—John, a natural collector of curiosities, wanted to oblige them. In Nevada, the image of a colorful snake captured his attention. "Stop at the Desert Zoo," the billboard ordered. We stopped.

"Let's buy a California king snake," John remarked casually as we watched a multicolored, graceful reptile about two feet long slither up the side of its cage.

"Buy a snake?" I was intrigued. Snakes had always fascinated me. As a child vacationing in the Catskills, I was one of the kids who caught garter snakes, killed them, and took their skins back to the city as trophies. Now here I was considering not killing but tending one.

"They are great pets," John said. "They eat only once a month—they swallow a mouse and then take a long rest—and you can play with them; they won't hurt you; they're constrictors and can climb up almost any surface." Thirty minutes later we left the "Zoo" with a California king snake patterned like a Navajo rug in ivory, black, and brown. John promised to build a terrarium for it when we settled into our digs in Berkeley.

Our cross-country pilgrimage ended in a San Francisco suburb, where we delivered the station wagon, newly washed. Then, with John once again on the backseat of the Vespa and the snake in a box on our luggage rack, we continued down the coast to Pacifica where John's brother Richard lived. As I wove along the coastal road, its terra-cotta sand hills bordering us on either side, their rocky soil sprouting a hardy welter of low-growing blue and yellow blooms, I felt once more the wonder of the West and opened myself anew to its raw power.

Arriving windswept at his brother's house, I parked the Vespa while John walked quickly to the front door and knocked excitedly. He had spoken of his brother Richard frequently, but when the door opened, I was taken aback by the strangeness of his face, paralyzed on one side, mouth twisted aslant. But his eyes twinkled with pleasure as he awkwardly embraced John and welcomed us with a big misshapen grin. For the rest of the afternoon, I could see how much the brothers were enjoying this reunion. Richard brought out the beer, and then, gazing at each other with obvious affection, both of them laughingly recalled anecdotes from their past while I listened, happy for John even though there was little room in the conversation for me.

But if Richard was delighted to see John, his wife Cory, a large thickset woman from the Midwest, clearly was not. And I fared no better in her good graces. Not only did Cory barely acknowledge John's presence when she finally entered the room an hour or so later, she quite blatantly ignored me, looking away whenever we crossed paths. She did, however, make her voice heard—and overheard. "I want them out of here," Cory shouted loudly that first night while John and I listened from the next room.

"Why is she so antagonistic to me?" I asked in the morning as John and I sat in the kitchen by ourselves having toast and coffee. I had my suspicions.

"It's because you rinsed your contact lenses in the sink," John said.

"What? You're kidding! That's crazy. There must be another reason." I paused, and then asked, "Is it because I'm Jewish?"

"No, of course not, it's just that she's ... I don't know, she's peculiar.... She didn't like your rinsing your contact lenses in her sink."

I didn't buy that. Having just traveled across what seemed to me clearly a Christian Midwest, I had become sensitized to my Jewish difference. Was I getting paranoid, seeing antisemites everywhere? More probably, Cory's antagonism toward us stemmed from our free-floating lifestyle, I tried to assure myself. After all, Richard was once also a light traveler.

"Cory must be worried about our influence on Richard," I told John, but my suspicions about her remained a stubborn irritant. We left for Berkeley the next day.

Being There

John and I rented a small semi-furnished apartment in an old Berkeley Victorian. Within the week, John had built a terrarium for our new pet, we bought a mouse to feed the snake, and I stared in fascination as the snake cornered the mouse, opened its jaws wide, and swallowed the mouse whole. Only a bulge could be seen as the mouse traveled down the snake's serpentine body, growing smaller as it moved along. I felt a pang of pity, but that was carnivorous animal life, wasn't it? "Nature, red in tooth and claw," as Tennyson had written. I was ready to accommodate.

We also adopted a long-haired black kitten with yellow eyes from the animal shelter. John named it Blackie after a London friend of his. It was a darling creature, tiny and defenseless-looking, yet much to my dismay, John enjoyed terrorizing the poor thing. He would pick up my guitar and, strumming it loudly, chase the kitten around the apartment or toss little Blackie up in the air and, laughing with delight, watch it somersault down to the floor, landing wide-eyed on its four little paws.

"John, you're scaring the poor cat. Don't do that!"

"Cats always land on their feet, Kitty. No need to worry."

John had another playmate and I a familiar totem. We were now a household.

Bohemia in Berkeley: 1959–61

Berkeley's bohemia existed on two streets—Telegraph Avenue, where alcohol was banned because of its proximity to the university, but coffee shops thrived as meeting spots, and San Pablo Avenue, which boasted two well-known pubs, the Blind Lemon and the Steppenwolf, both far enough away from the university for beer and wine to be sold. The Blind Lemon, named after the blues guitarist Blind Lemon Jefferson, was the place one went for folk music. John and I more often frequented the Steppenwolf where we drank beer and talked politics with the owner, Max Scherr. Max would eventually become the publisher of the *Berkeley Barb*, a weekly underground newspaper that became popular in the sixties for its counter-cultural politics. But in these early days of that turbulent decade, he was just a bartender-owner known for his Marxist political patter. Max kept a big glass contribution jar on the bar for progressive political causes, but John suspected that he actually emptied it into his own pocket each evening.

The most popular street in Berkeley was Telegraph Avenue, which attracted both students and disaffected emigres from elsewhere. The Avenue boasted a repertory movie house, the Cinema Guild and Studio, which published reviews of its offerings by Pauline Kael (she later became cele-brated as the New Yorker film critic), wife of the owner Ed Landsburg; a classy furniture store; a few secondhand bookstores; and several restaurants and coffee shops. Much to my delight, I discovered that Whitey, my old seaman friend from North Beach, now lived in Berkeley and had opened up a delicatessen next door to the Mediterranean, the Avenue's principal bohemian café. But business wasn't too good at the deli. Clueless about restaurant practices, Whitey had been serving old lettuce with browned edges to save on costs. A year later, he went bankrupt, puzzled—and hurt—by his failure.

The Mediterranean, a.k.a. the "Med" or the "Piccolo"—its name in the fifties—became my haunt. I often sat in the late afternoon with a group of under-employed intellectuals, artists and craftsmen who had their regular table near the front window. There was Big Milt, a tall, burly, self-employed architect with a sharp wit; Ed, once a history grad student and now an unpublished writer who enjoyed arguing politics; Herbie, a fast-talking, witty dental student from LA who served as our local stand-up comic; Don, a contractor of some girth occupying a chair almost every afternoon, who merely sat, listened but never said a word. And then there was my favorite duo: Harold and Peg. Weird and whimsical Harold, a bald-headed, reputedly brilliant mathematician whose rimless glasses lent him an alien aspect, Harold made cosmic pronouncements—"We glow in the dark, radiated even as we sit here." His wife, Peg—an artist with straight brown hair; a heart-shaped, clean-scrubbed face; and a whiplash wit—was the smartest of the bunch. Peg spent her hours in the Med playing Go, which was the rage in Berkeley.

I felt a bit awkward with Peg ever since her hand, placed under the table, had sought my knee. A surprise. I had silently removed it—nothing said. God knows I wasn't prudish about homosexuality. After all, John and I occasionally would sit at the Med's outdoor tables, taking turns evaluating the sex appeal of the boys that passed by, playfully imagining ourselves rivals competing for one of them. But in that game, I remained heterosexual; I'd never been inclined toward same-sex love. How naïve I was about *female* homosexuality. And how little I really knew of the private lives of my new coffee shop acquaintances. There was a comfort in the superficiality of our relations.

Academic Tactics

Having been accepted into the UC Berkeley English Department as a graduate student, I was looking forward to studying with Mark Schorer, whose essay "Technique as Discovery" had aroused my interest as an undergraduate. For Schorer, a writer's technique was the only means he had of exploring his subject. While poetry was usually understood by attending to its technique, novels were interpreted through content, attending to the plot and characters. Schorer advocated reading a novel as though it were a poem, examining its diction, its structure, in short, its "technique" through which its meaning would be revealed. That's what Mal had meant when he advised me to study literature rather than social work; that's where an understanding of human actions could be found; that's what I wanted from graduate school.

There was, however, one small obstacle to becoming a graduate student: the fee for a nonresident of California was seven hundred dollars a semester—an impossible sum for me—and only forty-eight dollars for a resident. I determined to apply as a resident, even though I had no verifying identification of residency—no tax record, indeed, no California documents of any sort. I wasn't surprised when the registration clerk told me to go down the corridor to the State Attorney's office to complete my application. I would have to bluff it out.

"Where's your California tax documents?" the man behind the desk asked.

"I don't have any."

"Why not?"

"I have never made enough money to file an income tax form."

"Well, how do you live then?" I could see he was hoping to trap me with this question.

"I have always had a boyfriend who pays my expenses," I answered, and gave him a sly, knowing look. He blushed; *I've got him,* I thought. After a few such exchanges, I left his office an official California resident, smug in my success at outplaying the system, and ready to begin my graduate student career. That's how I was thinking of it. A career as a graduate student. Unlike most of the students I met that first year, who seemed to move as a disciplined cadre toward an academic position, I had no ambition, no desire to *become,* but instead, just to *be* in the presence of ideas about literature. I wanted only the promiscuous pleasure of sitting around coffeehouses talking about books, hanging out with *les types bohèmes,* writing the occasional essay, and working only enough to support this way of life in beautiful Berkeley. At least for the present, this was Paradise.

John had taught me to be contemptuous of the work ethic. "There's nothing virtuous about work," he proclaimed. "They all just can't stand the idea that somebody isn't working while they are, that we don't buy their ethic." I bought his gladly, though I later came to believe that work *produces* energy, releases us to the aliveness in ourselves. Real work, not a job. John's mantra needed supplementation.

Of course, John could afford his personal ethic: he had his monthly disability check from the government. I needed an income, and so found a part-time job stacking books on the shelves in the university library. But it was boring, boring, and apparently, my tedium showed. "You don't smile enough," my supervisor told me, and wrote in her evaluation: "Attitude needs improvement."

Luckily, I smiled enough in my classes; there I talked enthusiastically, often surprised myself at how much I enjoyed interpreting literature, my attitude good enough so that at the end of the semester, my American literature professor asked, "Are you a TA?"

"TA? What's that?"

"Teaching assistant. You should be a TA," he asserted and taking my hand, walked me to the department office to apply. By the beginning of the 1960–61 academic year, I was a TA, grateful to the English Department for both educating me and offering me a financially supported niche.

While I was taking classes, John found his own ways in the world: puttering around the apartment fixing things, or building them; browsing the bookstores (he was a great reader of esoterica); socializing at the Med; or going into the city to Vesuvio's, where I would find him ranting about the HUAC hearings while dispensing a pitcher of beer to his mates. Sometimes, as the sun was lowering on the horizon, John and I would ride my scooter across the Bay Bridge to a pub near the Art Institute on Chestnut Street, where his brother Richard taught history, our king snake in a basket tied to the luggage rack. The snake was a big hit with the art students; they would fix their gaze on it as it squeezed its way up my arm, spellbound by my snake charmer performance. Sometimes Whitey rode into the city with me on my Vespa, sitting on the back seat, terrified, knowing the snake was right behind him on the luggage rack. I couldn't help but gloat: this burley seaman was cowering behind me while I drove boldly on.

Except for the tedium of my part-time library job, which, gratefully, was short-lived, the academic year passed quickly, agreeably split between being a graduate student—Mark Schorer's praise for my paper on the narrowing of Melville's perspective from *Moby Dick* to *Bartleby the Scrivener* gave me a real high—and being a Berkeley bohemian, living a lifestyle made popular in the literature I was reading. Living with John meant playing with conventions, trying for the untried, and for a time, we played in Berkeley together. I even allowed him to bleach my hair blonde one afternoon with one hundred percent peroxide given him by a lab tech friend.

Me as a blonde with Blackie

It changed my aspect so completely that even my own mother, who flew in from New York to visit me a week later, didn't recognize me when I went to pick her up at the airport. I stood in front of her as she sat waiting, and she, aware after a moment of someone's presence, looked up at me, puzzled by this stranger's stare. And then I laughed, and the spell was broken; she knew me by my laugh. Uncanny, a mother's face, the first mirror of the self, according to psychological theory, here ironically shattered by my mother's lack of recognition. Playing with reality—disorienting, but also holding out the enchantment of transformation.

But a whiff of disenchantment was in the air.

At Vesuvio's, Henri still showed the same postcard projections of another time and place; the women in bathing suits were still "itching to get out of Portland, Oregon." Yet the Beach was not what it used to be. Tourists had begun to swarm through the streets made famous by the Beats. Vesuvio's was drawing too many Montgomery Street suits. The artists and poets and teamsters and con men that once sat at the bar were rarely there.

If my pub diversions were wearing thin, so was my patience with John's once charming impishness. I was tired of hearing him say, "I'm going to pick up a carton of milk. Be back in half an hour," and then returning three days later. I no longer bothered to ask where or why since his stories never made sense.

But when his singer friend Bobby Blue came to stay for a few days, along with his big, intimidating German shepherd, and he and John sat around drinking themselves into a stupor, I finally blurted out, "I've had it, John. I want them gone, man and dog, gone." Cory's words in my mouth! Echoing her disapproval! The next day, I returned from class to the apartment to find excrement smeared across the wall of the living room and a big "Fuck You" scrawled on the bathroom mirror. The apartment had been trashed, but at least man and dog were gone. John himself was not to be seen for several days.

In June of 1960, after many spats, John and I finally split up. He went off to Alaska to fish, having convinced some of the students from the Art Institute to follow him: "There's a bundle of money to be made fishing during the summer." (They in turn would be followed annually by a growing flock of art students taking John's advice and prospering). I was relieved. Although I was still fond of him, after a year of living with Peter Pan, now become the Pied Piper, I'd had my fill. We parted friends, and when, the following year, he married Sheelagh, a free-spirited English biotechnician working in a canning company lab, and became somewhat domesticated, I was delighted. I was not losing a lover; I was gaining a friend.

Routine Replacements

On my own again, sitting in my living room, listening to Frank Sinatra singing "April in Paris" with Blackie curled up beside me on the couch, I let myself melt into the music of the past while I awaited the next turn in my life story. I assumed it would take the shape of a new romance, as it had so often in my life. But I was becoming aware of a paradox. At the same time that I thought myself an independent woman, freely and actively pursuing my automobility, I seemed to need a romance in order to drive my lifeline forward; otherwise, I remained in a state of inertia, taking seminars, playing my guitar, hanging out at the coffee shop, waiting for something to happen.

Nevertheless, the rest of the world still turned, and some small excitement was added to my life when a domestic drama, the result of an adulterous affair, had its climax outside my apartment door. The characters: James, a dandyish Classics student who lived next door; his wife Thérèse, a small, French, birdlike creature from Egypt; David, who lived across the hall; and Susan, his pretty, young blonde wife. Apparently, James and Susan were, as one said then, "carrying on." The affair, uncovered one evening by Susan's husband David, erupted into a loud altercation that I could hear going on in the hallway. I opened my door just as David knocked James down onto the floor and, standing over him, was threatening to beat him to a pulp. James quickly scrambled up and escaped into his apartment before that could happen. For several hours, silence reigned. Around two in the morning, I was awakened by a knock on my door; there stood James and Thérèse, suitcases in hand; they had come to say goodbye before quietly stealing away. But, as Thérèse whispered furtively to me, they were leaving Sappho, their black cat, and her newly born kittens in their apartment. The following day, Sappho appeared at my open kitchen window holding a kitten in her mouth and, jumping through the window, dropped it on the floor, hopped back out again, and returned a few moments later with another one, repeating the process until all the kittens were transferred.

There was no father cat in the picture. A dramatic example of instinctual mother-love.

For humans, however, such mother-love was not always benign.

In Schorer's literature class, I had been again reading *Sons and Lovers*, a brilliant representation of the emotional coils of family life that centered around Paul, the son embraced and ensnared by his mother's powerful love. Clearly, I identified with Paul, the story's protagonist, rather than with Miriam, the young woman who loved him but feared sexual passion. At the same time, I felt the need for a literary counterpart; I knew that daughters as well as sons needed to fight off the sticky embrace of family, and especially of maternal love. Paul was supposedly freed at the novel's conclusion to find his way in the world, but Lawrence, I suspected, remained tethered in spite of his worldly success. How tethered was I? I called home with some regularity, but always felt a wave of guilt each time I heard the sad longing in my mother's voice as she asked about my life. I never told her the truth; I didn't want to upset her. My father never spoke on these calls; he remained a silent adversary in the background. My parents—intimates whom I had made strangers.

My classmates, on the other hand, were strangers fast becoming friends—among them a young, recently-married couple, both poets, who had just returned from working as forest rangers in the Sierras; a tall, dark-haired Israeli woman with a cosmopolitan mien; and an attractive Hungarian refugee, who sold low-cost stylish clothing on the side, some of which I bought. The women—all better educated than I—were astute literary interpreters; all had a passion for literature; all would reenter my life years later, one as a feminist filmmaker, the others as colleagues. I suspect I valued their friendship in good part because it added to my own sense of self-worth. Friends were those people that made you feel better about yourself.

In this sense, Blackie was a real friend. A street cat now as well as a house cat—he had grown exceptionally large and fierce-looking—he always welcomed me home with loud meows and, blinking at me with his bright yellow eyes, kept me uncomplicated company. Occasionally and unexpectedly, Blackie would bite—an act which I attributed to his having been made neurotic by John's sadistic play. Valerie, who visited me periodically, also teased Blackie for her amusement, strumming my guitar with a gleeful expression on her face while chasing the terrified cat around the apartment. But one afternoon, Valerie got her comeuppance: as she was lying on my couch reading, Blackie, sitting on the arm of the couch, suddenly turned and bit her in the head. Blackie, affectionate but unpredictable, could hold a grudge.

While life as a graduate student was agreeable in those early years of living alone, sporadically, I would fall into a deep well of depression and withdraw from the world, taking to my bed for days at a time, until a spontaneous urge to make a phone call to a friend told me that my dark descent was over. It came in waves, this familiar feeling of emptiness at the core of my being that swept over me, but I didn't question it. I knew it was just a matter of riding the waves, then sinking down, down, down into fathomless depths, where no thought reigned, until an urge to reach for the telephone a few days later brought me back up again, into the light.

As if to complement my mood swings, the *nouvelle vague* of French cinema swept into Berkeley in the fall of 1960. Fragmented in structure, slow-moving, experimental, the films at the Cinema Guild and Studio, chosen and reviewed by Pauline Kael, seemed uncannily to project my own moody iconoclasm. Godard's *Breathless*, with Jean Seberg wandering the streets of Paris hawking the *Herald Tribune*, even depicted my own earlier actual experience. Sitting in the darkness of the theater as the screen lit up my life in two dimensions, I felt myself in tune with—or was it in advance of—the times. A tumbleweed, as George Whitman would say, or as my parents said less flatteringly, a trumbernick. Like the heroine of *Breathless*, I had felt most alive when I sensed danger hovering near: the mind raced; the blood flowed quickly; the breath was held in suspense. In the movie, Belmondo, playing Seberg's criminal lover, betrayed by her, is killed: À

Bout de Souffle. Breathless. Double meaning of the word itself: life heightened, lived at a fast a pace, always running. But also without breath, dead.

I saw *Hiroshima Mon Amour* on my first date with Max Lovitt, a jazz drummer from Lincoln, Nebraska, that I met one afternoon in a coffee shop. I always thought Max was a Jewish name—my father's name, after all—but there was no mistaking this Max for Jewish: he was as different from me as the French woman and the Japanese man were from each other in *Hiroshima Mon Amour*. Six feet tall, reddish blonde hair, a boyish freckled face with an upturned nose, laconic in his movements, but with a quick dry wit, he looked like the quintessential Midwesterner—though he too, like John, had run away from its ethos. What was most appealing was his consummate understanding of both jazz and classical music which drew us together. Sitting in my small cozy apartment, Blackie curled in a corner, incense burning in the little Indian brass turtle on the top of the oak bookcase, the candles on the coffee table flickering, shadowing the room, Max and I smoked grass and listened to Miles Davis playing *Kind of Blue*, to Coltrane's sound-bending saxophone solos on *Giant Steps*, to the young up-and-coming drummer, Tony Williams, whom Max pronounced a prodigy.

"Listen to the conversation among the instruments," Max explained earnestly. "Good jazz is a conversation. If you can't hear the instruments talking to each other, it's not working." I listened and learned to hear the conversation. And so, in the following months, once again, I found myself sitting at a side table in a club, adoring a musician. Only this time it was the drum talking, rhythm-talk: in love, in love, in love. The beat went on.

Of course, it didn't. The music of that year ended the following summer with a dying fall. The proximate cause: jealousy. Unlike my toleration of John's sexual peccadillo with the Bulgarian princess, I became easily jealous with Max, whether I had cause or not. Spinning out scenarios of betrayal in my mind—Max with his ex-wife Mary Alice, Max with his old girlfriend Risa—I was stuck in an awful groove. I couldn't stop obsessing about Max not loving me enough. Max. My father's name. Was this a replay of the ancient triangle—Oedipa unleashed, seething, seething? But never could I imagine that the last painful turn in the downward spiral of my romance with Max would be caused by the visit of my best friend.

The critical scene still lingers in memory: Valerie, Max, and I were sitting in my living room, I happy to have her finally meet him. I'd told her so much about my falling for him, but also about not being sure of his feelings for me. As we sat conversing, I saw Max's eyes light up with interest and pleasure whenever Val spoke. And why not? With her sea-green eyes, olive complexion, and full lips, Valerie was not only extraordinarily attractive, but naturally eloquent, her voice impassioned even in casual conversation. How seductive was a passionate voice! I saw the rapt effect of Valerie's words, and of her intelligence, which seemed immediately to assume literary form. It was music to his ears. And Valerie was flirting openly with Max! I felt a wrenching in my gut as I saw Max respond to Valerie's unconscious—it had to be unconscious!—overtures: her hand touching his, her look connecting with his, her eyes laughing.

In spite of what I told myself, that men and women were sexual creatures who liked to flirt with one another, I couldn't seem to accept that fact with Max. I wanted, I *needed*, to be the only object of desire of the man I loved. Nor could I openly acknowledge my feelings. My best friend and my lover? There was too much to lose by raising the issue openly. Ashamed to show my neediness, painfully swallowing my anger and my hurt, I decided to withdraw silently from the field of competition—and from Max. A devastating sense of loss swept over me, but I knew there was nothing to be done. Like those dark waves that periodically overwhelmed me, this anguish too would pass.

To distract myself after Valerie's visit, I thought of taking a trip to LA to visit my CCNY friends. How convenient, then, that at a Berkeley garden party a few weeks later, Roger, a friend of Max's ex-wife, offered me a ride down to Santa Barbara in his MG convertible.

"It's a glorious ride along the coast," he told me. "I've got a big house near the beach, and you can take the bus from there to LA the next day."

I checked with Max before I accepted the offer: "Is it okay to ride down with Roger and stay at his place? Is he trustworthy?"

"Sure," Max said, with an indifferent shrug that pained me. "He's a good friend of Mary Alice."

It *was* a glorious ride, the sun shining, the waves of the Pacific cresting and breaking softly as the convertible wove along Highway One with its top down, and when, a bit windblown, we finally arrived in Santa Barbara, he *did* have a big house on the outskirts of the town. We had a drink before dinner, wine with dinner (he had some food in the fridge that he quickly prepared), and why didn't I recognize the signs? Surely, I must have noticed, as we sat on his couch talking and sipping California brandy after dinner, that he was getting too cozy, sitting too close. Nevertheless, before I fully registered what was happening, he was trying to embrace me, awkwardly, drunkenly, starting to pull at my sweater, saying, "There's no one around. . . . No one can hear you. . . ." as I started to scream, "Stop it, stop it," full volume, thinking, *Mary Alice's friend, he knows Max, Max knows him, why didn't Max warn me, he's trying to rape me in his big house in Santa Barbara!*

But he was a slight man, short and thin, and weakened by alcohol. It was late, it had been a long drive, and so, changing my tactic, I babbled on about Mary Alice and Max—"What would they say if they saw you now?"—as I squirmed in his grasp, fending him off until he leaned back tiredly, eyes closed, listened to me chatter for a few minutes—drowsed—and fell asleep! Moments later, having swept up my few belongings, I found myself running down a dark road with my small suitcase, running, breathless, away from the house toward the light of the town.

Running, always running toward the light.

When did it start, this frightening, familiar flight from a menacing male? And how responsible was I for the situation? As a teenager, hitchhiking with my best friend Florence to Quebec and recognizing the inherent danger in being girls on the road, we both vowed to be cautious: "We won't get in if there's more than one man in the car, right?" So why, in Trois-Rivières, as dusk fell, did we accept a ride with two men? From the backseat, we watched nervously as the driver took a flask out of the glove compartment and, after passing it first to his friend, offered us a swig. Before we could strategize an exit, the car turned off the main highway onto an isolated road that ran through hilly farm fields. And then it stopped. As the driver and his friend were opening their doors, Florence and I jumped out. But then, they too were out of the car. For a moment we four stood facing each other across the trunk of the car. I broke the silence first and, mustering all the authority I could find, insisted the driver open the trunk so we could get our luggage. Amazingly, he actually followed my orders, opened the trunk, and then, standing there looking stupefied, asked: "Don't we get anything for taking you this far?"

Irrationally, I had blurted out: "My father will send you a check!" My father? I wondered at the absurdity of my outburst even as Florence and I breathlessly hoisted our heavy suitcases out of the trunk and, strengthened by the adrenaline coursing through our bodies, ran with them away from the car up the hill toward a farmhouse, whose light was barely visible in the dusky distance.

And again, years later, as a grad student, there I was, foolishly hitchhiking alone, when somewhere around Bakersfield, with the last rays of light fading from the sky, the driver who had picked me up turned off the highway onto a dirt road alongside a grassy field. My panic swelled as the car bounced along a narrow road barely illuminated by the headlights. Then the car stopped. Terrified, my thoughts racing to find some possible escape, I pushed my elbow frantically against the door handle just as the driver, looking crazed, reached across the front seat for me. Thankfully, the door opened to my pressure, and pulling myself out of the car before he could grab me, I ran stumbling across the grassy field into the unknown darkness, aware of my pursuer's headlights slowly following behind, fearful that he would catch up. But then, amazingly, there were lights in the distance moving slowly in my direction. Headlights! I ran toward them through tall grasses, a truck taking shape out of the darkness, and when I reached it, two young farmhands inside who were eager to rescue me, and just as eager to catch and punish my pursuer. Grateful for their outrage but fearful of its potential violence, I persuaded them merely to give me a ride to a nearby motel. That night, alone in a safe space, I repeatedly played out the evening's harrowing moments, awed by the fact that I had survived yet again.

The Breaking Point

In the early summer of 1961, deciding to break my obsessive affair with Max, I drove back across the country to spend the summer in New York, this time with Blackie on the seat beside me. Exhilarated by being on the road again, with the help of Dexamyl, I drove three thousand miles in three days, breaking only to sleep in my car for several hours during the night in some small-town, deserted square. I ended my freewheeling cross-country jaunt at my parents' apartment in the Bronx. They were ecstatic to see me, and I was happy to give them the pleasure of my company in small doses. They even welcomed Blackie, cat-sitting him while I spent most of my time downtown with my old friends, Valerie and Joan, now both working as journalists and living in the Village. Joan was my drinking buddy, and on those evenings when she and I caroused late into the night, I slept overnight in her apartment. Much to my delight, she'd turned a bookcase in her living room into a giant liquor cabinet, the mere sight of which gave me a feeling of warm comfort when I bedded down next to it on her convertible couch.

When I was not with Joan or Valerie, I'd lurk in a friendly Village bar, usually either the Riviera on Seventh Avenue, or the Cedar Tavern, a well-known watering hole for New York artists further east on University Place.

Sitting at the Cedar one night, nursing my Scotch on the rocks, I attracted the attention of someone who would unexpectedly take over my life for months to come. Curly dark hair, dark eyes, muscular, his biceps showing just below his rolled-up blue denim shirtsleeves, and a large ring of keys dangling from his leather belt, Brian walked in advertising his masculinity. I had been doing some advertising of my own that evening, gazing into my Scotch as if I were contemplating an unendurable loss. Out of the corner of my eye I saw him look briefly in my direction as he passed and then turn to nod to the bartender. I continued to stare sadly into my glass, waiting, and was pleased when he sat down on the barstool next to me.

The conversation started as usual, oiled by small talk. He asked what kind of work I did; I told him I was a graduate student considering what to do with "my life—this *thing* I had charge of that has come to a standstill." A flicker of heightened interest crossed his face when I called my "life" a "thing." That must have been the hook for everything that happened later.

And what more did I learn that first night? Born and raised in the Village, Brian now lived on the Lower East Side. His father was a Village artist—a painter—but he himself had no talent in that direction. He was a carpenter; he liked to make things. His voice took on a special intensity as he talked about the importance of labor to the spirit, and as we sat there talking, I felt the promise of something real emerging from our conversation.

He was, he told me, a follower of Gurdjieff.

"I've found my way to a greater self-awareness through Gurdjieff," he said. "Do you know his work?"

"I've heard the name, but don't know much about him. Katherine Mansfield, the writer, supposedly died in his arms at his institute—where was it, in France somewhere? He was a Russian mystic, right?"

"He was a lot more than just that," Brian said, sounding a bit irked. He took a long draft of his beer, and then, as if I had tapped an underground spring, he pressed on: "Gurdjieff believed human beings are only partially developed, that there is a higher state of consciousness that is not given to us freely but must be acquired by intentional efforts." His voice was deep and yet soft, as if he were gently stroking the words before he let them go. I let them float around in my mind before I asked anything. I was intrigued.

"*Higher* state of consciousness? Meaning . . . ?"

He smiled into his beer as if he had waited for me to ask.

"Gurdjieff started a school to help people who were stuck in a groove reach a better level of existence." He paused and took a long look at me, and I felt in his gaze a penetrating appraisal.

"Consciousness, conscience, and will are not given to us freely"—his voice now grew more vigorous—"but must be acquired by intention, by work." As if to punctuate his remarks, he took another long look at me, and I felt myself caught in the intensity of his gaze.

A dangling woman without any goal of my own, I was a perfect foil for Brian's words, drawn to him by his impassioned certainties and my lack of them. Inevitably, our conversation on that hot New York summer night led me to climb the five floors to his Lower East Side tenement apartment. To my astonishment, I stepped into another world. He had remodeled the apartment, had knocked down walls and transformed the cramped tenement rooms into an open airy space. Bookshelves adorned one wall. Across the room, a bed, placed near two windows that looked onto the street; between them hung a large painting of a woman, its saturated colors demanding attention. As I stood admiring it, Brian reached out from behind and put his muscular arms around me, and I felt myself flow effort-lessly into the healing promise of the summer. *Yes*, I said to myself, it felt good to be enveloped like this; I needed this powerful swaddling.

And so it began. I would lie in Brian's bed on those July mornings, the air already shimmering with heat and humidity, my own body already wet with a summer sweat familiar from my Bronx childhood, and look out the dusty window at the tenements across the street. It was all so comforting, this heat and sweat and dust. It was New York.

The summer wore on, the heat continued to blanket the city through August, and I sank into it, spending more and more time with Brian in his bed than in my parents' apartment, our bodies gliding over one another in a compelling intimacy. But its more vital artery was the daily conversations we had about the nature of consciousness and the pursuit of meaning. The year before, I had been rereading Camus's *The Myth of Sisyphus*; its antihero rolling a stone uphill to no purpose had struck a chord of recognition. Now, with Brian, my interest in purpose returned. I learned that for Gurdjieff, our ordinary state of being was a "waking sleep," that there was a "Fourth Way" to a higher consciousness, a response to a modern ennui.

"Say more about this higher consciousness," I said to Brian one Sunday morning, lying next to him in his bed after making love. "How would I be more conscious than I am now, lying here with you, at peace with the world?"

Brian smiled, the kind of smile one offers a child, and pursed his lips for a moment, looking up at the ceiling. Then he spoke:

"When you achieve a state of higher consciousness, the mind is cleared of all the junk that's part of 'personality,'" he began, "and we come into contact with the real world of pure meaning. Now, we're cut off by our senses, by our needs and passions"—he turned his head toward me—"even by our pleasures. We'll become receptive to pure consciousness without thought, a state in which truth is revealed to us directly, without the use of words."

Disappointed by his response, which so little fit my own mood, I challenged him: "*Without the use of words?* How could I be conscious without the use of words? Aren't words the very tools of consciousness?"

I heard the disrespect in my voice and saw Brian flinch.

"Unless, of course, it's the here and now of body consciousness," I went on teasingly to mollify him, and reached out to finger the curl of hairs on his chest. For a moment there was silence. Then he smiled at me and, swinging his legs to the side of the bed, stood up and headed for the shower.

The summer passed by, our conversations recurrently returning to Gurdjieff's system of discipline in order to achieve higher consciousness. But the more I learned about that discipline, the less I liked it. I bristled when Brian told me that acolytes had to submit to a regimen of "intentional suffering"—to expose themselves to disbelievers—in order to strengthen their own psyches. Was I serving that function? Even more distasteful to me was the idea of being a disciple. I had always managed to avoid joining groups that demanded submission to a leader. Now, as part of my relationship with Brian, I seemed to be putting myself in that unwelcome position. I voiced my unease to Brian a number of times, but I could see that while he claimed to welcome discussion, his fulsome investment in Gurdjieff blocked out any real argument.

My growing aversion to Gurdjieff's discipline reached its climax in mid-August, at a private piano recital by the Gurdjeiff group's New York guru, Mr. Weiland. These concerts were given monthly by Mr. Weiland in his spacious Upper West Side apartment as an example, Brian explained, of the creative freedom one acquired through the Gurdjieff discipline. Invited to attend as a special favor, I was welcomed by a tall, slim, gray-haired man with chiseled features, piercing blue eyes and an exceedingly calm demeanor, and took a seat in his light-filled living room along with twenty or so others. The room became hushed; the concert began. Mr. Weiland's fingers ran dexterously across the keyboard as he poured his thoughts into a flight of notes. And then, involuntarily, I coughed, and all eyes in the room turned toward me accusingly. Higher consciousness brooked no coughing. Feeling assaulted by their eyes, I turned to Brian for support, but there was the same sour disapproval written on his face. He was with them, not me.

By Labor Day, when a cool thread of wind in the air promised to blow away the summer's heat, I was ready to return to Berkeley. Brian's commitment to Gurdjieff's discipline was too complete. To avoid conflict, I kept silent about wanting to end the affair and equivocated: "I'll write." I didn't want an argument. As I told him before I left, at the very least, Berkeley offered a discipline I enjoyed, and more practically, a fellowship I could resume. What I didn't say was that I had no plans to resume this relationship.

But Brian had other ideas. A passionate acolyte, he was on a rescue mission, whether I wanted rescue or not. A month after I had driven with

Blackie back to Berkeley and settled into my classes at the university, Brian arrived at my door and moved into my apartment, intent on giving meaning to my life. And I allowed it. Why? Did I still long for that heady pleasure whenever he wrapped me in his powerful arms? Or was it rather his seductive words that had gotten at a truth about me: "You need to take yourself more seriously." Certainly, Brian seemed to be taking me more seriously than I had ever taken myself. That seemed reason enough to let him back into my life.

But living with Brian was unsettling. He didn't chat. There was no casual talk or playfulness, and little music except for the recorded piano improvisations of Mr. Weiland that Brian had brought with him from New York. Our conversations were always about essential matters. Truth. Knowledge. Meaning. Higher Consciousness. He was determined to convert me to that rigorous system of self-development that Mr. Weiland—always *Mr.* Weiland—called Work. "If you really want to Work," Brian instructed, "you're engaged in changing your life. You're engaged in admitting that what your life is at the present time is not right or not complete."

In New York I had found this vision compelling. My life certainly needed changing; I knew it; Brian knew it. But I also recognized an implicit devotion to authority in him that felt like chalk grating against the blackboard of my mind whenever we spoke. Now in Berkeley, I was experiencing that devotion at close quarters. Brian constantly tracked my thoughts, molding them into his vision of what I should or could be. He was the carpenter, and I was the raw material. Regularly, he would return after work—he had quickly found a job as a carpenter on a building project in San Francisco—and interrogate me about my activities during the day. What had I read? What was I thinking about? Did I read the Ouspensky book he left for me? I wanted to draw a line that said "this is me, not you," but I couldn't get the words out. Instead, I constantly needled him: when he quoted Gurdjieff, I spouted Camus; when he talked about Ouspensky, I talked about Rollo May. But such countermeasures could not shake his determination to mold me.

Strangulated by the force of Brian's personality, I literally dreamed my rebellion: *I am climbing the stairs of a New York tenement, climbing up to the fifth floor, Brian's floor. I knock on the door, open it, step inside. The apartment is empty, but sunlight pours in through the windows; the oak floors gleam in the sunlight. I look around, and there in a corner of the room, lying on the floor, is my favorite blue striped dress. On it, ugh, a huge, fat, ugly bug. Grabbing a broom that leans against the wall near me, I hit the bug with all my strength, hit it again and again, pounding it into a bloody disgusting pulp all over my dress and shouting the words: DON'T BUG ME!*

One afternoon, Brian walked into the apartment with his arm in a cast and told me he had fallen off a first-floor girder at his construction site. I laughed. Spontaneously. I saw him wince with the pain of my laughter and then flush with anger.

"Don't you care at all?" His question rang out and reverberated with meanings that mirrored me to myself appallingly. *I* was becoming a monster; *he* had to leave.

"Space," I said as firmly as I could, "I need my own space to do my schoolwork. You need to find your own place."

Surprisingly, Brian agreed and a week later moved out of the apartment. But as if forged in his iron will, our relationship continued; the tension accumulated. And then one evening, it snapped: he appeared in my apartment for "a serious conversation." The words I had held back for so long erupted: "You are suffocating me.... This has to stop. You have to go back to New York." He stiffened, and then, speaking softly, put his arm around my shoulders and led me gently but firmly to a chair.

"Please sit down, Claire. You don't mean that. You're just afraid to be vulnerable, and that's holding you back from being with me totally. We need to talk." But it wasn't talk that he wanted. It was interrogation.

"How authentic are you? How free, really? What do you think about the quality of your life? Don't you want more from life than what you have now? You've told me you feel empty. Aren't you capable of more than this emptiness?"

Standing in front of me as I cowered in the chair, his face a mask of tolerant concern, he hammered me with his words—the pressure was unbearable. My very self seemed to be shattering into broken points of light. I had to get away, but there he stood, blocking my access to the front door. But the small door to the balcony was open. He looked away for a moment. I jumped up and dashed through the door onto the balcony. Two stories to the ground: I could be killed, but no matter, I had to get out. I lifted a leg to climb over the balcony ledge, but there he was suddenly, pulling me back. For a moment we stood facing each other next to the ledge. Then, with a spurt of desperate energy, I broke from him, rushed into the apartment, opened the front door, and ran down the stairs into the street. There was my Vespa waiting at the curb. I jumped on the seat, pumped the pedal a few times, and took off. I could see Brian running to his car as I sped away.

But where to? In a panic, all I could think of was Cowell, the student hospital. It had taken care of me when I had the flu; it would perhaps take care of me now. I drove frenetically across campus, the road empty at this late hour, and pulling up sharply in front of the hospital building, ran up the front steps, rang the emergency doorbell, and when the door opened, fell into the arms of a nurse.

"There's someone after me. Please help me!"

A few moments later, the bell rang again, and when one of the nurses opened the door, Brian rushed in. The hospital lobby suddenly swirled with people, some holding him while he shouted—"I just need to talk to her"—and another swirl rushing me off to a roped-off area on the side. Immediately, the hospital staff called the police while I was ushered into a private room. Hours later, I was told that Brian had tried to run down a police officer in his effort to escape and had been taken to the police station. I was given a room in the psychiatric area of the hospital, behind locked doors. I remained there for a week, a Miss Dumpty trying to put the pieces of my mind together again, neither knowing nor asking whether my seclusion was voluntary. It was necessary.

Alone and unpressured, I mulled over the drama of the past year. Was I ever in any real danger? The police thought so; a month earlier a student had been shot in the university library by a rejected lover. But more importantly, what had happened to me? I, who thought of myself as committed to life in all its variety, had actually tried to leap off my balcony! Inconceivable in retrospect, and yet true. Exposed to my own radical vulnerability, to a mental fragility I had not thought possible, life itself now seemed more tenuous, death more real.

There was only one way that I could see to ease the immediate situation and reclaim my life. I called Mr. Weiland in New York; Mr. Weiland called Brian; and finally, it was over. On Mr. Weiland's instruction, Brian returned to New York, and I turned once again to my studies, my sense of self deeply shaken. Being a graduate student now seemed pointless. What was I doing in Berkeley anyway? I was a bohemian without an art, a graduate student without an academic goal. Could I seriously get a PhD and become "a professor"? I had no academic ambitions. Why then remain at the university?

I thought back over the last few years. UC had afforded me many gratifying moments, but they had little to do with serious scholarship. Mark Schorer's weekly seminar, conducted informally in the living room of his elegant house and ending always in an alcoholic haze for both students and professor, gave me the illusion of sophistication. My delight in such extraneous excesses of academia continued the following year when the inebriated Schorer introduced the equally inebriated visiting writer John Cheever, who, though barely able to walk upright onto the Wheeler Auditorium stage, could, once at the podium, stand upright and read soberly from his work to an appreciative audience. When visiting British critic Angus Wilson talked to us about E. M. Forster's closeted homosexuality, and its inhibiting effects on his fiction, I felt as though I were being inducted into a select society of cognoscenti. Perhaps most gratifying was the seminar I took with Aldous Huxley, one of the great British modernists whose work I had first read as an undergraduate, an experience crowned by my sauntering down Telegraph Avenue with Huxley after class one afternoon, conversing oh so very casually as we walked toward the Med for coffee.

"I saw that you blurbed the jacket praising Ouspensky's book, *In Search of the Miraculous*," I had said, furiously trying to impress him by showing off my knowledge of Gurdjieff and Ouspensky, momentarily grateful to Brian for having given me that esoteric education.

"I no longer think much of those who write about the other side of the moon," Huxley had replied drily, dismissing them—and my remark—with a wave of his long, bony hand. How foolish I had felt then, and embarrassed. Yet walking into the Med with Aldous Huxley and seeing the eyes at the front table turn toward me as he and I searched for an empty table— what an ego boost! And how I needed it that year.

But in the end, despite the friendships I had formed and the classes I had enjoyed and the unexpected moments of personal gratification, Berkeley in the early sixties was a small community. I wanted a larger world, a new start outside the academy, something more creative, more urbane. In the late fall, relying on my trusty amphetamines to keep my mind moving quickly, I took the exam for a terminal MA in English. But my thoughts were already elsewhere, across the country. New York. Perhaps a job in publishing. Perhaps....

6

Drifting:
Greenwich Village
Interlude
(1963–1966)

*People wish to be settled; only as far as they are
unsettled is there any hope for them.*

Ralph Waldo Emerson

1 965, New Year's Day, six in the morning. I am almost thirty years old, walking back to my apartment in the West Village after a party. The sun, not yet visible, casts a pale light on the horizon; the dark-gray tar-topped empty street that I walk on stretches out to meet it. Time itself seems to stretch out with no clear demarcations, no particular goals in sight, nothing which feels real, permanent. Thirty. Perhaps the first of those portentous numbers provoking serious intimations of mortality. And nothing to mark my existence these last few years in New York. Drifting.

I had come to New York in the summer of 1963 with vague dreams of working as an editor in a publishing house and living *la vie bohème* in Greenwich Village, where my two closest friends lived. The Village had been a magnet for us during our college years because of its association with the bohemian life of writers. As a small number of writers had proclaimed one cold January night in 1917 from the top of the Washington Square Arch, the Village was "a free and independent Republic," where men and

151

women could step outside the norms of the time. Sinclair Lewis had lived at 10 Van Nest Place, now 69 Charles Street, just doors away from Valerie's apartment. Edna St. Vincent Millay had lived near Joan's first apartment on Bedford Street, in the narrowest house in New York. When Joan moved to Bank Street, she was just down the street from Willa Cather's old apartment. At the White Horse Tavern on Hudson Street, around the corner from the apartment I rented, Dylan Thomas had drunkenly held forth when I was an undergraduate. Somehow, living among these literary ghosts always seemed to promise some opening to the arts. Valerie and Joan both were well on the way to having that promise fulfilled; both had become journalists of some repute. But I had still not found my niche.

Change was in the air that summer of 1963; politics colored the horizon. In August, I had marched with Martin Luther King in Washington, DC, and dreamed with him and thousands of others of a new day in America. In the autumn, I marched again with the Bread and Puppet Theater, this time against the war in Vietnam. Wearing a giant papier-mâché puppet mask that hid my face, I passed hard hat construction workers lining the streets and shaking their fists at me, shouting, "Traitor! Love it or leave it." Frightened inside my mask by this open expression of male rage outside me, I felt also exhilarated by the sense of danger, and not least, proud to be marching on.

But while I felt newly alive to the political moment, my desire to become an editor was an ambition soon squashed. "You're overqualified for office work," I was told by one personnel manager when I tried to get my foot in the door of a publishing company. "You're underqualified" by another when I applied directly for an editorial position. Miss In-Between. Still, I needed an income, and so I became a "Kelly Girl"—a glamorous title for a female temp worker—taking jobs that sent me spiraling down the social ladder, from a public relations assistant; to an office clerk; to a typist, typing addresses on labels in a button factory on Varick Street. So much for the value of my MA in English.

I was given a small reprieve from this psycho-economic misery when my application to become a substitute teacher was accepted at a local high school. Charles Evans Hughes was a tough place to walk into as a sub, especially for a young female with no visible claim to authority. "Where's your pass?" the police monitor would often ask when I walked down the hall, and I would have to raise myself to my full five-foot three-inch height and explain in my most assertive voice: "I'm a teacher!" As for exerting authority over the poor, street-smart kids whose own sense of agency lay in defying the teachers, a knife drawn by a young girl when I told her to sit down proved my lack in that regard. Each afternoon, at three o'clock, as I walked out of the school and down Ninth Avenue toward my apartment, I could feel the rigid mask that covered my face during the day begin to crack. As I crossed Fourteenth Street and entered the Village, the muscles around my mouth relaxed into something like a smile.

Settling Unsettled: My Village Life

My Greenwich Village home: a one-bedroom street level corner apartment with two living room windows facing Greenwich Street (the building's garbage cans were parked just outside these windows); a large commercial garage across the street, its trucks grinding their gears and waking me up at three in the morning as they left for their routes; a bedroom window around the corner that faced a local bar just across the street. Despite its unfavorable location, I relished living here, and had to bite my tongue when, on his first visit to my apartment, my father remarked: "Living on top of the garbage cans! Ach! Disgusting!"

Valerie and Joan each lived a few blocks away. Joan had become a successful TV news producer, often traveling to film stories about the undervalued rural communities of Appalachia. When she was in town, she and I spent our evenings either at the Corner Bistro, where I ogled the raffish Polish bartender, or at the Lion's Head, a habitual drinking spot for journalists. Valerie was writing for a small but influential journal and gaining fans rapidly. But her personal life had morphed into an unconventional romantic entanglement with a handsome African American wannabe actor who was, unfortunately, a liar, a compulsive gambler, and a thief. He even hocked her typewriter once to get cash for betting on a sure thing at the track!

And me? With no particular professional goal, nor any accomplishment to lean on for ego gratification, I relied mostly on my social life for feeling good about myself. Like Val, I too was in an eccentric entanglement with a professional gambler, and although Gene was neither a liar nor a thief as far as I knew, he did encourage my shoplifting predilections, once even mockingly challenging me to pilfer something from Klein's Department Store on Fourteenth Street. I shoplifted a belt to meet Gene's dare.

Since he lived only a few blocks away on Tenth Street, I saw Gene frequently, enjoying the friendship of someone whose interior life I couldn't begin to imagine. Sitting with him at a coffee shop, I'd listen as he told a story of some daily happening that hinted at his having underworld connections, but if I asked for more information, he would give me a long knowing look and change the subject. An enigma, he appealed to me; he was "different." Occasionally, I slept over at his apartment; on those nights, he would tell me, narrowing his ice-blue eyes in frosty amusement, to beware of his German shepherd.

"He'll attack you if you try to get out of bed in the middle of the night by yourself. Remember, wake me if you have to get up," he would warn with a sly smile.

Given Gene's sardonic personality, I was always taken aback when he encouraged me to be "a good daughter." But at his prompting, I became one, going up to the Bronx every Friday night to have dinner with my parents. I came to think of it as my Sabbath expiation for the anxiety I caused them. I would take the subway for an hour's ride to the North Bronx where they now lived, endure my mother's needy embrace and my father's awkward welcome, while guiltily observing my brother standing timidly in the background. In his last year at college, Albert had developed rheumatoid arthritis and, at the urging of my parents, had gone to work for my father in the candy store after graduating from college with a math degree. And he had grown obese. Each time I visited, I saw how cocooned in fat he had become, entrapped by their love into a grotesque filial dependence. That was always the most painful part of my visit, seeing how Al had been absorbed—cannibalized—by my parents. I felt I had abandoned him to their needs.

The Friday night ritual: After our dinner at the kitchen table, the four of us would shift to the living room to watch TV. I always winced silently as I took in the familiar baroque furnishings: the Italianate lamps on ornate end tables placed next to the Danish modern couch—one of two I had bought for Al and me to sleep on when I was a teenager. My father sank into the large easy chair in front of the TV and soon fell asleep. Al and I became mesmerized before the flickering screen while my mother, curled up in a chair, catlike, stared alternately at me and then at the TV. If it wasn't too late for the long ride back to the Village, I left after an hour or two, dazed by the soporific atmosphere. More often, I slept overnight in the living room on the familiar couch, my brother on its twin in his bedroom.

In my second year in New York, I forged a link with academia again: I became a lecturer at Queens College and a graduate student in English at Columbia University. But there was little to engage me in either of those institutions. As a commuting adjunct at Queens, I had no collegial contact with faculty and little with students. As a graduate student at Columbia, I was invisible to my two professors, who seemed invested only in their male PhD candidates. No surprise, then, that I resented riding the subway for an hour in either direction—to give classes or to take them.

The next year promised a sea change: I dropped out of graduate school and became a lecturer at Brooklyn College, where the salary was a respectable six thousand dollars a year, the students were brighter, the faculty more available to me as colleagues. I made friends at work and, having some wonderfully astute students, was happier in my teaching. Yet life was elsewhere. Locked in my apartment every weekend correcting freshman student papers with the world churning outside, moaning with Valerie about our mutual frustrations with men, or barhopping with Joan, who was rigorously committed to the hard-drinking life of "the reporter," I felt myself both personally and professionally at a dead-end. Only time moved forward.

Life in the Village: A Stranger Calls

My life took an unwelcome turn when a series of "break-ins" to my apartment gave me temporary notoriety in the city's tabloid *New York Daily News*—the newspaper that my parents regularly read.

Life in the Village, Or, a Stranger Calls

By LEONARD KATZ

Claire Katz, a young teacher of English who lives in a ground-floor apartment at 731 Greenwich St. in Greenwich Village, woke up screaming early today. There was a strange man in her bedroom.

The intruder seemed as badly frightened by the scream as the screamer.

He urged Miss Katz, who is in her mid-20s, to forget her fright. In a friendly tone, he said he meant her no harm. Then he began to remove his clothes.

Miss Katz began screaming again. She also fled, around the corner to the Charles St. Police station. There Patrolman Richard Maguire, was assigned to accompany her back home.

The two found the intruder in the living room, trying to explain his presence to two guests of Miss Katz—Mrs. Sheila Miller of Los Angeles and Mrs. Miller's sister, Jill Whittaker. The sisters were spending the night there before sailing for England today.

Arrested, the intruder identified himself as Robert G. Kearney, 22, a loader, of Jersey City. He told police he had "just made a little mistake and somehow got in the wrong apartment."

However, police said Kearney hadn't made a mistake at all but had entered the apartment through a window. He was booked on charges of burglarly and attempted rape.

New York Daily News clipping

Fortunately, they missed this story. Unfortunately, others did not.

Behind the headlines: Coming home one Sunday morning after having spent the night with Gene and the German shepherd, I entered my bedroom and, much to my surprise, found a slim young man lying asleep on my bed, naked, his clothes neatly hanging on the doorknob. He had apparently climbed in through one of the living room windows, as I could plainly see: a planter had been knocked off the windowsill and lay broken on the floor, its soil scattered amid clay shards. Tiptoeing quietly out again, I ran to the Charles Street police station two blocks away, shouting as I entered, "There's a naked man in my bed!" Such a remark could only draw laughter from the policemen on duty. Still snickering, two of them returned with me to my apartment, but the nude intruder had disappeared. Case closed, or so I assumed.

A month or so later, after a dinner party I had given, I awoke in the middle of the night to see the shadow of someone entering my bedroom. For a moment, in my sleep-dazed state, I thought it must be someone I knew, perhaps Gene returning after the party. I turned on the lamp near my bed, and there he was, the nude stranger, now fully clothed. "What are you doing here?" I asked, too groggy to think clearly. He just stood there looking sheepish, saying nothing. Irritated rather than fearful, I got out of bed, marched to the front door, opened it, and pointing to the hallway, commanded: "Get *out*." He obeyed and I returned to bed. A few minutes later, I heard a grating sound at the bedroom window. Springing out of bed more energetically this time, I opened the curtains and there he was, again!

"Oh, do you live here too?" he asked, seemingly surprised to see me. At which point, exasperated by his clumsy attempt to get into my apartment, I closed the curtains and called the police. Of course, once again, by the time they arrived, he was gone, and I felt myself dismissed as a hysterical woman.

To avoid a recurrence of any further break-ins, I had bars installed on the living room and bedroom windows, the bathroom window being too small and narrow to bother with. The apartment was now effectively impregnable, I assumed. That December, John's decidedly pregnant wife Sheelagh and her sister came to stay with me before sailing to England for Christmas. To amuse them, I told them the story of the break-in, warning them jokingly to be on the lookout for a naked man. Later that night, Sheelagh, who was sleeping on a futon on the living room floor, awoke to discover a stranger kneeling before her.

"Who are you?" she had asked, as she told me later.

"I'm Jerome," he had answered, but then, scrutinizing her face more closely, had added: "Oh, you're the wrong one!"

A moment later, I was awakened by Sheelagh's scream—"Kitty! Kitty! Wake up!" Jumping quickly out of bed, I rushed into the living room, and there he was again, that familiar figure, beginning to take off his clothes.

"Keep him talking," I whispered to Sheelagh, and grabbing my coat from the closet, I ran out the door in my nightclothes and into the street. The air was crisp, the snow newly fallen and powdery against my slippers as I ran the two blocks to the police station. This time, there was no joking; this time, we got him.

How had he gotten in? And what did he want? Unbelievably, he had managed to squeeze through the exceedingly narrow bathroom window. That took some doing. Yet "he meant no harm," I was told afterward by his lawyer. Apparently neither a burglar nor a rapist, but merely a drunken laborer from New Jersey, he had often seen me come home late—two or three in the morning was not unusual—and, after a few drinks, had on those several occasions drunkenly crossed the street and climbed into my apartment. And what was his intention? No one, including Jerome, seemed to know the answer to that question. Whatever his murky objective, I was "persuaded"—or rather intimidated—by his friends and family to drop the charges: attempted rape and burglary. (Of course, there really wasn't any attempted rape or burglary). One caller, pleading that Jerome's poor mother depended on his wages, even hinted darkly that moving forward with the case would augur badly for me. I dropped the charges.

While that problem ended, another ordeal began. The tabloid article had disclosed my name and address—a journalistic policy no longer allowed—and for months afterward, I suffered a barrage of notes, letters, cards, and not least, telephone calls blaming *me* for *his* criminal intrusion, excoriating *me* for living alone in the Village, for smoking, for wearing slacks. By merely being who I was, I had invited harassment. Yet I understood the accusation. It was still a fairly conservative time for women; I had chosen to live in the Village, where those who wanted an unfettered life tended to congregate. And an unfettered life brought with it certain risks. But as I came also to understand, I bore some personal responsibility; it wasn't smoking or wearing slacks that was risky, but rather the utter carelessness with which I pursued my freedom of action: the late-night drinking, the open curtains at street level, the offhand way in which "why not?" was my answer to most proposals—an answer especially imprudent for a woman living alone in the early sixties.

How imprudent that actually was became clear months later when I suffered a truly traumatic violation—an actual rape from someone I knew. It was an experience I secreted away in the shadowbox of memory for decades, keeping silent—for the shame of it, for the unwanted publicity that might follow, for fear of being blamed, and perhaps even more, for fear of a violent reprisal from the rapist himself. Within that shadowbox, like all trauma, the scene lived on in a continuous present:

"No, of course I don't mind," Doug says. "If this relationship is not working for you, I'm disappointed, but . . . Well, there's no point in going on. But . . . I was going to say, I wanted you to hear this fantastic record I just picked up, especially for you to hear: Miles Davis on a new track. . . . I tell you what. Why don't you just come over for a goodbye drink, and we'll hear this tune, and then, goodbye. No regrets. Okay?"

He's not angry! I'm relieved. It's been a month since he and I met at the Riviera Bar. We've sat talking and drinking at the bar a number of times, and last week, I went to bed with him in my apartment—why not? He's ruggedly handsome, dark hair slicked back, black lashes framing blue eyes, a brooding expression—very attractive. Yet despite this intimate contact, as with Gene, I don't know him. We've talked about jazz musicians, about living in California, about traveling, but whatever the conversation, I can sense something seething in this guy, and though that intensity was the hook that first drew me in, I don't trust its source in Doug. When my friend Roberta, a shrewd psychologist, raised her eyebrows the other day, surprised to hear I was still seeing him—"Big mistake, he's a powder keg," she said knowingly—I realized she was right. I have to back away.

So, here we are finishing dinner in a Midtown restaurant, and I've said as nicely as I can that it's not his fault, it's me, he's a great guy, but I can't handle any involvement with anyone now, so we'd better stop before our feelings get too enmeshed. He looks down at his empty plate, and then he looks up at me with such a sympathetic grin, suddenly boyish, and says he understands; people have needs. He does too. They don't always mesh. He's planning on leaving town soon anyway.

So okay, why not listen to jazz with him this evening? Why not have our brief affair end on a pleasant note. I'll have a goodbye drink with him, hear the new Miles Davis record, and we'll part in a civil way. Why not?

We each pay our share of the bill and, exiting the restaurant, I follow him down the subway stairs at the corner. On the subway, we chatter until his stop: Essex Street, the Lower East Side. We walk a block or two from the subway station to his flat. Up three flights, double bolted doors that open up to his manipulations, and we step into his one-room apartment. I've never been here before. I see a small room, a bed pushed against one wall, a small cooking range against another, and a small toilet in the corner of the room—the only separate area with an inner door in this uninviting space. The front door shuts behind me and I turn to see Doug bolt it again from the inside—crazy tenement building locks that have a steel bar running into the floor—and suddenly the face before me twists into a pure malignancy: "No one says goodbye to me before I'm ready!" He stands blocking the door now. There's a razor in his hand. Where did that come from? He holds it before my face with one hand and pushes me with the other into the middle of the room.

"Undress," he says, and then stands back, the razor still in his hand,

watching me, his blue eyes stone cold. "Take it all off or I'll slit your throat."
I shake with terror, thinking this can't be happening this can't be where I die
it can't end like this as I slip out of my dress, fumble with my bra, and try to
think beyond this moment. But there is no beyond. I am about to die, I know.
He looks crazed with rage as he watches me slip off my underpants, then pushes
me roughly onto the bed and stands blocking the only side of the bed open to the
room. He drops his pants, no underwear, and steps out of them, eyes fixed on my
body, then lies down beside me still holding the razor with one hand near my
throat, and whispers into my ear. "Bitch, cunt, you'll feel this, you won't forget
me." Then, grabbing my supine body with his other hand, he turns me over,
and unseeing, only feeling, I am torn apart with the pain of a forced entrance
that almost obliterates my terror, feel myself being ripped apart again and again
as he repeatedly penetrates me and mauls my flesh while shouting obscenities.
But as long as he does this, I'm alive. What happens when he gets tired or comes?
Will I be dead then?

How long this goes on I don't know. There is no time in a traumatic event,
no duration, but at some point, the assault stops, the pain stops, and lying
there next to him I hold my breath and don't move. After a while I hear his
long steady rasps of breath and realize he is fast asleep. I roll gently over to
the open side of the bed and slide off. He hasn't awakened. Naked, I grab my
clothes from the floor, unlock the door as quietly as I can, moving the floor bar
upright, thinking, expecting that surely he'll hear me and wake up. But no, the
breathing remains heavy and rasping, and still naked, I dash into the darkened
hallway and down the stairs to the open front door of the building. The night
sky is just beginning to lighten, a pink-gray dawn in the city, and I am still
alive! I dress quickly, there in the darkened doorway, not another living soul in
sight. I can't believe my good fortune. I'm alive.

I never saw Doug again, though I kept worrying I might. A few months later, I read a story in the newspaper about a man named Douglas who had kidnapped his son from his ex-wife and run off to California. In the story, she pleaded for him to return the child, who needed essential medications. That could have been my Doug.

Tripping

It was Christmas Day, 1965. Manny Funk was sitting opposite me in my Village apartment on his last night in town before he returned to Berkeley. I'd offered him an LSD cube, one of several that I had bought earlier in the year from Richard Alpert, a.k.a. Ram Dass. Manny was last summer's romance when I stopped in Berkeley after a trip with Valerie to Alaska.

The Alaska trip had been a fabulous adventure. Val and I had set out for Cordova, a small fishing village on Prince William Sound, accessible only by boat or plane, where John and Sheelagh's fishing buddies lived. Getting there was itself a feat. We took a driveaway car to Seattle, and after delivering it, traveled by bus to nearby Vancouver; then by train through the gloriously thick green forests and rugged mountains of Northern British Columbia to Prince George; and then by bus to Prince Rupert, a rough and tumble frontier town on the coast with an intimidating macho ambiance. The next day we sailed on the ferry through the Inland Passage—thrilling to the sight of the southern Alaskan coastline during the day, sleeping uncomfortably in lounge chairs on deck overnight. We disembarked in Sitka, and having had the assistance of the ferry's captain, who announced our need for a ride on the ship's loudspeaker, we met up with two young men who were driving to Anchorage. We rode with them through the Yukon Territory, a vast barren spread of land that offered no cover—not even a cactus bush—for relieving ourselves on this long and arduous ride; necessity taught us not to be modest. From Anchorage we flew on an old B-42 plane in a heavy rainstorm to Cordova, the turbulence so intense that it sickened even the flight attendant, who spent most of the flight discretely vomiting in a corner of the cabin. White-knuckled and green-faced, we finally landed in what looked like a nineteenth-century outpost, its wooden sidewalks in the town center declaring Cordova's rough-hewn character. But the surrounding landscape was breathtaking. Jagged snowcapped mountains rose up in the near distance; beyond the town, mudflats stretched out to Prince William Sound.

Downtown Cordova

We stayed with John and Sheelagh's fishing friends, two bearded, husky, hard-drinking men, Sully and Cal, and one wispy, well-named woman, Bird, whose sensitive face and gentle mien at first seemed out of place. But she too was a tough bird. After a few days of talking and drinking with Sully and Cal and chatting more intimately with Bird about her life in Alaska, Val and I observed a slow drift among our male companions, from good-natured bantering, to morose philosophizing, to a worrisome show of temper. Bird also looked a bit concerned, and so Val and I decided it was time to change venues. Val went out for a week on a fishing boat on the Sound with an Art Institute photographer turned fisherman whom she had known in San Francisco years ago; I decided to travel by road to Fairbanks, a trip that Bird helped me plan. She had a friend teaching in Fairbanks with whom I could stay; and since there were no roads out of Cordova, she contacted a bush pilot to get me to Valdez, where I could use my thumb again.

To Valdez on an Alaskan bush plane

I flew in a two-seater bush plane across Prince William Sound and landed in what had been Valdez. Although I knew it had suffered from a recent earthquake, it shocked me to see how it had been razed to the ground. As if in a dream landscape, I wandered alone in a heavy silence down what were once streets, now mere pathways along roped-off property boundaries of former houses, aware of being the only living person in this unreal city. Reaching the highway on the outskirts, I easily picked up a ride at a gas station with a friendly trucker going to Fairbanks. Both courteous and helpful, he stopped the truck en route to let me have the experience of walking on a glacier. And it was truly an experience. Gingerly stepping onto that ice sheet, with the snow crunching slightly beneath my feet, I walked alone for several hundred yards, conscious of an awesome and ancient solidity that nevertheless contained hidden cracks and crevasses.

Hours later, I arrived safely at the home of Bird's friend Linda. She and I hit it off immediately, and for the next several days, she showed me around Fairbanks and the surrounding area. During the evening hours, the sky dusky with summer light, we two sat in her living room and shared a bottle of wine while we talked about literature, about living in Alaska, about the ways in which the landscape stoked the imagination. A few days later, she dropped me back on the road near a gas station, where I again hitched a ride with another genial truck driver, this time back to Anchorage. Exhilerated by my Alaskan adventure, I flew to Berkeley, my last stop on this western excursion, in the mood for a summer romance.

Berkeley offered it in the person of Manfred Funk, a passionate jazz afficionado and also, to my surprise, a kindergarten teacher. Tall, slim, handsome in an epicene way, like Barney, he bore an uncanny resemblance to those images of Christ I had seen in Patsy O'Brian's bedroom as a child but with one distinct difference: Manny was one-eyed, having lost an eye as a teenager in a gun accident. He wore a black eye patch, and occasionally, a glass eye. I found the eye-patch sexy, the glass eye mesmerizing.

An amateur saxophone player, Manny introduced me to a different Bay Area jazz scene from the one I had known with Max—clubs in which music from the twenties and thirties still flourished. Having been wined and dined and enjoyed his company for the several weeks I was in Berkeley, I casually promised to write. He wrote first, asking if he could visit me for the Christmas holidays. Well, why not? And so there he was on Christmas Day, and there I was, having bought some sugar cubes from Ram Dass a few months earlier, offering Manny an LSD trip before he returned to Berkeley. I took a cube first. I thought I knew what to expect, having already taken one earlier in the fall and experienced its slight hallucinogenic effect. But LSD was unpredictable, I knew, and so, as a precaution recommended by experienced users, I asked Manny to be my guide for the trip, and then we'd switch places. But I had badly miscalculated.

Sitting across from him in my living room, I waited for something to happen. And then it did. Manny's face began to change, to melt at its edges; his mouth became rubbery, twisting out of shape; his one eye glistened with menace. "You look like my mother," I heard myself say, feeling a hot flush at the back of my neck, my terror rising.

"What's the matter, dear ...? Can I help you?" he asked, but his tone was devious, his offer, meant to calm me, didn't fool me. I knew he wanted to kill me. He got up from the chair.

"No ...no, no, don't come near me." I heard screams as he approached, but it was me screaming. Looking more and more sinister, he sat down again, a malevolent smirk spreading across his face, then freezing into a gelid mask, smile fixed in place. I knew I was in the room with a vicious maniac.

After a while—impossible to know how much later—a wave of clarity washed over me. Manny looked like Manny, the objects in the room had boundaries, I was back to myself. I recognized I'd been on an LSD trip. But before I could assimilate that fact, another wave of timeless terror swept clarity away, and there he was again, my mother's malicious agent, or was he my mother in disguise? Then another wave of normal perception, I was me, he was him. And then it started all over again, his face, my terror, his words, my screams. When would this nightmare end? Another wave brought a serpent, twisting this way and that, but then the serpent was no longer terrifying: it was gorgeous, its scales bathed in a golden light, a vision of the divine splendor of the universe, spiritually exhilarating. How privileged I was to be raised up to this exquisite level of perception, this unveiling of a godlike magnificence, infusing the universe with love and beauty.... And then ordinary reality broke in again, but it was no longer ordinary; it too was altered somehow, waves of stunning clarity more frequent, and even the hallucinatory ones no longer fearsome but glorious. And then ...

And then it was twelve hours later, according to the clock in the living room. The experience of hell and heaven was over. No more waves to sweep me away, but instead, a sense of having had the most intense experience of my life. And Manny had been part of it. We had shared an extraordinary intimacy; we couldn't be separated. "You look like my mother," I had said! An intimation of significance that I was not yet disposed to explore, but I knew that we were now bound together. Two as One. I would quit my job and drive to Berkeley to live with him. I would return to graduate school at Cal, where I had been loved, coddled even, by the English Department. Alma Mater. The future beckoned with a golden light.

7

My "Berkeley in the Sixties": From Psychedelics to Psychoanalysis (1966–1974)

From error to error, one discovers the entire truth.

Sigmund Freud

Driving across the country yet again, this time to live with Manny, I was riding high on my sense of a new life. It was winter, and so I took the southern route, down through the rolling hills of Kentucky, Tennessee, Arkansas, stopping at budget motels on the way. Light snow lay in patches along the roadside, but the highway was clear as I entered the flatter landscape of Texas, powdered with snow, surprising this far south, the roads slick and demanding my full attention as cars sped by, too fast. High on Dexedrine, driving into nightfall across the Oklahoma panhandle through New Mexico to Arizona, a magical shower of stars appearing in the dense darkness of desert sky as I headed straight toward the California freeway. No snow after Indio but a tricky fog enveloping me, more traffic joining as I headed north, crawling along slowly in a thick sea of whiteness, barely able to see the car in front of me. The fog lifted once I passed the farms and orchards of the Central Valley, and finally, after a few hours, there was the turnoff taking me to Manny's place in the Oakland hills, just outside the Berkeley line. The Bay glowed warm in the sunset as I found my way to his small cottage and glided into his driveway.

Two years after the Free Speech movement, Berkeley was still active with political purpose, its energy now turned toward resistance to the Vietnam War. A time of radical protest as well as radical sexual liberation—the Sexual Freedom League was clamoring for initiates—Berkeley's mantra, "Make Love, Not War," sang out on posters around the campus. I assumed it as my own. But my life with Manny had little to do with politics. Once again, having been accepted into the English Department's graduate program and given back my teaching assistantship, I was splitting my time between graduate studies at Cal and the local Bay Area jazz scene—this time not the cool contemporary jazz I had listened to with Max (who had since married, I learned sourly), but Manny's preferred domain: traditional jazz. Our evenings were often spent with a group of jazz record collectors who sat around listening to music of the thirties and forties and testing each other's knowledge: "Hey, that's Teddy Wilson on that side." "'It Don't Mean a Thing'—Ellington recorded that in 1932!" "Lady Day and Prez, so smooth together" "'Just You, Just Me'—that was Lester in 1948, his best time." They congregated either at our new place—after a few months of living in Manny's small cottage in Oakland, we had moved into a larger house in West Berkeley—or at a nearby jazz club we all frequented. On other evenings, Manny and I drove over to Montclair to spend the evening with Jack Vance, a Dixieland jazz aficionado. Big, burly, jovial, with steely observant eyes that twinkled behind rimless glasses, Jack was a writer of mysteries and science fiction as well as a talented raconteur. Sitting with him and his wife Norma in their woodsy, well-crafted living room in the Montclair hills, drinking beer and chatting about music or current events or the great outdoors, I often wondered why, although he was a writer, literature per se never entered the conversation.

Perhaps the person I was most fond of in Manny's social circle was his fast-talking, wisecracking DJ friend and drinking companion, Bob Houlihan, who hosted a jazz show on KJAZ. Red-faced and blue-eyed, Houlihan was by far the wittiest of Manny's cronies, always ready with a quick quip and the first to laugh at it. I'd never seen him sober, but nevertheless, I took him seriously. There was an urgency to his alcoholic self-indulgence, a ferocity to his laughter, as if he were driven to self-destruct.

Drinking was part of our lifestyle: gin martinis before dinner, wine with, brandy after, and then, if there were no musical evening out, Manny and I weaved our way toward sleep or sex. Occasionally, we ingested mind-altering substances—mescaline and psilocybin bought on the street—for an evening's entertainment. Then, as if in a trance, I stared at camera projections of saturated colors—red, purple, yellow, green sensually dripping down the wall of the living room in ephemeral patterns that seemed to open what Aldous Huxley famously called "the doors of perception" for each of us, alone. Or, with the lights turned down and Billie Holiday singing in the background, we ate brownies laced with grass, or we smoked it and then acted out sexual fantasies that Manny suggested. Naked, we floated around in a haze of sensual play that often ended in bondage scenarios that Manny composed: a flick of a tie—soft, not leather—against my bare flesh—sex almost on the edge, exciting.

Marijuana was always plentiful in our household, especially after one vacation in Mazatlán. Having brought back a large supply from Mexico, Manny and I cleaned, packaged, and sold it to friends. What a tableau we made, the two of us leaning over the kitchen table at night, the overhead light illuminating the pile of weed as we made up small five-dollar bags to distribute. I couldn't quite believe it, our ritual enactment of a criminal scene, knowing we could be arrested for dealing, even though we sold only small amounts, and only to people we knew. The benefits of our little joint venture: a little extra cash, but more than that, the pleasure of enacting an illicit drama.

A well-paid teacher in a Berkeley public school, Manny didn't lack for cash. Nor did he limit his pursuit of hedonistic pleasures in which I readily joined him. At least once monthly, we ate at the very best expensive restaurants in the Bay area, and I didn't hesitate to judge them.

Indeed, when we dined at the Le Trianon, I shocked even Manny when I told the chef, René Verdon—formerly JFK's chef at the White House—that his beef Wellington was too dry! I chewed on my comment with self-gratification for days.

Another great delight was sailing on Manny's new trimaran, and although I was prone to sea sickness, luckily, I discovered Marezine, which allowed me to enjoy fully riding the windswept waves of San Francisco Bay while glorying in the views of the city outlined against the sky to the west, Sausalito and Tiburon dotting the hills of Marin County to the north. On warm weather days, I would lie on the cabin top, sipping a gin martini over ice and occasionally helping with the jib—although Manny did the real work of sailing. It was a California idyll, sailing, eating in gourmet restaurants, going to jazz concerts on weekends, and attending literature classes during the week. What more could I want?

Manny on his trimaran

But as one year passed into the next, I was increasingly restless. *Shpilkes*, my mother would say. Gradually, the LSD effect was wearing off, and I began to realize that my commitment to Manny was based on a drug-induced illusion that had faded. Now my principal gratification came from my graduate seminars and from conversations with classmates who were fast becoming friends. Interpreting literature, always my strong suit for building self-confidence, was a wellspring of delight. Given my desultory lifestyle, I even surprised myself when, taking an undergraduate class in Early American literature to fill in my background, I became infatuated with the enflamed prose of the puritan writer Jonathan Edwards: "Strait is the gate, and narrow is the way." Not my way, yet the intense resonance of his voice moved me to consider concentrating on American literature rather than British for my degree!

That interest was strengthened when Marilyn Fabe, the reading assistant for that class, told me the professor had instructed her to "use the exam of the beautiful Jewess as the norm for an A." At first, I was pleased by what I took as a compliment of both my interpretive skills and my personal attractiveness. Yet the term "Jewess" rankled. I had always squirmed seeing the word in novels; it smacked of antisemitism, of an essentialist identity that I had refused. I thought of the well-known "Jewesses" of literature, dark-haired beauties like Scott's Rebecca, or Hawthorne's Miriam, exceptional women—strong, independent, smart—who, for the most part, were ultimately exiled or humiliated, losers in the game of life. I admired their strength but not their fate. Literature taught me that to be called a Jewess was not a compliment but an exclusion.

The more fervently I became engaged with literature, the less satisfying was life with Manny, and a familiar question began to obsess me: How could I get out of this unsuitable liaison without creating a scene? How even to broach the subject with Manny? "I want to be alone"? Of course, I didn't want to be alone. Or did I? I didn't know myself. There were times when solitude was deeply satisfying, when no one else was needed. But such an absoluteness of self was also frightening, and I moved away from that thought. More immediately, what I wanted was to get out of this coupling; I wanted more, not less, world. When I finally worked up the courage to say "I want to live on my own" (I didn't admit that I had already found a cute little cottage behind Sheelagh and John's house on Edith Street), it came as a shock to Manny. His response was a shock to me as well.

"You can't mean it!" he screamed at me, kicking over a chair in our living room. He stood there for a moment in the middle of the room looking wild—and then broke into tears.

"We can still see each other," I said uselessly, trying to calm him, although focused as I was on leaving, my sympathetic impulses were frozen. I watched him turn and disappear into the bedroom. Moments later, he reappeared in the doorway with a gun in his hand. I stood speechless as he stepped toward me spinning the barrel of the gun. Would he actually shoot me? When he finally stopped moving, the threat came at me aslant:

"I'll call your parents and tell them what a slut you are!"

My parents! They would be devastated!

"I'll kill myself and make you watch!"

He'll kill himself, not me!

Now I could afford to become angry as well as frightened. This was emotional blackmail. My mind was spinning like the gun's barrel, searching for a way to put a stop to his hysteria. I didn't blame myself. I didn't acknowledge my role in this scenario. As if from a distance, I saw his pain, but all I really wanted was for him to disappear.

"OK, OK, it's OK, stop, stop, put the gun away, don't act crazy, I'm not leaving. . . . We'll work something out. . . ."

Reiterating these sentiments in various ways, I eventually convinced Manny to put away the gun, but the only *out* I worked was to move out of our house surreptitiously the next morning while he was at work, knowing that this was only a temporary solution. I would have to deal in some effective way with Manny's mental breakdown and my part in provoking it. For the next few days, I slinked fearfully around the streets of Berkeley, not wanting to be seen. But I also called Manny's former psychotherapist, someone Manny had often spoken of admiringly, and explained the situation. Fortunately, he convinced Manny to voluntarily enter the psychiatric ward at Herrick Hospital for treatment. After a few weeks, Manny recovered his composure, accepted the end of the affair, and the LSD-generated drama was over.

But how similar was this situation to my history with Brian! I could no longer ignore the fact that I was inevitably drawn to men who needed me or something I represented—men who lived on the edge of breakdown. Was this what I unknowingly aimed for? Did I really want life to be a series of menacing scenes that I unwittingly encouraged and then left? And what of my own almost criminal indifference to the feelings of the men I had lived with? Was I exploiting them for my own selfish needs? It occurred to me that I exploited only men, not my women friends. My betrayals were profoundly gendered. How to understand that?

I was not enamored of these fragments of self-reflection. Confused by my own patterns of behavior, when a friend in analytic training at the Jung Institute in San Francisco told me of an eminent Jungian analyst at Langley Porter who was looking for graduate student subjects for a research project, I immediately made an appointment to see him for a consultation. I didn't like who I had become; I knew I needed help.

Toe-Stepping into Analytic Waters

A tall, handsome, well-dressed man in a tweed jacket, John Perry welcomed me warmly into his office, a plush wood-paneled room lined with bookcases and paintings, the ambiance exuding a sense of worldly knowledge. After a brief interview, he offered me a once-a-week analysis for two dollars an hour—an offer I couldn't refuse—but with the requirement that I bring in a dream every week. As ordered, I dreamt once a week.

Two dreams:

1) I'm sitting on a train with a cut in my finger. My mother sits across the aisle from me with a group of people who are watching a movie. The cut becomes infected, causing a huge swelling; I squeeze it and pus flies across the room, getting on people walking down the aisle. My mother sees me holding my finger and runs to me solicitously. I show her the cut, which horrifies her.

2) My family and I are sitting in a restaurant; the tables are covered with red and white checkered tablecloths. The Italian restaurant owner is sitting at a nearby table. He is a firefighter on the side. We converse, bonding because we're both from the Bronx. My father is very angry at my talking to this man; he associates him with "the underworld." I want to talk to him, however, and my family, led by my father, storms out. The restaurateur tells me the story of losing his restaurant.

Very Jungian, these dreams, Dr. Perry assured me. My mother, solicitous, but unable to help me heal; my father, enraged, unable to connect. Animus and anima. Both figures inside me, embattled. With great assurance, Dr. Perry offered a prescription for change: "Develop your anima." Apparently, as he told me, my animus was too strong.

So, cozy in my own little cabin behind John and Sheelagh's house, I tried to do just that. First, I had the hard clay soil in my small eight-by-twelve-foot backyard rototilled and good, rich soil added. Then I planted flowers—black-eyed Susans, zinnias, poppies, and a lavender bush—taking pleasure in feeling the soft, new, dark earth pass through my fingers even when it got beneath my fingernails. Mother Earth. But I did not abandon my animus; it was still thriving in my graduate work. I couldn't really imagine myself "a professor," but I seemed to be moving slowly in that direction.

There was, of course, good reason for moving slowly, for at the same time that I was trying to clean up the mess I'd made of my personal life, the political situation was heating up. Media reports on the Vietnam War showed the horrors of American involvement: images of napalm bombings, wounded soldiers, children aflame. On campuses across the country, outrage and anger swelled to bursting at the ravages we were causing abroad in the name of democracy, and nowhere more radically than in Berkeley. Teach-ins, street rallies, draft card burnings—the protests grew in seriousness and in fervor. My hands were colored purple from mimeographing leaflets that we passed out in the community. Classes were held off-campus. The ivory tower was collapsing.

1969: Make Love, Not War

It was not only the Vietnam War that provoked the students to political action. Under Clark Kerr, a liberal who seemed to have lost his way, the university administration had become an immediate target of protest for its collusion in American imperialist policy. The conflict came to a head when the university administration resisted the attempt by a contingent of young volunteers with picks and spades to create a People's Park on the site of an unused piece of property owned by UC. Inflamed by rumors that a basketball court was to be built on the site, a crowd of young people marched down Telegraph Avenue vowing to protect this "People's Park." In response, Reagan called in the National Guard, who entered Berkeley like an occupying army, bearing arms. They had their own way of "protecting the park"—with a cyclone fence and bayonets. Not surprisingly, their presence promoted more protests, in which I participated. As I looked into the faces of these national guardians, it was obvious that many were young recruits who didn't want to be there. Some of us tried to engage them in conversation, and taking our cue from the Haight-Ashbury flower children, offered them flowers. I shoved some black-eyed Susans from my yard into the fence, and a young guardsman smiled at me good-naturedly.

But Reagan had told the local police to do "whatever it takes" to suppress the protest movement. Worse yet, he called in the Alameda County Sheriff's Department, a police force more brutal than the National Guard. They too had guns.

In the midst of this turmoil, Valerie came to visit me. Her second marriage had ended in disappointment, and she wanted the comfort of our friendship. We had arranged to meet in front of the student union, but the campus had become a war zone. Students were fleeing helter-skelter pursued by uniformed troops, tear gas was being released from a helicopter flying above the union. Given the campus tumult, Val and I retreated to the Mediterranean Café on Telegraph Avenue, at some distance from the acrid smell in the air and the turbulent fray on the ground.

We had just sat down with our coffee when suddenly the owner of the Med dashed out from behind the counter, waving his arms as if shooing away a horde of flies and shouting, "Everyone out, everyone out." Confusion spread quickly; through the café's large plate glass window, I could see people running down the street. A moment later, Val and I were unceremoniously hustled out into an already crowded entranceway. Immediately, two Alameda County sheriffs, standing in front of the doorway facing us, shot tear gas directly into our faces. Blinded, my eyes burning, I felt a wet towel thrust into my hands by strangers from a volunteer aid brigade: "Hold this to your eyes. Don't rub. It'll help." We were lucky. Someone was shot and killed a block away.

People's Park protest, Telegraph Avenue 1969

Strategic Relations

A few months later, political actions having abated over the summer, I received a telephone call from an acquaintance of Manny's, Erik Henderson, a physicist who worked at the Lawrence Radiation Laboratory, the citadel of nuclear science overlooking Berkeley's campus.

"I hear that you and Manny are no longer a couple. I thought you might like to have dinner some evening."

And so it began again. With the Vietnam conflict ratcheting up, I entered into a relationship that would absorb me for the next several years. But this one was different, I hoped. I wanted it to last. I had my own agenda. I was thirty-five. I wanted a child.

At first, I was delighted by Erik; he was not only handsome, but also a reputedly brilliant physicist, fiercely committed to finding a nontoxic source of energy—fusion rather than fission—as well as a devotee of contemporary music with an extraordinary knowledge of its avant-garde. In fact, there were so many interests we shared, and I was so attracted to him physically, that for the first time since my aborted love affair with Barney, I began to think of marrying. Up against the clock and absolutely determined not to miss the experience of having a child—that's how I thought of it, an *experience* rather than a commitment—I fixed upon Erik as the very man to fulfill my desire. With him, so my logic spun out, I could have an *ideal* child: one who incorporated both our physical traits—Northern European and Southern Mediterranean—and our complementary intellectual abilities—scientific and literary. In short, I was imagining an *Übermensch*. Magical thinking, no doubt, yet I believed my desire was imbued with genetic probability. My task: to make this relationship work.

As it happened, my parents were coming to California for a long-deferred visit. "I should have never allowed you to go to college. That was your ruin," my father had bellowed at me not so long ago, his face set in a habitual scowl. My mother's face, on the other hand, regularly blazed with love and concern even as she worried aloud at my unmarried state. Now, curious about my lifestyle, they were coming to see it for themselves. And now I worried. Determined to introduce them to Erik, how could I do it without arousing their old prejudice against my having a non-Jewish boyfriend? How could I manage the inevitable awkwardness of a meeting between an American physicist of Scandinavian ancestry and two suspicious East European Jewish immigrants? And then I hit upon an answer: I would ask Erik to give them a tour of his workplace, that nuclear physics research edifice sitting impressively on a knobby promontory overlooking the campus. Since their interaction would be structured around the tour of an imposing national site, conversation would necessarily be limited. *Take it step by step*, I told myself.

The first step in wooing my parents: a few days into their visit, after I'd shown them around the Berkeley campus and given them a tour of the hills with their panoramic views of the Bay, I invited Julie, my tough Jewish friend from Brooklyn, to have dinner with us in my apartment. I meant to reassure my parents that I had Jewish friends, but I hadn't counted on the obvious: both Julie and my father were aggressively dogmatic; both asserted rather than conversed. That evening, the talk around the dinner table quickly turned rocky as my father and Julie, well-matched in their obstinacies, disagreed on every issue. I shuddered as the dinner party hovered on the verge of a precipice. Julie called me the next morning to tell me what I already knew: "Your father is like a two-ton truck in conversation; no opposition tolerated."

The next day, as planned, I introduced my parents to "my good friend" Erik, who was going to give them "a tour of the Lawrence Radiation Laboratory, where he works." Erik drove us up the steep canyon road to the Rad Lab and once in his element, walked us through the lab and the cyclotron, explaining in layman's terms their operations. As we made the rounds, I watched my father's face change from its initial impassive expression to one of awe. His eyes actually opened more widely as he began to grasp Erik's—and thus my—proximity to this formidable center of American prestige and power. Even my mother, who understood little of Erik's talk, seemed full of wonder at this apparent rise in her daughter's social status.

They never asked me if Erik was Jewish. The visit was a success.

But as the intimacy between Erik and me unfolded over the year, certain quirks in his persona made me uneasy. For one thing, whenever he attempted to articulate an idea or express an opinion, he searched with difficulty for the words he needed—a situation that put a strain on our conversations and limited our intellectual exchanges. For another, when we attended concerts, he often was so moved by the music that tears freely flowed down into his beard while I sat self-consciously beside him, discomfited by his lack of emotional control. But most disturbingly, he often projected his own thoughts or perceptions onto me, insisting they were mine so convincingly that at times I became uncertain of my own mind. Had I really thought or said what he said I said or thought? Unsettled by this mental porousness, I found myself at times running to friends to verify my separate sense of reality.

And yet, I loved looking at him, being held in his arms, imagining him the father of a child that would be both brilliant and beautiful. On long weekends, we would drive down to Baja California, stopping along the way to make love outdoors in a national park with the redwoods literally at our backs or in the car along the highway, his ardor wrapping me in a blanket of pleasure. Crossing into Baja, we would explore the empty beaches along the coast, camping out on glorious moonlit nights; or we would drive up into the mountains on rough terrain to a hidden hotel—a dangerous ascent for his Toyota that made the outing an adventure for us both. When he suggested we move into a small nineteenth-century cottage in San Francisco on Telegraph Hill, with a dramatic view of the Bay Bridge, and live there together for a year, I quickly agreed, despite my qualms.

And so, filled with ambivalent anticipation, I settled with Erik into our cottage on quaint Napier Lane, accessible only by way of the steep Filbert Street steps, and played at marriage. Each morning, Erik went to work at the lab in Berkeley, I read for my seminars, wrote my papers, and grew tomatoes in the planter on the front porch—animus and anima in balance. Each evening, we sat at the kitchen table, often in the nude, looking at a glorious view of the Bay Bridge, drinking good red wine, holding up our glasses to the future.

On one such warm evening, feeling especially content, I brought up my desire to have a child. Erik's response was dismaying: he adamantly refused to be a father. He already had two children from a previous marriage and had no desire to have another. Disheartened, I dropped the subject, but not my desire, thinking he might yet change his mind once he saw how well we had fit ourselves into a satisfying domesticity. I should have guessed then that our seemingly easy relationship would become increasingly burdened by my wish, and his refusal.

Several months later, we were standing in the kitchen after dinner, finishing the last drops of wine before doing the dishes, and once again, I brought up the subject of a child. Once again, Erik threw cold water on my desire, but this time, leaning against the sink and twirling his wineglass, he casually remarked, "Anyway, I don't think you'd be a good mother." The words cut sharply into the softness of the evening. In an uncontrollable rush of hot anger, I threw my wineglass at him with all my strength. It crashed against the sink and shattered into shards near his naked feet. I froze, appalled. The past tore into my consciousness and ripped it open, revealing a time-warped repetition of my mother's impulsive responses when she was thwarted. I saw now that I'd constructed a fantasy about some Edenic domesticity with Erik that didn't match our reality. In the ensuing days, one truth about the future became clear: Erik would neither father my child nor remain my partner. By the end of our year on Telegraph Hill, the word "love" had disappeared from our conversation, and we moved back to Berkeley—to separate quarters.

Earthquake Sounds

While the affair with Erik was winding down, the second wave of feminism was sweeping into the Bay Area, bringing with it the new practice of consciousness-raising groups, perhaps the most effective strategy to emerge from feminism for women like me. Sitting around with a group of friends and acquaintances in Berkeley in the early seventies, all highly educated middle-class women of my age, I discovered how much personal experience I thought was mine alone was actually a shared condition among us. How many of us felt the need to have our fathers' approval and, like me, muted our own voices to get it? Or felt guilty if we didn't? How inhibited especially were our *public* voices, our uncertainty of our own authority, our fear of humiliation as women in a man's world? *Take her back and bring me a boy.* Words still worming their way through the folds of consciousness.

Even the most trivial aspects of our daily lives became a group revelation. Like wearing high-heeled shoes. As my friend Marilyn complained, "I wore them to feel attractive, but wearing those damned heels totally unbalanced me!" Unbalanced me too, as I confessed, remarking on the sad irony of habitually wearing high-heeled shoes despite having inherited my father's bad feet, my painful corns and calluses a daily reminder of our congenital bond. And how incongruous a demand high heels for women were, we sophisticates all agreed, since it was primarily a male fetish, proof that male desire dominated our fashion models, and thus us.

But even more consequential was our new understanding of the feminist mantra that the personal was the political. Seeing my experience as a common condition of women was the key to resisting my often self-imposed silence by swallowing my outrage. Indeed, these feminist insights began to alter the very shape of my relation to the world, and so, inevitably, my future. I began to take myself more seriously as a scholar who was not just playing but working toward a serious profession. What remained constant, however, was my increasingly obsessive desire for a child. As it turned out, the question of having a child became a controversial issue in our group, and ultimately resulted in a book co-authored by my friend Marilyn Fabe and Norma Wikler: *Up Against the Clock.*

Since my failed first love affair with Barney, when we had playfully planned to have nine children, I had put aside any desire for a child for the sake of a free and easy "automobility" that included sexual relations. Like many other women, at the age of twenty, I had been fitted for a diaphragm at New York's Sanger Clinic, and even when, in the heat of passion, I hadn't inserted it (without the diaphragm, sex was another kind of exciting risk), luckily, I had never gotten pregnant. Unlike several of my friends, I had never needed the services of the amateur abortionists who practiced in the shadowy alleyways of New York or California. When the birth control pill appeared as an option, pregnancy was easily avoided, saving me and many women from the deleterious consequences of illegal abortions. But ironically, while living with Erik on Telegraph Hill, I had fallen through the rotten floorboards of our cottage porch and developed a blood clot in my leg, and so I had had to stop using the pill for medical reasons. Compelled to return to the diaphragm, a less secure wall against conception, I thought more seriously about having a child. Already in my late thirties, I needed to allow a breach in the wall soon.

If feminism and child-bearing was a hot topic among my friends, psychoanalysis was the hot topic in the English Department. Frederick Crews had initiated a new course on psychoanalysis and literature that quickly became the most talked about graduate seminar in the department, and I decided to take it. Although initially resistant to the pronouncements of the father of psychoanalysis—surely infantile sexuality did not control our adult destinies, nor did penis envy characterize women's development—I found myself persuaded by Freud's theory of the unconscious and its corollary, that unrecognized wishes stemming from the parent-child relationship directed our present behavior. Earthquake sounds, cracks in the foundation.

The consequence of this new understanding: I determined to write a dissertation about a contemporary American woman writer using aspects of psychoanalytic theory that melded with my new feminist insights. Looking into the published fiction of the past decade or so, I came upon the work of Flannery O'Connor, a Southerner and a Catholic, whose comic-grotesque fiction was little known as yet in the academy. After reading a few of her stories, I knew I had found my dissertation subject.

O'Connor's fictional concern was narrow; recurrently, she depicted enraged characters, mostly parents and children insisting on their self-sufficiency, but locked into fierce attachments that ended only with a violation so intense that they were forced to recognize their essential dependence. "I'm doing alright by myself," an O'Connor character says in an ironic allusion to Paul's warning in the New Testament against believing in self-help. Echoing Paul, O'Connor repeatedly overturned that assertion through some unexpected act of violence that opened them to change.

Although O'Connor's avowed intent in portraying violent acts was to shock her readers into a religious awakening, her psychological portraits as well as her sardonic wit drew me, a secular reader and a Northerner, into the heart of her fiction. Her skill in caricature, her ability to capture the essence of a character with just a few strokes of her pen, as well as the unexpected violence at the climax of her stories—this was writing just begging for a psychoanalytical reading. Almost as important to me was that O'Connor had produced a relatively small body of work—two novels and two collections of stories. I would not have to do enormous research; I could probably finish the dissertation in a year or so. Up against the clock, I needed to finish quickly if I were ever to get a job—and have a child.

Yet somehow, I couldn't seem to begin the actual process of writing. Months passed; I stared at the blank page in the typewriter and smoked incessantly, filling the huge ashtray I had bought especially for the occasion. As I read and reread O'Connor's stories, I found myself again and again interrupted by increasingly obsessive thoughts. Shouldn't I be "producing" a child before it was too late instead of sitting alone in my apartment trying to produce a dissertation? Was I going to miss this crucial female experience? And even if I wrote the dissertation, why would anyone hire me, already in my mid-thirties, when I knew that academic departments were looking for young blood? I felt the future shrinking as my anxiety swelled. To add to my distraction, Erik dropped by periodically, and though we were no longer a couple, we always ended up in bed. I couldn't seem to cut the sensual cord that kept me tied to him.

A Snake in the Family

In the midst of my struggle to write, I received an unexpected call from my mother: "You must come home. Albert is very sick, he sits around and cries and won' get up or out. We don' know what to do.... Oy, oy, I'm so afraid for him. You must come home and help him. I don' know how." I hung up the phone with a heavy heart, and a wave of guilt swept over me, as it had in the past; I had abandoned my brother; I had made my getaway early from my needy parents; he had been caught in the tentacles of their love. Now, from what my mother said, he seemed to be on the verge of a psychological breakdown, crying and refusing to leave his room; now he really needed my help. Having been studying

Freud, I thought I knew exactly the kind of help he needed. I immediately arranged to fly back to New York.

Confident in my diagnostic abilities, as soon as I arrived at our Bronx apartment, I began to search for a psychiatrist who specialized in psychosomatic medicine. Unable to get an appointment with the preeminent doctor in that field, I accepted his office's recommendation for a substitute and took my brother by the hand, literally, for his first few appointments in mid-town Manhattan. Speaking with overweening hubris, I gave the psychiatrist my diagnosis of my brother's condition: his symptoms were a version of oedipal repression, I informed him, and I lay out its narrative scenario. What the psychiatrist thought of my presumption I never knew; but under his treatment, Al not only improved in mood during the next few months, but within the year, he had taken a computer course to learn programming, gotten a job with the city of New York, and moved into an apartment in Manhattan. A year later, he met a sweet-tempered woman who adored him; she moved in and eventually became his wife.

But my role in his radical change of circumstance cost me a terrible scene with my father that would haunt me for years to come. I still vividly recall sitting in the living room of the Bronx apartment encouraging my brother to move out when my father, overhearing me from the adjoining bedroom, burst into the room livid with rage: "You nogood selfish *choleria*, you snake!" he spit out at me, his face contorted with hatred and disgust. "You're always against the family!" His words thundering forth were hammer blows pounding me to bits. Utterly devastated, I cried for forty-eight hours without being able to stop. Without being able to look him in the face for years. *I* was now the *choleria* in my father's eyes.

Returning to Berkeley exceedingly distraught after that scene—I had to take a Valium in order to stop crying—I knew I too needed help.

A Rage of Vision

Help arrived initially from an unexpected source: a semester-long clinical seminar offered by the San Francisco Psychoanalytic Institute to interested Berkeley graduate students and faculty. Reading Freud with clinicians rather than literary critics made a huge difference. Clinicians presented actual case histories: mothers and fathers, daughters and sons, families locked in antagonisms permeated by erotic desires, idealizations, and disappointments. Listening to those case histories, I began randomly to associate to my own family conflicts, and I soon realized that an analyst could use these "free associations" to help me make sense of my writing block, my tie to Erik, my obsessive desire for a child. Here in the seminar were the institute's luminaries, experts in aiding such self-understanding. Surveying the group, I set my sights on the only woman analyst at the table. She seemed both intellectually confident and warmly personable—the very features I admired and envied. At the end of the seminar, I tentatively approached her. To my great relief, she agreed to see me once a week for a discounted fee. Moving out of my apartment into a furnished room so that I could afford a weekly therapy hour, I began the intimidating process of self-discovery—this time with an analyst who would not dismiss my animus.

For the first six months, I went on faith. I drove weekly across the Bay Bridge to San Francisco, and although I would periodically miss the freeway exit leading to my analyst's office, I also missed the uncanny implications of these "mistakes" that Freud had described as unconscious detours enacting unwanted confrontations. Of course, since psychoanalysis was "talk therapy," I talked—about my inability to leave an unworkable relationship, my foundering dissertation, my ambivalence about the future.

Nothing that was said in that room seemed to open new doors of understanding. Except one thing: my psychoanalytic hour seemed more a bibliotherapy than a psychotherapy. As my analyst wryly pointed out one afternoon, whereas most patients would bring into their talk associations to family members and family history, I would free-associate to an O'Connor character, a fictional situation, a text. I could talk about the maternal figures in O'Connor's stories who aroused the rage of daughters, but had little to say about my own mother, whose emotional outbursts bore no apparent relation to O'Connor's prim matrons. I could point to a fierce paternal authority that haunted an O'Connor character but was unable to free-associate to my own father and the judgmental role he continued to play in my psychic life. Apparently, exploring my personal history meant projecting it elsewhere—into the fiction of a writer as different from myself as anyone I could imagine.

One day, unable to find a parking space, with my hour coming up, I decided to pull into my analyst's driveway. Since it was time for my session, I reasoned, my analyst most likely was in her office and wouldn't be using her driveway for at least the next fifty minutes. *Fait accompli,* I hurried to the waiting room and waited for the usual buzzer that signaled me to enter her office, but the room was silent. No buzzer sounded. A short time later, to my great surprise and discomfort, my analyst herself appeared in the doorway of the waiting room, her eyes narrowed into a cold stare.

"Is that your car in my driveway?" she asked sternly.

"Yes."

"Please move it right now; I can't get into my garage."

Embarrassed, but also irritated—I was losing my hour to this parking fiasco—I rushed out, drove around for what seemed an interminable time until I found a space, and returned to the office harried and angry, with only ten minutes of my hour left.

As we discussed this incident, I felt annoyed with my analyst for making such a fuss. Why was my parking in her driveway such a big deal? After all, I hadn't known that she hadn't yet arrived. Yes, I freely admitted, there were other special privileges I took: double parking when I couldn't find a space—who would care if I were there only briefly? Parking next to a fire hydrant—who would be harmed? No fire would break out in the short time I intended to be parked. Although these minor infractions felt both trivial and justified by the demands of the situation, I could hear the disapproval in her questions, and I swelled with indignation at her using up my valuable time with this petty interrogation. I said nothing about these feelings during the brief remaining minutes of this botched session, but when I got back to Berkeley, I told every friend I encountered how furious I was at her self-righteousness. The following week, with my rage safely spent, I went into my session and told my analyst how angry *I had been*.

If I thought that was the end of it, I was mistaken. Like the closing remark of *Portnoy's Complaint*—"now vee may perhaps begin"—this recognition of my rage was the real beginning of my psychoanalysis. For shortly after this confrontation, almost as if a curtain were parting to reveal a secret drama being performed in some hidden corner of my mind, at moments of relaxation, disquieting visions involuntarily flooded my mind; vivid, erotic, and violent scenes appeared before me as on a screen, interposing themselves between me and the real world, even in the midst of a casual conversation. One evening, saying good night to Erik at my door, suddenly I saw him standing before me stripped naked and vulnerable, his flesh bloodied, and then falling backward, fragmenting, his body parts decomposing. I forced myself to push these images out of my mind, to close the inner curtain and continue with ordinary life. At the same time, my dream life took on an extraordinarily transgressive charac- ter; now, family members frolicked before my inner eye, seducing me into orgiastic pleasures from which I awoke in a panic. No longer confined by O'Connor's mediating fictions, my inner life seemed to be displacing my outer life in intensity and even duration. Without increasing her fee, my analyst increased the number of hours I saw her.

What happened next I did not anticipate: I began seriously to write my dissertation. The words flowed effortlessly; the argument was strong. My psy- choanalysis was apparently working, and although I didn't know why, I did know it had something to do with my past habit of swallowing rage. "Make Love, Not War," the slogan floating around Berkeley, had lost its antithetical quality; the line of difference had blurred. Something was happening.

Perhaps the most curious evidence that I was undergoing a psychological change occurred one afternoon when, after leaving my analyst's office, I stopped at Macy's before heading across the Bay Bridge. I almost always stopped to shop after a therapy session, a compulsion that often ended with my shoplifting some trivial item. Usually, I shoplifted small items: sweaters, hats, sunglasses, belts—nothing I really needed but things I suddenly wanted. Now, at Macy's, I spotted a lovely blouse, tried it on in the dressing room, and then walked out to see myself in a larger mirror on the main floor. *Yes, this looks good. . . . I'll buy it.* I looked around for a salesperson, but not one was in sight. Annoyed by this lack, I followed my old rationalizing logic: *Oh well, since there's no one around, I'll just walk out wearing it.*

But as I stood there in front of the mirror, hand on hip, with that rationale in mind, I heard my analyst's voice: *You are an adult; take responsibility for what you are doing.*

I shifted my weight to my left foot and looked in the mirror again, thinking: *But there's no one around; there should be a salesperson on the floor. Not my fault if there isn't.* I shifted my weight onto my right foot: *You should take responsibility for yourself and not blame your actions on someone else. You are grown up now.* After shifting back and forth—left foot, right foot, left foot, right foot—I returned to the dressing room, took off the blouse, and left the store, blouse-less and blameless.

Two years later, I had completed my dissertation—appropriately called "A Rage of Vision"—broken the bonds of my fruitless erotic tie with Erik, and was ready to apply for an academic position and assume a responsible place in the world. How that had happened, I still had no clear idea, though when I complained to my analyst about my lack of understanding, she said: "Why don't you trust that good work is being done unconsciously?" Certainly, I was proof that it was. Somehow I had taken her perspective inside me; somehow I had been made purposeful under her watchful eye and resonant voice. Now, I thought, with my feminist and psychoanalytic supports in place, I could take on the fathers.

But could I? The academic job market was notoriously competitive, with few tenured women in English departments. Despite the new affirmative action policies, I knew that I was beyond the age limit for acceptable hires. In order to get beyond that hurdle, I lied about my age: a strategy of dissembling I had learned from my brother, who had lied to get his first job. And it clearly worked. I received eleven interview offers, an inordinately large number compared to my classmates. The next hurdle to overcome: to present myself in person rather than on paper as a desirable candidate.

But whatever the outcome of the academic interviews, one thing I was sure of: I would no longer shoplift.

8

Loosening the Paternal Bonds, Listening to the Mother Tongue (1974–1994)

The stories we tell ourselves about our private pasts shape how we come to see our personhood and who we ultimately become.

Maria Popova

Chicago, 1973: I am a woman graduate student about to be interviewed for a position as an assistant professor in the eminent, though unconventional, English Department of SUNY Buffalo. I know from the academic grapevine that this year they must hire at least one woman; affirmative action is now the law. But the requirement itself may put me at a disadvantage, for in this department of seventy-five members, seventy are men who will likely bristle at having to bow to this external demand. As I stand outside of the door of the interview room in the carpeted corridor of an elegant Chicago hotel, I can hear raucous laughter coming from within the room, and my anxiety level goes up a notch. Then the door opens, a fresh-faced young man of about my age ushers me in, and I enter a smoke-filled room crowded with men—fourteen, I learn later—of varying ages sitting around a conference table. Several of them are puffing on cigars; others are still laughing from some earlier joke and talking to one another. Noticing me, one of the talkers invites me to take a seat at the table. After a few moments, the buzz quiets down and the questions begin.

Questions I can do, and I feel myself relax, feel a surge of confidence as I begin to respond. Then the first hint of trouble: playing with his cigar, the most famous scholar in the room, whom I recognize immediately, leans in and asks provocatively:

"So, you're a psychoanalytic critic?"

"Yes, I've written a psychoanalytic study of Flannery O'Connor's fiction."

"So, give me an example of what you do. Psychoanalyze *As I Lay Dying*," he commands, and sits back in his chair, cigar in hand, watching me, vaguely amused. If he's looking to trip me up, he has struck gold: though I love Faulkner, I have not read that novel.

"Right now?" I ask.

"Yes, just give it a go."

I remember my MA orals years ago when I was asked to talk about a Dickens novel that I hadn't read. My mouth had gone dry, and I had become unable to speak until the questioner had given me some water. Then, I had recovered enough to continue, and luckily, the interrogator had moved on to a different text. Now, ten years later, I am being asked about a book I haven't read but should have. Ashamed of my academic inadequacy, but this time not panicking, I quickly ferret around in my mind for a defensive maneuver and find one:

"I am a close reader and can only do an analysis of a text when it's before me. It would be fraudulent to do an analysis without the text in hand." Fortunately, as I say this, I find I really believe it and so can speak with conviction.

"Do it anyway," he says, getting more assertive.

"No, I'm sorry, but I won't. I need the text before me to do a reading. That's how I work."

"We'll forgive your broad strokes; just give me the outlines of an analysis."

"No, I'm sorry, I can't do that. It would not be a legitimate analysis."

Our obstinacies are well-matched, but he has the power, and I am about to give up on this interview when one of the younger professors breaks in:

"Leslie, get off the dime. Let's move on and see what she knows."

I am relieved but also angry. In spite of my culpable maneuver, I sense I've been inappropriately assailed in some undefined way.

Later that evening, at a reception for job candidates, drink in hand, I confront Leslie.

"Why did you keep insisting that I answer a question I thought illegitimate?"

He leers at me impishly and leaning toward me says conspiratorially: "C'mon, you loved every minute of it, didn't you!"

And in a flash of illumination, I understand the nature of our interchange: it had been purely sexual, as was his remark now. He never would say this to a male candidate. Furious, I turn on my heels and walk to the other side of the room.

Yet in spite of my refusal to accept his bait, I did get the job. Or was it *because* of my refusal? Was it because I had stood up to him, had not swallowed my outrage, that I had not lost the job offer? Had he enjoyed my resistance? Didn't I also enjoy sparring with a powerful paternal figure? Too intoxicated at the time by feminist insights into the nature of patriarchal power to attend to my own role in that interchange, I didn't acknowledge its seductive lures. I too had been aroused—an easy mark for such paternal seductions. And not just me. For while there are women who, understanding how the erotic allure of male power supports their own disempowerment, refuse to respond to it, many others enjoy the provocation. It's a kind of mutual tease.

Whatever the complicated nature of that exchange, I vowed to use that little duel in my first feminist theory course to demonstrate, QED, the sexualized ways and means of power in the professions—how senior male colleagues could exert an eroticized authority that allowed them a good measure of control over their junior female colleagues, let alone their graduate students. This uneven entanglement, I came to argue, was a distorted reflection of the old father-daughter affair, culturally supported and rarely resolved. But if, as I thought then, I had finally freed myself from my childhood longing to please my father, even had, despite his scorning my values, finally completed my dissertation and was about to become a faculty member of a prestigious department, I was still in so many ways a daughter, still squirming against the paternal ties that bind. And somehow still amazed to find myself a week after my interview hired as a "professor."

Off to Buffalo I went then, determined to prove myself worthy of the position.

Shuffle Off to Buffalo: Professing as a Feminist

A rust belt, working-class city in serious economic decline, its motto "City of No Illusions" for its working-class pragmatism, Buffalo in the early seventies nevertheless sparked with creative activity. Nicknamed "the Queen City" (for being the *second* largest city in New York), it was the site of the relatively new State University of New York's star campus, funded in the sixties by Governor Rockefeller to compete with UC Berkeley as a public institution. It had as a consequence become home to a good number of prominent artists, writers, and critics in various fields connected with the university. The music department hosted the famous Budapest String Quartet as well as the more avant-garde music of Lukas Foss's Creative Associates. Its maverick English department boasted a diverse community of illustrious writers and critics, among them Leslie Fiedler, whose pioneering *Love and Death in the American Novel* had greatly influenced my understanding of American literature, and Robert Creeley, whose *For Love* turned the very process of breathing into poetry. John Barth, whose great American comic novel *The Sot-Weed Factor* I had just read, was leaving the department, but the writer John Coetzee was coming in, and René Girard, Michel Foucault, and Jacques Derrida, leading French theorists of

the time, were frequent visitors to the English department's comparative literature program. Not least, Norman Holland, the leading psychoanalytic literary critic in the country, oversaw a program within the department on literature and psychoanalysis—my principal reason for wanting to teach there. Needless to say, I was thrilled to join this community—and more than a little intimidated.

My interest in Buffalo had been first aroused at a Christmas party in Berkeley the previous year, when I had asked the poet Bob Hass, who was teaching in Buffalo that year but was in Berkeley for the holidays, to describe the difference between Berkeley and Buffalo.

"Well," he said after a moment's consideration, "in Buffalo, when you walk down the hall of the English department, you run into clusters of people and hear heated conversations. In Berkeley, when you walk down the hall, you hear typewriters." He was not exaggerating: the department I had come to was alive with talent, energy, and experimentation, and I, a single woman with a spotty academic history, was ready to dive into that maelstrom and make a place for myself.

But it wasn't easy. For one thing, with seventy men and five women comprising the faculty, the actual *mael*strom was effectively male; for the most part, the few women professors quietly attended to their own affairs. And for another, I arrived in Buffalo bearing a new name: I was no longer Claire Katz, the name under which I had been interviewed and hired, but Claire Kahane, a name I had newly adopted after learning from a Hebrew scholar friend in Berkeley that Katz was not the German-Yiddish spelling of "cats," as I had always assumed, but a diasporic acronym for Kahane Tzedek (Ka-tz), a linguistic pointer to the family line of descent from the high priest Aaron, the brother of Moses (Kohen, or Kahane, meaning priest, Tzedek meaning most righteous). Following a feminist practice of the time, I decided to discard my given patronym and assume a more euphonic version of the paternal moniker: Kahane. (*Tzedek*, i.e. "righteous" I could do without). It was a surname that still marked me as belonging to the Katz family line, but I myself would choose the link.

After all, I was in the midst of reinventing myself, so why not imagine myself the daughter of a Jewish high priest rather than an uneducated Jewish immigrant who disapproved of my lifestyle?

Imagine my surprise then, when entering the department's mail room (perfidious ubiquitous homonym!) on my first day of teaching, I ran into Leslie, his eyes rakishly twinkling as he remarked: "So, you have decided to announce your ancestral relation to the high priest!" How ironic: only he who had tormented me during my interview had recognized the historical allusion; only he understood my symbolic act.

Still mulling over that irony, I went to face my first class on the modern English novel. As I entered the classroom, the professor from the previous class—a tall, elderly gentleman with a surly expression on his face—was picking up his notes from the lectern. He paused and looked at me as if I were disturbing him. I introduced myself:

"Hello, I'm Claire Kahane, a new faculty member. I'm about to teach my first class here. On the modern English novel."

"What writers are you teaching?"

"I'm starting with D. H. Lawrence."

"Lawrence was no novelist," he grumbled testily and marched out of the room, leaving me open-mouthed. And so my initial class as an assistant professor began.

That first winter in Buffalo, with its endless days of sunless skies and leafless trees, its bitter winds blowing off Lake Erie icing the walkways, its urban palette a relentless dull gray and muddy brown brightened only by snowfalls, I cried myself to sleep each night, shrouded in loneliness. But inevitably, the spring thaw came. Social links began to be forged, friendships began to blossom with women from other departments as well as with my male colleagues in the Literature and Psychology program (in which I was the only woman). Happily, the program itself offered me new knowledge in the form of British object relations theory, which unlike traditional Freudian theory, was all about the early mother-child relationship, when mother and infant are locked into an experience of oneness that makes developing a separate self an often lifelong pursuit. Thinking again of my dissertation, I realized how much more apt British theory was for interpreting the ringing "I ain't you" of O'Connor's angry child characters. By the end of that first year in Buffalo, not only had the misery of the lonely cold winter melted away, but these new psychoanalytic insights fired me up to teach literature written by women. I had an inside track to their conflicts.

In 1974, only a few women writers were being taught in English departments despite the growing feminist movement. With my own interests becoming more defined, I began to fill the gap in my department, not only by offering courses on women writers, but also by adding female psychology and feminist-psychoanalytic criticism to the graduate curriculum. In 1980, I organized one of the first academic feminist-psychoanalytic conferences, "The Creative Use of Difference," a title I cribbed from a speech by the Black feminist poet Audré Lorde. With the financial support of Norman Holland, who held a funded chair, I brought to Buffalo feminist scholars from around the country, among them Vivian Gornick, Dorothy Dinnerstein, Susan Gubar, and Jane Gallop—names that would become well-known in feminist studies over the next several decades. The conference papers were so fresh in their approaches that Madelon Sprengnether, a conference presenter, and I decided to collect them for a book she, I, and her colleague Shirley Garner would edit.

I and my co-editors at work on The M/Other Tongue

Several years later, *The (M)other Tongue: Essays in Feminist-Psychoanalytic Interpretations*, one of the first of such collections in this new field, was published. Clearly, by 1980, I had found my niche in the department.

I had also, by that time, found a more personal niche.

A Domestication

On a beautiful Sunday afternoon in the summer of 1975, a new friend from the Slavic Studies department asked me to go with her to visit someone she'd been dating, Rainer Hanser, a professor of German literature and an amateur cabinetmaker. She wanted, so she said, to see his latest piece of furniture—a high desk he had designed for a colleague with a bad back who needed to stand when working. But, as she confessed coyly to me, she didn't want to go alone. "Anyway," she added, "I want you to meet him. He's so worldly and so interesting." I went.

He opened the door, a tall, sandy-haired, blue-eyed man, and I was taken aback by how handsome he was. He eyed me with obvious pleasure as he showed us his new piece, an ingeniously designed walnut desk. That evening he telephoned and asked me to have dinner with him.

"I really can't," I replied, uncomfortable at being put in an awkward position. "You're seeing Emma; it would be inappropriate."

"Would you change your mind if she tells you it's all right with her.... We were just casually dating, nothing serious."

I hesitated, and then said, "Yes."

A short time later, Emma called me: "It's okay, Claire. Go out with him. He's really taken with you."

That evening we went to one of Buffalo's better restaurants, and although it quickly became clear that Rainer was seriously courting me, I remained somewhat ambivalent about entering into a relationship with him: he seemed a bit too formal on our first date, a bit too European, a bit too . . . what can I say, a bit too *German*. He very quickly proved himself an exciting lover and a generous companion. His desire kindled mine; we saw each other constantly, and when I discovered I was pregnant, he, delighted at the thought of having a child, proposed marriage.

Reader, this time I married him! But the reasons for my marrying were not purely romantic. Of course, Rainer was such a good prospect: handsome, sexy, intelligent, a lover of classical music, a connoisseur of literature—how could I not be attracted to him? A refugee from Nazi Germany, Rainer had entered the US at the age of eleven, along with his father, mother, brother, and sister. Having relatives in the Bay Area, they had first settled in San Francisco and then moved to Vallejo where his father, a pediatrician, intended to set up a medical practice. But Vallejo had a naval base, and since they were German nationals, despite being Jewish refugees, they were classified as enemy aliens and not allowed to live near military installations. Ultimately, they found a home in the quiet little town of Napa—neutral territory, where Rainer quickly learned to be an American teenager, even becoming Napa High's football star, and where his father became Napa's only pediatrician, to be revered for over forty years.

Having fled Nazi persecution, Rainer never wanted to live far from a border—just in case, and so Buffalo, on the border with Canada, seemed a good choice. At the same time, he never lost his attachment to, and longing for, his lost homeland. As an undergraduate at UC Berkeley, he had studied German literature. Not only did he make it his life's work, but he also developed personal relations with members of Group 47, a circle of well-known contemporary German writers who, like him, were intent on rescuing the German language from its debasement by the Nazis. At home he surrounded himself not only with German literature but with German classical music. His record collection contained works by all the important German composers; he himself played the piano—Beethoven, Brahms, Bach—but with such passionate intensity that it would often seem to me a painful protest as much as a pleasure.

Now, here he was, wanting to marry me and have our child. How could I hesitate?

Yet I knew there were other more pressing motives for my saying yes, all stemming from my unwavering resolve to have a child. I had become pregnant once before, toward the end of the affair with Erik, before I was to leave Berkeley. But the timing had been out of joint, and I had had an abortion. Fortunately, abortions were legal in 1974. Instead of slinking around a dark alley to some unknown, incompetent provider, as several friends had done, I had the procedure in a bright, clean medical facility surrounded by sympathetic staff, who, babying me, gave me ice cream when it was over. Now, here in Buffalo, forty years old, gainfully employed, and pregnant—there was no way I was *not* going to have this child!

I confess that when I first discovered I was pregnant, I considered becoming a feminist heroine and having a child on my own. But almost immediately, I had a vision of my father and mother crying "oy vey," and jumping out of their third-floor apartment window, each in turn. In my saner moments, I knew that at least my mother could be brought around to accept me as a single parent. Her children were her life; she wouldn't—couldn't—withdraw her love. But my father! Again, my father: he would never be able to tolerate the humiliation of having an unmarried daughter with a child. It was a *shanda* (shame) that he, Meilach, the King, would not be able to bear. He would cast me out.

If it was mainly fear of familial exile that pushed me into marriage, it was also love—but more for my parents than for Rainer. I longed to give them the gift they had wanted for so long: a Jewish husband and a grandchild, their line into the future untainted by shame. Rainer came to the rescue; he was enthusiastic about marrying me, and how grateful I was that he made it so easy. "After all," he assured me, recognizing my hesitation, "I've been married four times, and I never left my wives. They left me." Rather than worry about this marital history, I was relieved. Just the kind of marriage I could actually enter into. In short, while I knew I was not "in love" with Rainer as I had once known "in love" to be, I married him, and the amorous adventures of my earlier life came to rest in a domestication I had for so many years managed to avoid. I became not only an English professor specializing in feminist-psychoanalytic criticism, but a wife and soon-to-be mother, living out the contradictions I was analyzing in the classroom.

At first, I seemed to have nothing to regret. After interrogating me on the phone—I had lied to her so often that she didn't quite believe me when I called and said, "Ma, I'm pregnant but, don't worry, we're going to get married, and he's Jewish"—my mother glowed with an iridescent satisfaction when I introduced her to Rainer. As for my father, he couldn't quite forgive Rainer for being German despite his being also Jewish, but he too welcomed my reclamation. And so did I. Rainer was a loving, considerate partner, sharing the tasks of my pregnancy, even attending Lamaze classes in natural childbirth with me. There we were, a gray-haired forty-nine-year-old husband and his forty-one-year-old wife, among a goodly number of twenty- and thirty-year-olds, bravely following the instructions—I rhythmically breathing, Rainer massaging my back and keeping me focused. I did have one disconcerting moment when I learned from amniocentesis that I was carrying a male fetus; somehow, I had assumed I would have a girl—a being like myself, whom I could teach what I had learned. But that moment passed quickly. Having a boy betokened another kind of adventure that I came eagerly to anticipate.

There was, however, a real worm in this apple I had not anticipated: having put on twenty-five pounds—"a fat mother means a happy healthy baby," my obstetrician had pronounced wittily—I saw not only my own body radically change during the course of my pregnancy, but Rainer's manner toward me as well. As my body swelled, he withdrew sexually. One evening, at a small dinner party, he openly flirted with the colleague who had first introduced us while I fumed silently. Confused and hurt by the change in our relationship, I confronted him:

"What's happened to our sexual life? You seem to be turning away from me."

Looking uncomfortable, Rainer confessed that he was put off by my altered shape. "I can't help it. Seeing your pregnant body . . . I just don't . . . can't feel sexual. . . . I know it's stupid, probably has something to do with my mother. I'm sorry, I just don't feel any desire." And he turned away.

What can I say? I was hurt, angry, disappointed, angry, depressed, angry. My maternal body, it seemed, had expelled me from a romance narrative that I had finally determined to inhabit and put me instead into a depressing domestic fiction I had not foreseen. I tried not to dwell on that fateful twist in my marriage, but it dwelled in me, rankling each night as I lay in the bed I shared with Rainer.

Still, during the day, I gloried in my pregnancy: my skin glowed, my colleagues were delighted, my old sense of having magical powers returned despite Rainer's sexual distance. Yet tellingly, as the months went by, I found myself drawn again to the stories of Flannery O'Connor, now with an embodied understanding of her grotesque characters. "In pregnancy," as I wrote in a newly-minted essay during the last months of my pregnancy, when I dragged my heavy body from campus to home, "a woman's very shape changes as she feels another presence inside her, growing on her flesh, feeding on her blood. Pregnancy confirms a woman's identification with her own mother, and becoming prey to that intricate network of fears and wishes, rage and love that is the mother-child relation, she may be led to fear the fetus as an agent of retaliation, a mirror of her own infantile negativity."

I began to have nightmares, blood-soaked images of the death of my yet unborn son.

February 14, 1976. Valentine's Day. My wedding day. In spite of vague apprehensions that something would go wrong—I kept remembering the monster's prophetic warning in Mary Shelley's *Frankenstein*, "I will be with you on your wedding night"—my wedding day was not a Gothic tale but a comic farce. There I was, seven-months pregnant, my specially designed wedding dress draped prodigiously over my gigantic belly, not yet believing that this was actually happening, as I stood with Rainer before the rabbi in a small anteroom of the biggest synagogue in New York while my parents kvelled; my uncle and aunt and my father's friends conversed in stage whispers behind me, almost drowning out the rabbi's voice; and my friends watched with amused disbelief at the proceedings. I could hear Valerie and Joan shushing my relatives as I took my vows of fidelity and love. *Shh. Shh.*

A wedding cake photo of Rainer and me

In a final bizarre crescendo, as the wedding party entered the kosher restaurant that my parents had selected for the wedding feast, the jazz pianist playing in the center of the room took one look at me, paused for a moment, and then broke out into a riff on "Just in Time." The hilarity among my friends at this coded commentary only confirmed the surreal quality of the day's event. But I laughed too.

That evening, sleeping next to Rainer in Valerie's apartment, the comedy evaporated; I cried myself to sleep. I was married, but I felt monstrously alone.

Mothering

In late April, I gave birth to Jake, first almost killing him with my umbilical cord, which had tightened around his neck at each labor spasm so that I had to have an emergency caesarean section—so much for the much-anticipated "natural childbirth" that I had labored for months to have. In the days that followed, the nurse who brought him to me for feedings would regularly remark, "You don't have enough milk; the baby's still hungry." Leaving the hospital torn by anxiety about my ability to feed Jake and the physical discomfort of major surgery, I sat next to Rainer as he drove me home on a rainy April afternoon with the baby in my arms, terrified that we would get into a fatal accident.

For the next month or so, still suffering the effects of surgery, I was neither comfortable breastfeeding my infant nor able to do much for myself. Fortunately, Rainer had hired a professional caretaker who washed me, fed me, and fattened me with her tapioca puddings while I lay in bed like a baby myself. It was six weeks before I could get up and fully assume my new role as a mother. Rainer took to his fatherhood easily, washing Jake in the kitchen sink, cradling him more comfortably than I could in my post-surgery state, bringing him to me for feedings that I still worried about. Yet despite Rainer's being a doting parent and thoughtful husband, the relation between us continued to lack an essential element of intimate bonding: the sense of touch. Touch, a postpartum absence with my husband, a sensuous presence with my infant.

In June, with the underlying tension in our marriage unabated, yet unacknowledged openly, we bought a lovely old three-story Victorian house near the Olmstead-designed Delaware Park, a neighborhood popular with other academic families for its green lawns, quiet streets, and big back-yards. Having never before owned a house, I was excited enough by this new experience to close my eyes to my marital disappointments. Rainer and I took such intense joy in the baby that it was enough for the time being. I still harbored the fantasy of eventually "having it all"—the joys of motherhood, a gratifying career, and a happy marriage—improbable as that might seem.

Rainer and me with Baby Jake

One morning, in the middle of moving packed boxes from our old apartment into the new house, Rainer came into the kitchen carrying a carton of books with his face drained of all color. Immediately, I knew something was seriously wrong.

"You look sick. I've never seen you so pale. You need to see a doctor right away."

Without arguing, Rainer agreed to stop off at our doctor's office on his way to the new house. An hour later, a phone call from the doctor informed me that Rainer was in the middle of a major heart attack and had been taken to the intensive care unit at Buffalo General Hospital. Had he not stopped at the doctor's, he would have died that very day. Hanging up the phone, I couldn't help but wonder if the unspoken strain of our marital relations had caused a disorder of the heart. I felt guilty.

The next months were difficult, both physically and psychologically. With Rainer in the ICU, I moved alone into our new house with my three-month-old infant in my arms. Luckily, I had help: two of my colleagues from the Lit/Psych program made the move easier—Murray installed a shower for me over a claw-foot tub in the upstairs attic; David set up a sound system so that music could be heard throughout the downstairs rooms; I settled into my new home, now virtually a single parent.

During those stressful summer months, I often telephoned Valerie and Joan for emotional support. Good friends, they decided to fly up for a weekend to buoy me up with their presence—a mistake. While I ran around the house getting dinner ready with one hand and tending the baby with the other, they sat on the back deck drinking wine, talking, laughing, and occasionally asking if there was anything they could or should do. It was not a question I could answer. Valerie seemed irritated at my preoccupation with household tasks, Joan puzzled by my inability to relax. I swallowed my hurt and resentment at their lack of understanding. They now belonged to a different life—one that excluded me. Their easy freedom from domestic obligation seemed itself an accusation, and I was not unhappy to see them go. Alone was better.

Six weeks later, Rainer was released from the hospital, still needing care. At home, his invalidism created new sources of tension.

"What's that smell?" he would ask irritably at least once a day.

"What smell? I don't smell anything," I would answer, exasperated by his irascible obsession with odors, by having to coddle him as well as the baby. (Only years later did I learn that heart patients often suffer from various sensory distortions.) The seeds of alienation that had been planted during my pregnancy took easy root during that first thorny year of marriage.

To add to the household tension, at my invitation, a Berkeley friend who needed a Buffalo residence for a year in order to get her PhD moved into our attic space along with her dog. She was writing a dissertation. And flirting with Rainer. I said nothing to her or to Rainer; I was determined not to rock the marital boat, at least for a while. I couldn't give up the profound gratification that came from our shared delight in our beautiful boy. Jake. A gift.

Mother and infant in mirror stage

Yes, a gift but also a revelation, for much to my astonishment, my infant had aroused a feeling in the core of my being that I had never experienced before. In the past, survival at any cost had been my secret mantra; now I was awed by a novel recognition: *I would sacrifice my own life to save Jake's.* So this was maternal love! And it was this love that sustained my marriage. Rainer took such delight in Jake's existence that for the next several years, my disappointment in our relationship seemed more than balanced by the profound pleasures of parenthood that we shared—pleasures bolstered by our family travels: to New York to spend time with my brother and his wife as well as with my friends; to Oberstdorf, Rainer's beloved childhood vacation spot in the Bavarian Alps, where Jake, Rainer, and I biked through flower-strewn meadows and hiked down mountains or along deep gorges; to California, driving across the country to visit Rainer's father and sister in hot and sunny Napa, his brother and sister-in-law in the Berkeley hills, and his daughter from his first marriage across the Bay in Marin County. (I liked his daughter Alexa so well that I vowed to bring her more intimately into our family circle, and made sure we stayed in contact over the years). And although I myself had no relatives in California, my old Berkeley graduate school friends—Marilyn, Carol, and Margret, now married with children of their own—as well as Julie, the displaced Brooklynite, took the place of family. So my love of travel, an enduring desire I had satisfied in my single life, was gratified in my married life also.

Yet even as my body resumed its normal state and our sexual life revived somewhat, the tension of that unhappy first year remained a burr in the corner of my consciousness for years, putting a pall on our intimacies and conversations. Too ashamed of my neediness to voice my discontent openly, I clamped shut as I felt the emotional gulf between Rainer and me widen, the spaces in our big Victorian house grow larger and more silent when we were alone. When, in 1979, my father died, and nine months later, my mother, I could not share my grief with Rainer. The walls around an inner emptiness grew higher.

In 1982, having just gotten tenure at the university, I decided to take a sabbatical leave, not only from my teaching duties, but from my marriage. There were questions to be answered, decisions to be made, both personally and professionally. Should I leave this marriage, a move which I believed would devastate Jake? (Would he scream, red-faced and helpless, at the loss of his familiar world as I once did as a child?) Should I stay for his sake? Or was my dissatisfaction a flaw in my character—an illusory belief in the perfect soulmate that I had reluctantly surrendered when I married? With Jake in tow, I returned to Berkeley and to my old analyst, determined to clarify my feelings and decide on my future. As it turned out, I had to dis-inter the dead in order to make the most of my life.

Bringing Up the Bodies

On April 9, 1982, I left my analyst's office in San Francisco and walked into a tree. Head-on. A meaningful accident when I thought about it. It was the anniversary of my mother's death, a death linked in my memory to her story of *her* mother's death—a virtual murder by a Russian soldier— and of a tree so essential to that story. Oddly enough, although it was the anniversary of my *mother's* death, I had spent most of the hour talking about the night my *father* had died. I couldn't remember his actual death date—a significant lapse—and so had to deduce it logically by remember-ing it was also the night of Valerie's birthday party. That night stretches out in my memory like the long corridors of the hospital in which my father lay gasping for air. My father. My mother. Deaths. Births. And Valerie, mixed up in this mental muddle. How to sort it all out?

Valerie's birthday was June 14; my father's death then, I calculated, must have been in the early morning hours of June 15, 1979—circuitous deduction, circumambulation around a blind spot. He had suffered a heart attack several weeks earlier and was still in the intensive care unit at Columbia Presbyterian, gravely ill, as the doctors had informed me. I had just flown in from Buffalo to visit him, and feeling a dread descend upon me as the plane landed, I decided to stop first in the Village. Valerie was having a birthday party, and I needed a little cheering up. It would be good to see old friends. And after all, my father wasn't going anywhere.

* * *

"So how does it feel to be middle-aged?"

My voice sounded hollow to my ears as I greeted the familiar face I had known for twenty-five years with a kiss on the cheek. She leaned forward to reciprocate, her breath heavy with the odor of tobacco.

"I suddenly saw these lines around my eyes this morning that I swear I didn't have yesterday!" She laughed girlishly at her own remark, and I gave her the ironic appraisal she had come to expect from me. Loving her, I didn't mention the brightly rouged cheeks, the blue line drawn too darkly and artificially around her beautiful green eyes, the glisten of moisturizer shining unnaturally on the surface of her skin. *My harlequin sister, what can I say?*

"You look terrific, Valerie, only forty, I swear."

"Forty!" She arched her eyebrows in mock horror and turned to Joan, who had come up to us, drinks in hand. The doorbell buzzed again. Valerie's cue.

"Take care of this traitor, Joan, she's given me only four years for my birthday."

Valerie went to the door, and Joan handed me a drink, her smile undercut by the tight lines at the corners of her mouth and by her sad, heavy-lidded eyes. Her face had gotten puffy this last year—marshmallow cheeks. Too much good living, I thought, downing the Scotch in my glass in one swallow.

"How's your father?" she asked. There was that pained look that crossed her face whenever she said the word "father." Hers had died a few years ago, leaving her his debts and the vivid memory of his failure as a parent. A gambler, a womanizer, a charming cad: he had once even made a pass at me. I'd never told her about that.

"Last I heard all was quiet on the eastern front."

"This must be really hard for you, Claire." She squeezed my arm. "I still have nightmares about those months *my* father was in the hospital, hating him and not wanting him to die. . . ." She pursed her lips. "Fucking bloodsucker."

"Mine is too, sort of. Different style, though." As I said this, I remembered my father's angry outburst during my last visit to the hospital: "*Why can't you find a doctor that can help me? What, you're too busy? You don't have the time?*" How much time was enough?

"Well, if ever we were justified in boozing, tonight's the night," she said gamely, reaching for the bottle on the side table. "More Scotch?"

"Yes, thanks. That's fine." She poured, clicked her glass to mine, and I took a sip, more slowly now, taking pleasure in its lovely golden color, feeling the tension in my back ease as it slid warmly down my throat and stroked my chest. I leaned back against the wall and looked around. Away from New York too long. I recognized only a few of the faces in the room. Just the right mix for a lively party, though.

Immediately, I was ashamed. My father, struggling for life in the hospital, me at a party. "His life would have ended mine." Virginia Woolf's line kept returning to me these last few weeks. She had suffered under her father's emotional demands; I was suffering under my father's judgments. "*Selfish, you are selfish, always thinking of yourself first. You don't care about us. A troublemaker from the beginning. Just a good time you want.*" Unfair, dammit. Unfair. Yet here I was.

"Not a good time for me to be interested in partying," I said.

Joan squeezed my arm again.

"You can't stop the merry-go-round just because of a parental heart attack."

"But what would my father say!"

We both laughed conspiratorially and clicked our glasses again.

Heart attack. An odd word. It wasn't only his heart that had attacked him. What was it? His brain, unsatisfied with what it had thought for seventy years? His eyes, their vision confined by a wall of obstinacy? His blood, too proud to risk any humiliation? Internecine warfare. And humiliations there must have been aplenty. As when he failed the New York driving test. "You mean to tell me that 'cattle crossing' means 'cows crossing the road'? A bunch of real idiots, asking me about a sign like that. What a ridiculous thing, that test. Who needs to know about cattle crossing in New York? They have dreck in *kop* (shit in their brains).... So, I won't drive. Who needs it? This is New York. Who needs to know about 'cattle crossing'?"

Indeed, who needed to know? Knowing didn't always help.

Looking out the window, I could see occasional little squares of light in the windows of buildings stretching across the street beyond, leading to the river, dark and shining. And in the sky, a June moon.

"How's your mother holding up?" Joan asked.

"Oh, she's a bit frightened by the whole thing, but it gives her something to do, taking care of him and not being rebuffed."

Joan nodded, and in her face, I saw my mother's face when she was younger: the same look of pained sympathy, the tears welling up in the eyes. And for what? A dog run over by a car. A stray emaciated cat. A plant that had died, wilted in the ashen air of the Bronx. Joan, like my mother, always empathizing with the cast-offs. She gave my hand another squeeze and walked across the room to Valerie, who was setting out several more bottles on the sideboard. Joan said something to her, disappeared into the kitchen, and a few moments later, reappeared holding a cake with one candle lit. The buzz of conversation ceased.

"Toast, everyone, to Valerie. With a glass half full, and never empty."

Glasses were raised, Valerie laughed, there was a burst of shrill accompanying laughter and applause. I clapped too, but felt numb. What was there to applaud? Valerie's neck sunk more deeply into her shoulders as she embraced a friend who was rumored to have breast cancer. Joan was now absorbed in earnest conversation with a young man who, judging from his crumpled clothes and his swagger, was short on cash and big on ego. They would probably end up in bed.

Shivering suddenly, I imagined the hospital corridors cold and dark. I had to go.

* * *

The hospital, built on a precipice overlooking the Hudson River, reared up in the moonlight as my taxi approached from below. It was quiet inside the lobby, but when I got to my father's floor, the corridors seemed to echo with the clatter and moan of some hidden despair. As I rounded a corner, my mother and brother appeared, panic in their gestures as they approached me.

"There's no doctor or nurse around, and he can't breathe!" my brother said, his voice quivering. "He tried to get out of bed, and I think he had another heart attack!" My mother groaned and looked around desperately for someone to materialize, but the hallway was empty. My mind started to race wildly as I heard my father's shout down the hall—"I can't breathe." I ran to his room and saw the look of absolute terror on his face as he turned toward me and gasped: "I can't breathe. Do something. Help!"

How could I help? What could I do, knowing as the doctor had told me last week that he probably wouldn't live out the year—and now, perhaps not even the night. In a panic myself, I dashed frantically out into the hallway and ran down the corridors. No one. I took the staircase to the next floor. A resident wearing a yarmulke was sitting at the nurse's desk. He looked up as I approached him.

"Come quickly, my father can't breathe. He's just had a heart attack and he can't breathe!"

Without hesitation, he picked up his medical bag and followed me down the stairs to my father's room. After a quick glance at my father's medical chart and his contorted wheezing face, he administered an injection that calmed him. My father lay there, breathing with difficulty now, but breathing. The resident and I stepped out of the room. My mother and brother were sitting in the corridor and looked anxiously at us.

"There's nothing more I can do," the resident said nervously. "I gotta get back upstairs to my station."

He left, and we three remained outside the room, waiting. By now, my brother and I had gleaned the truth: this was a death watch. "He may not last the night," I told my mother, trying to prepare her, but the mere suggestion triggered a frantic expression and loud moaning. How could I say more?

Then the wheezing and shouting from inside the room began again: "I can't breathe! I can't breathe!" Again I ran upstairs to find the resident, myself now in an unthinking panic. He was still sitting there at the desk.

"You must do something; he's suffering again. You must do something!" I cried.

He followed me once again, reluctantly this time, saying, "I've given him the limit of morphine that's safe. I can't do any more."

We entered the room; my father, chest heaving, wheezed the words "help me, I can't breathe!"

"You must do something," I begged the resident, desperate to ease my father's suffering. "You must!"

"It's dangerous," he said, hesitating, but then, yielding to my urgency, shrugged his shoulders and gave my father another injection. Again, my father calmed down. For a few minutes. And then he began to wheeze again, this time more deeply than before. This time, the resident left the room abruptly and quickly returned with two other young men in white coats. They ushered me out of the room. Again, we three sat outside the room, now silently. I tried to imagine the scene behind the closed door. What was happening? Finally, unable to bear the suspense, I got up and entered the room surreptitiously.

No one noticed me at first, and I froze in place before the scene: my father, struggling to breathe, while the residents shocked him with an electric device, jolting his body. His eyes bulging, grotesque and unseeing—white eyeballs, veined with red; his mouth, open, gasping like a fish, drowning in air. Not my father, but a fish, glassy-eyed, thrashing, and then, suddenly, with a few shudders, he fell back, stilled. I stared in horror as they begin to pump his chest manually; I must have gasped for air myself, for suddenly, I was noticed and brusquely told to leave the room. Moving like a robot, I joined my mother and brother again, but this time, I knew what was happening. A short time later, as my mother anguished beside me, rocking back and forth, moaning inconsolably, her hands covering her face, and my brother sat silently staring at the wall, they wheeled out a gurney with a figure under a tarp. Only the big toe showed, a tag hanging from it: Max Katz.

Dead Souls

Long after his death, my father's gut-wrenching ghost sat inside me, refusing to be buried. I had defied so many of his injunctions, had given him so little pleasure, had so often forfeited his love. As a child, adoring him, I had felt his raised voice far more hurtful and frightening than my mother's angry hand. As an adult, I had been devastated by his scathing judgments of me: *"A snake! Selfish!"* How many scenes with my father had ended with that unjust word? And now, as I lay on the couch talking to my analyst, that relentless memory returned in full force, and I felt myself reliving that awful moment years ago when my father exploded at me for trying to rescue my brother—*"You nogood selfish choleria.... You're always against the family."* Was I? Forever wrestling with that brutal negation, with my contradictory desires: to be separate and independent and also part of the family, to be a good daughter and also like my father. The underlying ironies of that traumatic scene lost on me for years: my father, who as a young man had left his family in Europe, wouldn't allow his adult son to leave him. His daughter, the snake, was proffering his son the inducements of an independence, from which his own beloved sister, the communist who refused to leave Poland, had died. Forbidden fruit, this desire for autonomy. No way for me to receive the paternal blessing on that road. I knew in my bones why Emerson was so appealing to nineteenth-century women writers. Paternal as he was in his pronouncements, his inflation of the independent self had released women as well as men from the injunctions to duty, from submission to social demands.

Only when I married a Jewish college professor and gave birth to a son did I see myself restored in my father's eyes. His relief that I had miraculously become respectable, and even more, the pleasure gleaming in his face as he played with his grandchild—"What a smart little boy, what a good little boy," he would croon—was more than matched by my own pleasure in finally having given him something he wanted from me. But now he was dead, and I was contemplating divorce. It was a slap in his face—his dead face.

Al, who had been my father's companion for so many years, had his own way of assimilating his loss. Over the next year or so, he seemed to incorporate my father, taking on more blatantly his way of speaking and telling jokes, even exploding in anger at his wife just like my father though Al was really a gentle soul. But my mother proved unable to survive the empty center her husband had left in her life. She did try for a while, agreeing to move into a new apartment in Manhattan near my brother, allowing us to buy her a new dining room table and chairs that we hoped would somehow draw a nurturing circle around her—though neither my brother nor I knew how that could happen in Manhattan when she was herself so much a piece of the Bronx. How bitter the irony that soon after my father's death, she developed stomach pains and complained of indigestion. The dining table would remain unused. Nine months later, she was dead, consumed by a cancer she didn't know she had.

Yet almost prophetically, before anyone knew of that fatal gestation, she had begun to tell stories about the death of family members and friends— her cousin Gussie, dying of stomach cancer; my father's friend Ralph, who had regularly brought her dresses from his workplace, felled by a stroke, his wife Tillie, by breast cancer; Fischel, my father's younger brother, dead of a heart attack on the same weekend as my father. And her brothers in Russia, disappeared in the Holocaust. It was as if the death of my father had opened her to other death-saturated stories that had lain unarticulated, buried until now. And at the core of her new storytelling impulse was a story I hadn't heard before, one that she was now ready to tell:

"When my mother married him," she began, "he had already two children, and I was like nothing to him. A drain on the little that was. 'Send her to the cousins,' he told my mother. 'They need help in the house.' 'She's young yet,' my mother said, 'and besides, she can help here.' I was standing outside listening. My ears were ringing. My head hurt. I felt cold like the stars. 'We have enough help here with Yankel and Yussel,' he said to her.'"

We were sitting at the small kitchen table in my mother's apartment. She reached toward a green prickly plant on the windowsill, some sort of displaced cactus, and felt the soil, rubbing a few grains between her thumb and arthritically misshapen forefinger. As always, there were plants on the windowsill, veined green leaves and twisted stalks struggling for sun in the shaded Bronx apartment we had all once lived in, carefully tended by her as if they were her children.

"The next morning, I was sent to my mother's cousins in another shtetl, to live and help them with the cleaning, the farm, a little of everything. I was already a *balabosta*. I'm not sure how long it was I stayed there. I worked hard, mostly outside, there were two children about my age, they were very nice to me. When I needed something to eat, they made sure I got it. I remember one day a young bully," an American word she pronounced with a special vigor, "from the village took away the basket of blueberries that I was all morning picking. They complained to the cousins, and the thief had to pay me for my work. Of course, I missed my mother. I was so young, what was I, about nine? Once in a while she came to see me, my mother. I used to wonder, would I ever live with her again in our house? Then I was sent to live with my grandfather, who worked at a nearby dairy farm. I learned to milk cows. I remember hiding in the barn once when the Cossacks came. I watched. I was scared. They made him get down on his knees, and they cut off his beard."

I waited for the end of the story, watching her compose it.

"Then one day, maybe it was a year, maybe two years later, I don't remember exactly, a cousin came to tell me that my mother was dead, and already buried. She was killed by a Russian soldier who was looking for food. He wanted potatoes; she opened the cellar door to show him she had no potatoes; she was pregnant. He knocked her down the cellar stairs. Killed her for not having enough."

She paused again, staring, her brow now furrowed, her eyes moistened by memory, and then continued telling her story, how she ran miles down roads and across fields to her mother's new grave.

"There was a tree nearby the grave, and I put my arms around it. I hugged the tree and I cried."

She rocked back and forth, holding her elbows, cradling her sorrow, her eyes closed, a little humming sound coming from her that buzzed around the room. Sounds from another world, more real than our present one. I envisioned the tree with spreading branches.

"I can still feel the tree pressing into my skin, after all these years."

Her mother, the tree. She rubbed her arms with her rough hands, a soft scratchy sound that sent a shiver up my back, and with a sigh, rose up from her chair and walked to the stove. The sun was streaming through the kitchen window and lit up the blue veins of her arm as she reached for the *chanik* (kettle) on the stovetop. The rest I already knew—that at the age of fourteen, sponsored by her aunt in America and helped by the Hebrew Immigrant Aid Society, she had traveled on her own from Rakow, in Minsk Gubernia, to New York, carrying her heavy losses with her. Unspoken presences, they haunted the life of her children in turn.

Six months after my mother told me this story, she entered the hospital, her abdomen bloated, as if she were carrying some wondrous child. The diagnosis: peritoneal cancer, although for months the doctors had attributed her abdominal pains to pathological mourning. Maybe it was that also. Who knows how dynamic the mind is, how potent its reach? Every day for the next few weeks, I would sit at her bedside, staring at her swollen torso, watching numbly as it was turned several times a day by the nurses, lugged first this way, then that way, like a beached whale. Every few days her body would be drained of the fluids that kept filling her up.

After the first week, she asked me to call her few remaining friends and relatives to tell them where she was, and several came to visit. But no one spoke of dying; no one said "cancer," least of all me.

"You'll be all right. It's an intestinal disorder. The doctors are treating it. Don't worry. They just need to find the right combination of medicine."

Don't worry. Did she know I was lying, as I had always lied to her, when I assured her that she would recover soon? I couldn't mouth the words that might cause her pain; she seemed so vulnerable. Don't worry. But she always had anyway. She must have known what was incubating inside her without my saying the word.

As the days passed, she grew increasingly silent. What was she thinking as she lay there, staring back at me? Perhaps she continued to tell herself stories about people she loved and had lost; perhaps that's what kept her engorged day after day. Then one day, the noise coming out of her mouth became louder, a deep guttural snore from the center of the earth. I knew there were no stories that could survive that sound. I sat beside her for several hours that day, wondering how long she could last, leaning in close, watching for a sign, fearful that I might not recognize her death when it came. But there was no mistaking the moment, for when she finally gave up the ghost, it was bright red, and it spilled from her mouth.

Later that evening, my long watch over, I returned to her apartment. The furniture familiar from my childhood—the oversized chairs and the Danish modern sofa, the baroque Italianate lamps on their end tables—seemed grotesque witnesses to the heavy absence at the center of the apartment. I walked into the bedroom and lay down on the familiar twin bed that was hers, bought when she and my father finally had been able to have their own bedroom. And as I lay there, curled up in a fetal position, it seemed that my body was shrinking. A skeleton, desiccated, I lay inhabiting my mother's aged body that felt like my own.

Death scenes. They inevitably accumulate as one grows older and become the seeds of new stories, as if death itself generated new life. Death demands a narrative. Trauma requires a story. Events that happen *to* us, that we cannot set aside or readily forget, demand to be composed and passed on as a legacy. This old truth was newly resurrected for me after the deaths of my parents, which left me with memory-images of mortality so vividly corporeal, so horrifically embodied, that I needed to put them into language to contain my feelings and make memory serve me. Just as my mother had told me the story of *her* mother's death and her exile from home as part of her mourning, so almost immediately after my mother's death, feeling benumbed and unable to talk about such matters with Rainer, I sat down, pen in hand, to write her story and to think about my long and self-imposed exile from her presence.

But before I could set down the first words of her story, an image entered my consciousness: as if in a cinematic close-up, I saw two feet, shod in sandals, walking on desert sand, and I knew these were the feet of my mother when she was a young woman. And then I heard her speak, telling me how hard it was to walk through this dry parched land, how the hot sands burned her feet, but how she had to go on. Assuming *her* first-person voice, I began to write, my "I" telling of *her* struggle—as a child, as an immigrant, as a wife and mother—to go on, to survive.

A week after walking into the tree, I was telling her story to my analyst, but I was asking a new question: Whose feet did I see walking, whose words was I giving voice to? My mother's or mine? That question surely was not an innocent one, nor strictly personal, as I myself had argued in writing about the mother-daughter relationship—though personal it was also. In how many past scenes did I suddenly find myself playing the part of my mother? Arguing with Erik in the kitchen that night in San Francisco, and like my mother, when words failed me, throwing whatever object was at hand. Making a guggle muggle—my mother's delicious concoction of egg yolk, milk, and honey—when my own child had a cold, and miming my mother's incantations as I whipped the egg yolk: *guggle muggle guggle muggle,* her magic now mine.

Walking into a tree on the anniversary of my mother's death? How could it not signify? My mother, who had longed for her mother's embrace, had embraced the tree; I, blindsided by my need to distance myself from that embrace, had crashed into it. What a headache this dramatic enactment had given me! How it spoke, without words, of a conflict about being a mother and a wife, as well as the daughter of a mother whose own mother had sent her away. I could now see that her history had triggered her own overwhelming need for her children. Again, the sad irony: her need to have us close increased my strong desire to be independent!

But I was also the daughter of a father who had excoriated me for that desire, for contradicting his wishes and voicing mine. How ever would I, a "professor," find a confident voice of my own with that censorious paternal judgment in my ears?

Six months after I had raised the ghosts of my parents with my analyst and explored the reasons for wanting to leave my marriage, my parents' estates were finally settled, and I came into my inheritance, my first experience of having a bundle of cash. Determined to use it to make a difference in my life, I decided to realize an old wish: to buy a little piece of Berkeley, a "real estate" that would be mine alone to use as and when I chose. "Pie in the sky," my analyst called it when I complained of not finding anything to my liking that I could afford. Maybe it was, especially since the actual grounding of my life was in Buffalo. But hadn't I always sought "pie in the sky" and sometimes even found it? What was so wrong with following a dream, with trying to realize a wish?

In midsummer, Rainer arrived in Berkeley and courted me again. We had dinners with Berkeley friends animated by good conversation, nights during which he was passionate and tender, and congenial visits to his sister and father in Napa and relatives up the coast. Although I waffled at first, by summer's end, not only had I bought a small bungalow in Berkeley with Rainer's blessing, but we had agreed to try to make our marriage work. And so Rainer, Jake, and I returned to Buffalo, more a family than when I had left.

Domestic Reconstructions

For several years, I felt I had made the right decision. Rainer and I seemed more attuned to one another, more considerate in our daily dealings. Our sexual life picked up again, and for the most part, our home life satisfied us. By the time Jake was eight, we had added a cute black kitten with white spots to our household. Jake named him Millen, a name whose origin neither Rainer nor I could fathom, nor Jake explain at the time. (Years later Jake confessed that it was the first part of the word "millennium.") How he loved the cat, *his* familiar now, with the passion of an only child! But love can produce its equal in pain. One morning, after Jake had left to catch the school bus on the corner, I heard heart-wrenching screams and, rushing outside, saw Jake running back toward the house, hysterical. He had found Millen lying by the curb of the school bus stop, crushed into a bloody pulp, while the other kids, pointing at it, were laughing. It was his first real confrontation with a horrifying loss, the shock made worse by the laughter of his peers. Rainer and I comforted him as best we could, recovering Millen's remains and then allowing Jake to watch tearfully from a second-floor window as Rainer dug a shallow hole in the backyard that "would hold Millen's spirit forever," as I told Jake, spewing forth yet another lie to protect him from the ravages of reality. How grateful I was to have Rainer there to support this ceremony of innocence, to be Jake's good father.

Ceremonies: I value them. They bind a family, a community, a nation together; they help heal the wounds of experience. During my marriage, for Jake's sake, I made sure that we celebrated holidays: Thanksgiving, Christmas, Chanukah, and even the Passover Seder, a Jewish ritual that my feminist group had turned into an ecumenical gathering of like-minded political progressives celebrating liberation from slavery as a universal principle. (No matter their religious origin, we secularized the holidays, as did the popular culture.) When Jake, at age twelve, asked to have a bar mitzvah, Rainer and I were taken aback. It was a request that seemed to come from nowhere. Nevertheless, we didn't object; we may even have been secretly pleased. And so I set about making this ancient ceremony happen. I hired a Hebrew tutor—a wise scholarly woman with a philosophical bent—designed a service with the help of friends, and found a rabbi—the Hillel rabbi at the university, a tall robust figure with a flowing white beard—who agreed to hold a ceremony at Hillel House. On his thirteenth birthday, Jake was confirmed as a Jewish man.

As it turned out, so was Rainer. Before a room full of family and friends, Rainer, normally guarded about his private life, declared how pleased he was that Jake was taking a different path from his own and then, in a tremulous voice, confessed that he hoped Jake would find happiness in a heightened sense of community rather than feel, as he himself did, estranged from both his Jewish heritage and his native and adopted homelands. "How relieved I feel that my isolationism has not taken full root in your personality, Jake," Rainer said in a voice shaking with emotion, "for this has not been a source of great happiness in my life." As he spoke, many eyes in the room moistened, including mine, moved as we were by his emotional uncovering of sentiments long kept closeted. How courageous, I thought, to confess them publicly as a father's lesson to his son.

That day, and in the days that followed, it seemed to me that we three came together in a common spirit of family feeling, sparked by the bar mitzvah and what it had elicited from each of us. But Rainer's spurt of emotional availability did not last, at least for me, and I began again to feel the old gnawing sense of dissatisfaction with my marriage. I wanted to be actively, visibly desired. I wanted to be wanted. I wanted passion. *Pie in the sky?* I was even flirting with a handsome unmarried Buffalo colleague who was flirting back, both of us titillated by the allure of illicit possibilities. For a time, he and I met for drinks and conversation; for a time, I walked to and from my classes with a lighter step, humming old songs. Yet for some reason I couldn't fathom, I was reluctant to turn this incipient romance into a mature reality. Why? Perhaps because I knew it would be a transient gratification. Perhaps because my colleague was a New Englander from an old American family, his upbringing too distanced from my own. For whatever reason, when eventually, in one of our by then romantic assignations in his apartment, he pressed me to get serious and go to bed with him, I ended the flirtation. I could still hear my father's ghostly indictment: "*A snake in the family.*"

Conscience and Consciousness

As the ties of my marriage wore thin again and Jake, a teenager, no longer needed, or wanted, my supervision, I sought my principal gratification in work. One of its most satisfying benefits was the opportunity to travel on my own every summer to a small academic conference held in various European countries, at which I always presented a paper. Despite the occasional waves of dissatisfaction with my marriage, I was always grateful to Rainer for being at home, overseeing Jake while I was away on these professional jaunts.

PSYART conference in Pécs, Hungary 1983

Generally, I remained in the conference country for a week or two afterward, continuing to travel for the sheer adventure of it, as if I were still testing myself and my ability to be on the road alone and self-reliant. There were times when I clearly failed. In Italy one evening, entering a restaurant as a middle-aged woman alone and asking for a table, I drew questioning stares from the waiters. Feeling freakish, I ate my dinner without gusto and returned to my hotel room in a pool of melancholy. Yet I recognized that this annual plunge into an anxious singularity yielded psychological benefits. It forced me to meditate on what aloneness meant to me, to distinguish between alone and lonely, and to better understand myself at this stage of my life—fragments of self-knowledge wrested from solitude, not always pleasing to my self-image, but valuable.

The most vivid of such learning experiences occurred during my teaching stint in China in the autumn of 1988. It was an exciting time to be in China; the country was still animated by the iconoclastic energies released in the long aftermath of the Cultural Revolution. Exchange programs with the West had been encouraged, and having applied for a teacher exchange between the University at Buffalo and the Municipal Authority of Higher Education in Beijing, in late August of 1988, I found myself lecturing at Beijing Teachers College on Walt Whitman and Emily Dickinson before a class of students in training to teach college English.

After my lecture, several students gathered around me, and as if nominated, one of them asked, "What do you teach to graduate students at your university?"

"Freud and feminist theory for the most part," I replied.

"Our last foreign professor taught us about Whitman and Dickinson," she asserted politely. "We would like you to teach us about Freud and feminism."

As I discovered, Freud had just been published in Chinese, and the students, exhilarated by the intellectual freedom of the post–Cultural Revolution era, were eager to learn about psychoanalysis. Although I had brought no relevant books with me for such a course, for two hours once a week, I lectured from memory, surprising myself at how much theoretical material I had retained.

When I wasn't teaching, I explored Beijing. Early mornings, I biked happily on my newly acquired Chinese bicycle (which I bought on the streets in a heated negotiation with the help of my assigned aide) to a park where I attended a Qigong class that promised to relieve stress through physical movement. To get there I had to circumvent the smelly honey bucket truck making its early morning collections. Often, I would ride my bike downtown, with fellow teachers or by myself, along streets crowded with hundreds of other bikers, ringing my bell to warn that I was a new rider.

Occasionally, I explored hutongs—ancient neighborhoods consisting of rows of single-story houses built along narrow lanes and alleys—often nodding a greeting to an elderly man or woman sitting on their front steps, who would stare quizzically at me as I rode by. Periodically during my solitary excursions, I would stop my bike in the middle of a street to look around and marvel at my situation, amazed to find myself on this other side of the globe, confident, even joyful.

Beijing street market scene with bikes

No matter how alien some of the customs—the queue-less pushing to get on buses and trains or to buy tickets for performances, the corrupt black market money dealings (which I took advantage of), and more disconcerting, the cooking of dog parts by vendors on the streets and the squealing of pigs lashed mercilessly to the backs of bicycles—China satisfied my old desire for exotic experience.

Eating bird at a Beijing banquet

Yet before my China adventure was over, I was filled with remorse for my own actions: I had carelessly put someone who had offered to help me into a dangerous situation because of a selfish whim.

At the end of my term, the foreign guest office of the college arranged an exit trip: I was to travel from Beijing to Guangzhou along a route from north to south that included visits to Suzhou, Hangzhou, and Shanghai. Although I was initially anxious about my inability to communicate in Chinese, it proved no real obstacle. For in each city, whenever I pulled out my *Rough Guide to China*, some nice young man would approach and asked if he—it was always a "he"—could help, if he could "practice his English," if he could "walk with me." I soon discovered that "walking with me" meant that, like a tour guide, the stranger would not only tell me about the wonders of his city but show them to me as well.

One day, standing with my *Rough Guide* in downtown Shanghai, I found myself in such a situation. On a street crowded with people weaving around me and a river of bicycles and trucks flowing nearby, I was approached by a polite young man who asked if he could help me and also practice his English. I replied gratefully, "Of course," answering his smile with my own. But this time I had my own agenda.

We introduced ourselves—his name was Wang—and speaking slowly to make sure he understood, I showed him a citation to an exotic-sounding restaurant listed in the *Rough Guide* and its mapped location, and asked: "Can you tell me how to get there?"

He took a moment to read and then shook his head slowly: "It's too difficult for you. I think you should not try to go there. It's too far."

Not one to be thwarted so easily, I persisted: "But I'm really eager to try the food there. Can you take me there? If you can, I'd like you to be my guest for dinner." He hesitated, looking distressed, and after a moment's pause, said: "It's not allowed for Chinese to fraternize with foreigners. Very sorry. I can't go there with you; I can't eat with you."

I pouted at his polite refusal and, putting my desire above his caution, pleaded with him to reconsider: "I so much want to go there. And who would know?" He looked even more distressed, but I continued to press him until finally, with the courtesy of a host, he acquiesced.

How many streetcars we took to get there I can't recall, but a good hour or so later, we entered a featureless building in a rather shabby neighborhood and climbed the stairs to the red-curtained alcove entrance of the restaurant. After waiting for two seats at a table—Chinese restaurants have large tables at which strangers as well as friends and family are seated—we were led through the curtain into a spacious high-ceilinged room crowded with people noisily talking and furiously eating. As we were being seated at a round table in the center of the room, I took note of the group of rowdy, intoxicated soldiers in uniform at the table next to ours and was grateful to be with Wang.

With Wang's help, I ordered dishes recommended in the *Rough Guide* and ate heartily with relish, more so than he. When the check came, I reached for the small black shoulder bag I had hung on the back of my chair. But my hand encountered only the wooden chair frame. Discombobulated, I cried aloud to Wang and to the room, "My bag! My bag's missing, my passport, money—everything I need is in it."

"Oh no. Are you sure?" Wang, eyes wide, froze before me.

"Yes, I hung it on the chair and now it's gone! We have to call the police."

Once more, a look of extreme distress crossed Wang's face as he leaned toward me and whispered, "Maybe the soldiers took it. . . . I think the soldiers took it." By this time, the soldiers were gone.

"We have to call the police," I repeated, my hysteria rising. "Can you do that? You have to do that. Or get the restaurant owner to do that. . . ." Looking increasingly miserable, he shook his head from side to side, and I burst into tears. That seemed to activate him; he rose from his seat and, promising to call the police, disappeared across the crowded room.

About half an hour later, with Wang still gone, a curious trio appeared in the door of the dining room: a wizened but dapper elderly gentleman, in a cream colored jacket, wearing a purple bow tie, accompanied by two strapping young men in dark suits at his side. *At last, the police*, I thought. They made their way to my table. One of the men brought the old man a chair, and once seated in front of me, he began to converse in English:

"You came here with a friend to have dinner?"

"Yes, I did."

"You are American?"

"Yes, I'm American."

"What are you doing in China?"

"I came to teach in Beijing and now I'm on my way out of China."

"You have lost your money?"

"Yes, I have lost my money. Someone stole my purse!"

"You have lost your papers?"

"Yes, I have lost my papers and can't leave China without them. And I have a flight tomorrow."

Given this rhythm of query and response, I had no doubt I was speaking to a very polite senior policeman, and so when the old man concluded, "I'm very sorry you have lost your things," arose from his chair, and bowing to me, left with his two companions, I was puzzled. What had just happened? Who were they? A short time later, Wang reappeared. When I described this mysterious visit, he informed me that the gentleman was probably an elder whose function it was to pay due attention to foreigners upset by a local experience. An old tradition. Not the police.

"But the police should be here soon," Wang assured me as my panic returned. "I called them from the kitchen." Sometime later, as he and I sat silently at the table waiting, several men walked through the curtain into the restaurant and, waving their arms lustily, ordered the staff to clear the restaurant, as I understood from seeing waiters scurrying around ushering people out. No ambiguity here. The police had arrived.

I was led into an office on the side of the dining room and seated in front of a tall, slim, cold-eyed official. I was immediately put on edge. He began to ask me questions similar to those asked by the elder, but in a voice without any emotional valence. Wang was seated next to me and translated between us. Some fifteen minutes into the interrogation, the door opened and another plain-clothed policeman walked in—dangling my bag in the air! A surge of relief—"That's my bag!" I shouted to the room, but no one responded. The policeman gave my bag to my inquisitor, who looked through it and then returned to his questioning:

"Is this your bag?"

"Yes, that's my bag."

"Describe its contents."

"My passport, my wallet . . ."

"How much money did you have?"

I tried to imagine how much I had and came up with a number: "About four hundred yuan and one hundred dollars in American cash."

The inquisitor looked at me icily and intoned, "Think again."

How much? How was I to remember? The pounding of my heart interfered with thinking clearly. I walked backward in my mind.

"Oh, yes, I forgot. I bought film this afternoon. Three hundred seventy-five yuan and one hundred dollars."

"Think again," he intoned again, stonily.

Panic. I tried to remember. Oh, yes, the little statuette. . . .

"I forgot something else I bought. I think maybe three hundred yuan?"

That seemed to satisfy him; he handed me my bag and, turning to Wang, said something in Chinese I didn't understand. Wang translated: I had to go.

"But what happened?" I asked. "Where did they find my bag?"

"While we were waiting, they searched the houses of all the restaurant workers; they found your bag in the apartment of one of the waiters. Now you must go."

I rose, but he didn't.

"Wang, aren't you coming too? I need your help to find my way back to the Teachers College," I heard myself implore.

Wang looked down at his lap, and said softly, "I have to remain here. Please go."

Waves of guilt washed over me; in Beijing I had been told that crimes against foreigners were often punished by execution. What would happen to the waiter? And Wang, who helped me when he shouldn't have! What would be his punishment?

"Please go," he said again quietly.

I made my way out of the empty restaurant and onto the dark, deserted street. A nearby streetlamp cast a long shadow on the sidewalk. It was close to midnight by my watch. I had no idea where I was or how to make my way back to my quarters at the Teachers College. I was considering whether to crouch in a doorway until morning when, as if in miraculous answer to my need, a taxicab pulled out of the darkness and stopped near the corner, and a young woman hidden in another doorway ran out to meet it. Without hesitating, I ran after her. The cab was full of other young people, apparently workers who had arranged for these nightly pickups. I pleaded with them to take me too, gesturing, repeating the few Chinese words I knew—"*Wǒ shì lǎoshī*" (I am a teacher). Wondrously, they understood I was staying at the Teachers College and had me driven there.

But Wang? Whatever happened to Wang? In a country like China, in which social transgression was not a game, what consequences had my single-minded pursuit of pleasure done to him? Never had I so clearly recognized my instrumental use of the exotic Other. Again, a piece of self-knowledge wrested from a solo journey; again, not pleasing to my self-image. *Selfish*. My father's judgment would echo in my memory for years to come.

9

A New Millennium: Carpe Diem (1995–2006)

Throw your dreams into space like a kite, and you do not know what it will bring back, a new life, a new friend, a new love, a new country.

Anais Nin

The Other Woman. How could I allow myself to be humiliated by actually living out such a domestic cliché for so long? But there she was, an intrusive presence hovering over my marriage during this last decade of the twentieth century. I had known for several years that Rainer was having an affair. Actually, I was fairly certain he was having two affairs, one with a newly discovered cousin in Germany, whom he visited twice a year—she had miraculously survived World War II—and one with Madeline, the former wife of a colleague who lived, conveniently, across the street from us. As the Other Woman, Madeline was the greater irritant, her proximity allowing her to make greater demands on our daily lives. Often, as Rainer and I were about to get into bed, the phone would ring, and after answering it, Rainer would turn to me and say matter-of-factly: "I have to bring the *Times* to Madeline. She didn't have time to get the paper today and wants to read it."

"At eleven thirty at night?"

"She's too tired to go out, and we have it, she doesn't."

Indeed. Although I was more exasperated by Rainer's refusal to acknowledge the affair than by the affair itself—"She's just a friend," he would repeat whenever I asked about their relationship—I had decided, mainly for Jake's sake, neither to accuse nor to act on the knowledge, but rather to swallow the humiliation until Jake had graduated from high school and had gone off to college. I wasn't prepared to put Jake through the pain of dismantling the world as he knew it, at least not while he lived at home. I had not yet acknowledged that letting go of this marriage would be difficult for me also, unfulfilling as it was. I had been Claire Hanser as well as Claire Kahane for twenty years now, with all the history that those names implied.

But if, as "the betrayed wife," I was caught like a fish thrashing around in a torn domestic net, in my life as a feminist scholar and critic, I felt purposeful, stimulated, fulfilled. Work was such a relief from my domestic disappointments—invigorating and self-affirming. A book of essays co-edited with a favorite colleague, Charlie Bernheimer, had achieved the notable distinction of going into a second edition, and the monthly meetings of my feminist writing group, women of academic accomplishment in various fields, was nurturing my new work. Carolyn, a philosophy professor, was writing a book on taste in artistic production; Betsy, an architectural historian, was writing about the kitchen as a household space associated with women's domestic role; Liz, an anthropologist and the chair of women's studies, was readying a book on the working-class lesbian community of Buffalo; Isabel, a law professor, was lecturing on the pervasiveness of domestic violence in Eastern Europe; and Carol, an art historian, was researching the depiction of women in modern and postmodern art. Galvanized by the group's collective enthusiasms, I was working on a book arguing that the powerful voice of nineteenth-century feminist orators psychologically unsettled turn-of-the-century Anglo-American fiction—a theme my own past subjection to a powerful male voice had opened up for me. Who had the authority to speak? It had been a formidable question for me, and the writing group helped me answer it.

By that last decade of the twentieth century, not only had most of us published significant books, but our conversations had led to our co-teaching new interdisciplinary courses that invigorated our respective curriculums. The three of us—Carol, Carolyn, and I—standing in front of a class called Feminism and Postmodernism in Art and Literature and engaging one another in dynamic discussion was an education for our students as well as ourselves. The energy in the class was palpable, the papers that emerged creative. When, in the spring of 1994, Isabel arranged with colleagues in Poland for the six of us to go to Kraków to give a seminar on the impact of feminism in the American academy, I was thrilled. Teaching about feminism at Jagiellonian University, the second oldest university in Central Europe! It seemed a great distinction; it felt like a radical contribution. And surely, it would be a relief to leave my conflicted domestic scene for a few months.

But on second thought, going to teach about feminism in Poland, the country where my father was born, gave me pause. Had he been alive, he would have spurned my "return" to the land where his family had been murdered: "*Don' go. What's to go for? A* farshtunken *land ... Fahged aboud id.*" Commands—actual or imagined—ignored, defied. And as if it were yesterday, I felt again the mortification of losing my voice a decade ago because of an unconscious paternal interdiction: my father's "no."

It was December 1985, the year of the publication of *The (M)other Tongue*, a critical anthology that took patriarchal literature to task for silencing women's voices, and I was standing before a microphone in a large hall, facing an audience of five hundred academics at a major professional conference. I had agreed to be the respondent to a panel of papers, but having received them just before leaving for the airport, I had had no time to review them. *I'm accustomed to extemporizing*, I remember thinking. *I'll just browse through them on the plane.* Once on board, I pulled the first paper from my case and looked it over. It was a highly theoretical analysis, and much to my distress, I understood nothing of its claims. The other two were more accessible, and so I formed a strategy: I would avoid saying anything about the one I didn't understand and generalize about the other two from notes I would take during their presentations.

But that afternoon, as I sat on the platform listening to the papers, I couldn't seem to focus my attention. I heard the speaker's voice but couldn't assimilate the content. When it was my turn to step before the microphone, my heart began to hammer, and out of my mouth came a garbled remark about the paper I understood least! As I babbled on compulsively, my mouth became increasingly dry, until finally, with no saliva left, my tongue actually stuck to the roof of my mouth, and I could not speak. I could do no more than open and close my lips like a fish gasping in air. And why? As I came to believe through my psychoanalysis years later, the very act of public speaking as a feminist had been for me a kind of unconscious theft of paternal authority. My father, an uneducated immigrant, had lost his mother tongue. I had used mine to take down the patriarchs. And I had built a career on that subversive stance.

Now, no longer self-silenced—years of insightful therapy in Buffalo had freed my voice—as I packed for this trip to my father's hated homeland, I could hear him contemptuously dismissing my feminist project in Poland, just as he had dismissed the value of my trip to Germany years earlier, his words brimming with disgust. *What's to go for?* As it turned out, there was much to go for. And to take back.

Becoming Jew-ish, Again

Since childhood, when I had seen my father break down in a fit of sobbing after getting the news that his family had been locked in their home and burned to death, the fate of my parents' families in Eastern Europe had been part of my shadow-life, a submerged knowledge that periodically surfaced to remind me of the Nazis' final solution and the simmering antisemitism in Europe that underlay its realization. Certainly I knew from my own earlier experiences that antisemitism was a fact of life in the United States. Wanting to protect myself from further humiliations, over the years, I had increasingly distanced myself from "Jewishness." *No, no, not me.* Not an admirable stance, perhaps, but assimilation as "an American," a cultural ideal promoted in the mid-century America of my youth, became my goal.

College had encouraged my assimilation as it had for so many other first-generation Americans, promoting a love affair with the English language and its literature that would last a lifetime. More insidiously, I found myself attracted to men who looked like that portrait of the fair-haired, lightly-bearded, epicene youth suffering on the cross that hung on the bedroom wall of my childhood friend Patsy. Barney McCaffrey had been the first, but not the last, avatar to fit that description. Indeed, with the radical exception of Brian Altieri, that dark-eyed prophet from whom I had fled in a panic, my lovers over the years seemed like recurring mirror images of the non-Semitic-looking Christ of both working class kitsch and high Renaissance art. Ironically, I eventually married a German Jew who appeared, as he himself testified, the very likeness of the pure Aryan of Nazi myth—tall, slim, light-haired, blue-eyed! (His brother, who resembled him, had been pulled out of his high school class by a visiting Nazi official and exhibited as the perfect Aryan.)

Now, I was going off to Kraków, a city of catastrophic significance for the fate of the European Jews. For despite its reputation as a center of early modern knowledge, Kraków's modern history was darkly tainted; it had been the official site of the Nazi government in central Europe, chosen, because of its central geographical position, to facilitate transport for the extermination of the European Jews. Auschwitz was only a half hour away. And so, under the pressure of place, at the end of our first week of teaching, the four of us who were Jewish found ourselves passing under the archway bearing the inscription familiar to me from so many films—*Arbeit Macht Frei*—into Auschwitz, the camp.

We entered the first building with some measure of apprehension that only increased as we made our way through the exhibits—a mass of ghostly hair cuttings, a mound of eyeglasses with thin bent frames, old shoes piled up higher than my sight line, and most especially heartrending for me, a mountain of suitcases seemingly thrown at random, one on top of the other, each suitcase chalked with a person's name, country of origin, birth date. Faced, at this "tourist site," with the actual physical remains and belongings of the hundreds of thousands murdered here, I found myself weeping as I had not wept in a long time, mourning not only the loss of a world I knew only obliquely, but also the deaths of my parents years earlier and *their* losses—their parents, brothers, sisters, uncles, aunts—familial ghosts, all unknown to me, all consumed. Ashes.

Even before my visit to Auschwitz, traveling by train from Warsaw to Kraków, my own ghosts had appeared in the Polish landscape. My mother appeared in a *babushka* leaning over to pick vegetables in her garden, in a young girl carrying a pail down a country lane. My father in a laborer angrily spurring on his horse as he drove his cart down a muddy street, in a large grim-faced man standing next to me in the train corridor, who reached over my shoulder with lips clenched to close the train window after I had opened it. Auschwitz converted these apparitions into material remnants of the past: hair, glasses, suitcases.

Of course, there was more to my experience of Poland than its vestiges of the past, horrific or otherwise. In its post-Communist euphoria, Poland was reinventing itself as a bastion of a progressive European culture, a stance that would reverse itself years later. Our younger Polish colleagues enthusiastically welcomed us as American feminists and arranged speaking tours for us at other universities. On the other hand, the older colleague assigned to smooth my departmental path seemed more ambivalent about my presence. As we walked to my first seminar, she interrogated me about my background: where, when, who my parents were.

"My father was Polish," I told her.

With a slight smirk, she remarked: "He was not really Polish, but Jewish, yes?"

By the month's end, in what I thought of as a profound irony, Poland, the country most associated with the Jewish genocide because of Auschwitz, had awakened in me my own Jewishness *precisely because there were so few Jews in the country.* As we traveled from Kraków to Wrocław to lecture on feminism, or visited the resort area of Zakopane in the Tatra mountains, or in a further act of witness, toured the infamous Majdanek concentration camp situated before all eyes in the middle of Lublin, I felt the palpable presence of Jewish absence—an absence insistently marked by the seemingly ubiquitous representations of Jews. I felt it in the piles of Jewish folk art dolls laid out, one on top of another like corpses, in the market square of Kraków; in a Yiddish theater in Warsaw with no Jewish actors; in a tourist restaurant decked out as a nineteenth-century Jewish inn with a costumed faux-Jewish waitstaff; in newly published translations of books by dead Jewish-American authors; and more darkly, in antisemitic graffiti—"Żyd *idzie do domu*" (Jews go home)—scrawled across the walls of buildings in Lublin where there were no Jews left. Even more, I discovered an analogous absence in me that I had not previously acknowledged, a gap instead of a living connection to my parents' conspicuous Jewish identity. Surprisingly, I found myself wanting to know Yiddish culture more intimately, to acknowledge my parents' passing by digging into their material past, and into the past of *their* families.

Auschwitz aroused similar feelings in my Jewish colleagues, and so, after our final week of seminars, four of us agreed to travel farther east on a pilgrimage of sorts, each of us compelled by the uncanny familiarity of the sheer names of places—Pruzhany, Grodno, Minsk—to uncover the actual sites of our family histories, long buried by the Holocaust. Two of us were able to find material evidence of ancestral places—a lumber mill in Ukraine once owned by Carol's grandfather, a shtetl in Belarus where Liz's grandmother had lived. "The Jews just went away during the war," an old woman who lived there told us in all seriousness. "They left. Nobody knew why." But my own journey to Pruzhany, my father's birthplace, uncovered only Judel, the last Jew left in the city. Sitting with him in his living room while his wife, a former USSR officer wearing a housedress and a hair ker-chief, served us tea, their family photographs plastered all over the walls, I felt myself eerily back in the Bronx, and even more so as I listened to Judel tell his story, in a familiar Yiddish accent, of surviving Auschwitz only to be sent by Stalin to a Siberian labor camp because he had survived.

"If you survived, Stalin said you were a collaborator," he explained, his voice dripping with a bitterness that sounded exactly like my father's. Same intonation, same way of laughing. Ghosts. But he hadn't known of any family named Katz. Dead end.

Traveling farther east to Minsk, hoping to find some evidence of my mother's past, was even less rewarding. Although a burly Israeli from the Joint offered his help, I didn't have enough information to discover the site of her shtetl or find any record of her existence. Apart from the few stories she had told me, her material history would remain, like Freud's "dark continent," (his comment about women's sexuality), a mystery.

Yet the trip had itself been a success of sorts. We returned to Buffalo with a sense of mission: to teach what we had learned about the Holocaust and its effects. In the fall of 1994, I offered a new course, The Holocaust and Its Literature, not only to enlighten my students about this darkest of episodes in modern history, but also to keep the intensity of my own confrontation with it alive. Jankiel Wiernik's *A Year in Treblinka*, Elie Wiesel's *Night*, Abraham Sutzkever's "Frozen Jews," and for me most powerfully, Paul Celan's "Death Fugue"—no one could read these horrific accounts written by survivors and close the books unravaged. Celan's words especially echoed loudly in my ears: *Black milk of daybreak we drink it at evening / we drink it at midday and / morning we drink it at night / we drink and we drink . . .*

Apparently, I needed, even wanted, to keep the shock of the Holocaust alive in me. And why? Was it because by immersing my students and myself in such excruciating depictions, I somehow thought I could honor my parents' experiences of loss vicariously? Because "never forget" had been internally mandated? Or because this literature answered to a sense of catastrophe, a black milk I had drunk as a child? Did I do well to teach this traumatizing literature when, for some students, its emotional charge went beyond what they could bear? Some complained about the angst raised by reading Tadeusz Borowski's *This Way for the Gas, Ladies and Gentlemen*; several ran out of the class in the midst of a documentary I showed on the liberation of the camps—even though it had been shown on *Frontline* in 1985. Was it right for me to subject my students to such painful representations because of my own need for acts of witnessing?

Certainly, I hoped they would benefit from what I deemed a moral imperative, and yet I suspect that there was also an illicit pleasure in the frisson of repeatedly re-experiencing through literature "the horror, the horror." Casting a cold eye on my motives, I still wonder: was I acting out a repetition compulsion and taking a perverse pleasure in psychic pain? Or was my immersion in Holocaust literature a legitimate way of mourning the immensity of such loss—first the shudder, then the letting go? Whatever the warren of motives, after Auschwitz, I no longer felt distant from my family lineage. I could be *also Jewish*.

Letting Go: Further Variations on a Theme

Letting go of the past: a theme in my life that grew in general importance during the decade before the millennial turn. Among academics, "The End of History," the final stage of civilization's political and social evolution, had become an obsessive theme. In my own small orbit, I too was apprehensive about the sense of an ending. In 1995, I turned sixty, a disturbing number. My son was away at college. My marriage was in tatters. I had to restructure my personal life along different lines if I were to have another—and most probably last—chance for a more satisfying life. As winter was turning into a cold Buffalo spring, one chilly morning, I entered Rainer's study and, taking a deep breath, proposed that we get a divorce.

Rainer did not appear surprised. Rising from his desk with a slow nod, he walked to the window and stood looking out at the leafless trees outside. I waited, not knowing what to expect. After a few moments pause, he said, turning toward me, "I understand, but divorce may not be such a good idea. Remember, if we divorce, you'll lose the benefits of our joint income and linked retirement accounts."

As soon as he said this, I breathed a deep sigh of relief: this conversation would not be antagonistic or hurtful. Rainer was concerned about my welfare. We had a history. We were still family. And what he pointed out was true: given my modest salary, my financial safety net for the future would be seriously torn in a divorce. Yet I had to leave this marriage. I knew I could survive any economic downturn, but perhaps there was another way....

"We should also think about what the effects of a divorce would be on Jake," Rainer continued. *Yes*, I thought. Jake, such a sensitive child—the look of anguish on his face years ago when he had heard Rainer and me heatedly quarrelling. He was no longer a child, but still, I knew he would be distraught if we divorced. How could I toss him from the train just as he was accommodating to college life? The thought of Jake's response had paralyzed me before, but I determined it would not do so now. Was there a wiser way to proceed?

As the cold morning light filtered through the study window, an idea took shape in my mind: why couldn't Rainer and I share our house, but live in it at different times of the year? I could have it in the fall and teach while Rainer was in Germany—he had already been spending several months a year there with his cousin. And in the spring, he could return and I could go to Berkeley and live in the small cottage I had bought years ago. We could come together as a family for the longer holidays when Jake was home from college, sparing him the more disruptive consequences of our separation. To my great delight, Rainer agreed!

I was proud of our negotiation and the civilized resolution it achieved—especially since I wouldn't have to give up anything. My Buffalo house, my relationship with my husband, my social and professional connections in both Buffalo and Berkeley, my desire to live on my own as a single woman. Pie in the sky!

The plan worked fine for a few years. Every January, I took a leave without pay from the university and went back on the road as I had years ago, my spirits soaring as I drove across the country along a route that became increasingly familiar, stopping each year at what I came to consider my "stations." First stop, after a typically harrowing drive through Ohio's winter ice storms: Lexington, Kentucky, where a dear Buffalo friend had gone to teach and where we caught up on academic gossip over dinner and a good bottle of wine. The next day, driving along the snow-powdered highways of Tennessee, then dipping down in a detour to Austin, Texas, where two former Buffalonians always delighted me by roasting a whole pig in their backyard as a welcome. The next day, back up to the interstate again, clay-colored mesas becoming visible in the distance as I continued on the road to Tucson, Arizona, anticipating a walk in the Sonora desert with another former Buffalo colleague, and a visit to a favorite spot, the Desert Museum. Back on the road—passing Phoenix and entering a multi-lane highway with its ubiquitous malls that told me I was now in Southern California, stopping overnight at a dreary motel in Indio, and then onto the insanely challenging freeway system of Los Angeles for a friendly visit with another former Buffalo colleague, now a feminist historian at UCLA. On the last day, I'd either head up the Central Valley, past the stench of stockyards—poor beasts, standing in their own shit—and the fruit orchards further north, or allow myself the luxury of driving up the serpentine coast road, the roiling sea visible below, finally arriving at my own small cottage in Berkeley, exhausted and exhilarated.

After a night's sleep, I easily resumed my West Coast life with my academic Berkeley circle. Marilyn now taught film at UC; Margret and Carol had both become translators. But I also looked forward to seeing friends like Sheelagh, who, no longer John's wife, was now a professional fisherperson with a boat of her own; she fished in Alaska every summer with her second husband, but still had a house in Berkeley where she lived during the rest of the year. Julie, my old Brooklynite buddy, was now a lawyer making professional use of her pugnaciousness. My days were typically spent writing papers and preparing new courses for Buffalo, my evenings having dinner with friends, or going to a movie or the theater, or reading and listening to music at home—alone but not lonely.

But something else was happening that surprised me. As if Berkeley had turned on a spigot of youthful desire, I found myself actively looking at men that I passed on the street and feeling pleased when I saw them looking back. Apparently, I wanted a new romance, or at least male company. And so I joined an internet dating service, a new and popular means of social engagement. The result that first year: a few dinners with a few men, all without consequence, but curiously satisfying. Playing the field. Stimulating a buried aspect of myself.

During my second year's leave, I actually found a new romance—a handsome retired historian who literally swept me off my feet on our first date. After a beautifully served candlelit dinner in his tasteful San Francisco apartment, we danced in his dimly lit living room while the moonlight filtered through the tall windows, casting our shadows together. He was a good dancer; he gazed appreciatively at me; I felt myself melting into his arms and feeling what I had never expected at this time of life—that I was falling in love, and with someone who seemed to me sexy in spite of his being seventy-three. So sexual attraction and a love affair could still happen in these later years! Smoke and mirrors, as it turned out; the romance didn't last past June, when he broke it off, accusing me of publicly insulting him by criticizing his opinion in front of my friends. I cried for weeks, my tears mixed with righteous anger and disappointment. (Years later I recognized his complaint was justified; I had humiliated him in public, and the recognition changed my behavior.) Yet something else happened as a consequence of his rejection: each morning, out of my rage, I wrote a poem. Rage had provoked me to create something new; rage was productive—a fact I had forgotten, and for that reminder alone, I was grateful for the experience. Love could still happen; new work could come out of its loss.

Although I continued to relish my double life in Buffalo and in Berkeley, in January of 1998, I varied the pattern by accepting a teaching fellowship at the Hebrew University of Jerusalem for their spring semester, this despite the fact that the political situation in Israel was giving me pause. Tensions with Iraq were on the rise; thousands of Israelis were lining up at distribution centers to buy gas masks in expectation of a biological attack. Was this the time to go to Israel to teach? I wavered and delayed my flight. In the end, I took the risk and, by the end of February, found myself living in a small one-room cottage in the German Colony of Jerusalem and teaching a weekly graduate seminar on the Holocaust in American literature. Luckily, my cottage was just down the street from a poet and translator, Linda Zisquit, whom my colleague Bob Creeley had suggested I contact. She and her husband warmly welcomed me into their Modern Orthodox family life, as did my secular landlords, an arty bohemian couple with whom I became good friends. Animated by the articulate intelligence of my students and the lively intellectual atmosphere of the university, and befriended by people with contrasting beliefs, I couldn't have been better situated to experience Israeli life.

Although the "German Colony," as it was called, in which I lived was a "hip" area, the ubiquity of the Orthodox Jews elsewhere in Jerusalem, with their *payes*, strange-looking hats, and long black coats, disturbed me. I couldn't help but recall my father's expressions of distaste whenever he saw Orthodox Jewish men on the New York subway; A Jewish man himself, but with a fierce post-Holocaust commitment to modern secular values, he found the public display of their Jewish difference embarrassing, and perhaps even humiliating. It was part of a past he had defensively rejected. As a Jewish secular woman, I shared his feelings, if not his reasons. Their cultural values, especially their rigid separation of the roles of men and women, offended me, as did their assumption of a superior righteousness. At the same time, I was fascinated by the fervency of their public devotions. I still recall the sight of women throwing themselves at the Wailing Wall as if it were a lover while masses of men davened behind them with their own mad intensity. And the hats of the Orthodox men! Big Russian-style fur hats, large round brimmed hats, flat hats, tall hats—a crowd of hats fetishizing the Wall.

To counter my aversion to religious orthodoxy, I took walking tours that focused on Jerusalem's ancient history or went wandering through the colorful Arabic bazaar, seeking out its exotic treasures. One day, to my great pleasure, I came across a wise Bedouin trader whose insights led me to seek him out repeatedly. When we first met, he told me I had "a masked look"; but after a while, he said, "I see ambivalence in you: you have no deep roots, and therefore you are in danger of swaying in the wind." How perspicacious! I thought often about his remark as I sought out various excursions in Israel and beyond. I toured a Druze village in the desert and had lunch with a Druze family; I floated in the Dead Sea and luxuriated in its famous black mud baths; I commuted weekly by jitney to Tel Aviv, the more modern iteration of Israel, where I indulged my love of music clubs and the beach, dancing every Saturday on the boardwalk; I traveled with my Buffalo colleague Carol to Petra and Amman in Jordan, and walked among the ruins of ancient cities. But I never lost sight of the existing tension between Israel and its Arab neighbors, nor of the ever-present shadow of the event that rose up to stop traffic once a year, the catastrophe memorialized in Yad Vashem, the Holocaust Remembrance Center.

There was, however, one trip that almost proved to be a personal catastrophe: a four-day desert hike with the Society for the Protection of Nature in Israel. We were a small group: I the least physically fit , five companion hikers, along with Isak, our guide, and an armed security guard. As we hiked across the Judaean Desert, I marveled at the spectacular panorama.

Judean desert hike

The terrain kept changing. Long stretches of desert sand gave way to stark cliffs dotted with sandstone caves, and occasional streams with waterfalls at the bottom of canyons. As we wandered through spectacular scenic variations, I felt my own adventurous spirit expand to meet them. Some of the sites we stopped at, like the Monastery of Saint George of Choziba, a vertiginous cliff-hanging complex near Jericho with a difficult climb down, were astounding; some, like the comfortable kibbutz we stayed at overnight near the Golan Heights, a territory still in dispute with Syria, had compelling histories. But by the third day of hiking under a blazing sky, the intense heat had become a rival for my attention. I had suffered from heat exhaustion in the past and was familiar with its symptoms—headaches, nausea, physical weakness—and so, when my head began to ache, I worried. I knew heat exhaustion could have serious consequences.

On the fourth day, with the sun ceaselessly beating down as I made my way along the parched landscape, my headache became more intense; I felt dizzy and nauseated. I told our guide Isak that I was feeling unwell, but what could he do in the middle of the desert? "We're almost at our rest point, a river where you can cool off," he assured me. And so, pushing back my nausea, I continued to troop on as heat poured from the sky. When we got to the rest stop, with my head still throbbing, I managed to climb down the boulders to the shallow stream below. While the others frolicked in the water, I lay there quietly, supine in the stream, soaking my head until it was time to move on.

Cooling off at canyon rest stop

But the headache got even worse once I climbed back up to ground level. Head pounding, nausea repeatedly rising up, I barely was able to continue walking, but Isak urged me on. "Just a bit more, in less than a half hour, we'll come to an area where there's shade and you can rest again." The outline of a tree in the distance soon gave me hope, and when we reached it, I sank down in its shade and leaned back against the tree trunk, unable to move.

"Leave me here, Isak. I can't go any farther," I whimpered. Isak stood over me, looking anxious, not knowing what to do. At that moment, as if miraculously, a jeep appeared on the landscape carrying two men, the driver and one passenger. Isak flagged it down; there was room for me in the back. Explaining the situation, Isak gave the driver directions to our parked van, and told me to wait there for the group. Sometime later, barely conscious of my surroundings, I was dropped off in a parking lot near the van.

Unable to remain upright, I dropped to the ground next to the van and lost all muscular control; from every orifice of my body, fluid substances flowed freely. Sitting in a mire of excretions, I should have felt humiliated; I felt relieved. Time passed; the headache lessened; the group returned. Isak helped me to a public toilet in the parking lot and wiped me off with a wet towel. Recognizing how seriously dehydrated I was, he wanted to drive me to a nearby hospital, but I vigorously rejected that idea. I didn't want to be left alone and helpless in a foreign hospital on the Golan Heights. Instead, insisting that I knew what to do, I asked for a bottle of water and a straw, and for the few hours that it took to return to our kibbutz, I sipped water slowly, drop by drop, consciously trying to imitate an I.V. Back at the kibbutz, Isak nursed me for the next two days, and I recovered, feeling lucky to have survived without serious complications.

In late April, during the university's Passover break, I took a week-long jaunt to Istanbul, a city I'd long wanted to visit. Although I was frequently hustled by men on the street inviting me to have tea in their bazaar—shorthand for "let me sell you a rug"—or wanting to show me the historic sites, I recognized them as part of an endemic tourist culture, and never felt endangered. Indeed, I accepted the offer of one young man to be my friendly guide to the awesome Hagia Sofia and the Blue Mosque, and then took *him* for tea. On my own, I found a gorgeous blue-tiled 18th century Hammam in the old city, where I indulged in the sensuous pleasures of a Turkish bath. Happily, while bathing I befriended a young British woman also touring Istanbul. We met the next day, and together, took a daytrip by ferry up the Bosphorus, stopping along the strait to visit Ottoman historical sites, both of us delighted to have found a companion to experience this fascinating borderline between Europe and Asia. At the end of the week, having indulged myself in the sights and smells of Istanbul, I returned to Jerusalem to complete the semester. A month later, I was back in Buffalo, ready to draw on my Israeli experiences, both positive and negative, for my fall classes.

Retirement

I was in the midst of organizing an academic conference on Holocaust literature, to be held in the fall of 1999, when I was given an unpleasant surprise: my department chair insisted I return to full-time teaching. "We've lost some faculty. The department needs you back on a full-time basis." An impossible demand, given my domestic arrangements. After playing the income numbers—half-time work had kept me on a tight budget, but retirement would give me an almost full salary—I gave notice. Retirement, I discovered, would be profitable. Rainer could have the house all year; I would move into my Berkeley cottage, and although I still planned to return to Buffalo each year for family holidays and summer visits—Jake was now living and working in New York and came up to Buffalo regularly—I would construct a new life in the Bay Area, full-time.

With that plan in mind, I held my last academic conference, this one on Holocaust literature and invited scholars from various parts of the country to give presentations. But having set it all up, I watched it collapse as, on the opening day, a fierce snowstorm enveloped Buffalo, causing the city and its traffic to come to a halt, so that only the presenters, who had arrived the day before and were housed on campus, could attend. Needless to say, they were not happy, nor was I, to see my last academic project buried in snow. So did I retire.

Retired! A word that aroused such convoluted feelings. How many colleagues had I known who dreaded their last week of teaching? How mixed were my own feelings as I walked into my office after my last class and looked around at the small eight-by-ten space in which I had sat and worked for twenty-four years. My books, spilling out of shelves that were stacked from floor to ceiling. The gray steel desk, its disordered surface covered with papers, on top of which sat the telephone—a useful paperweight since there was no space for it on the desk anyway. Two large gray filing cabinets squeezed next to one side of the desk, filled with class notes and research articles. And a window that looked out on the red brick building across the way. Two years ago, I had painted one wall a lovely taupe in an effort to lighten the gloom of this gray space, but the institutional tenor of the room could not be erased. And yet here I had lived most hours of most days for most of twenty-four years. Here I met with students and advised them, here I did my research and writing, and here were stored the products of those years: books, class notes, published articles. Now all that would have to be boxed, bagged, removed, given away—even thrown away. Retired.

If I was saddened by this recognition, I was also elated. No longer would I be walled into this deplorably cramped space. The future lay before me like an open road. True, I was now sixty-five—not the customary age to start a new life or gamble on its being better than the old, yet I was doing both without any hesitation—and precisely *because* of my age. During the course of my life, I had periodically asked myself the question that was my yardstick for action: "If you knew this was the last day of your life, what would you most regret *not* having done?" For too many years, my answer had been "not leaving Buffalo and trying for a more satisfying life." Now, at age sixty-five, with mortality no longer a distant abstraction, and no reason not to act, I was eager to take up the challenge, to plunge into the future.

Plunge! Virginia Woolf's favorite word for capturing a sense of vital engagement with life—a word that resonated with me as a synonym for feeling alive. And what would make me feel most alive now that I was older? What plunge could I take now? The answer: challenging new work that would make use of my abilities and yet appeal to my desire for a change. And with that recognition, a casual wish from the more recent past took shape as a future goal: in the new millennium, I would become a psychoanalyst.

It was a natural, a new career linked to my academic expertise yet requiring a totally different posture. Instead of talking, I would listen. I imagined myself sitting in front of a fireplace, some young person in the chair opposite me talking while I listened attentively and, with all the knowledge gleaned from my past experiences, dispensed a healing wisdom. Caught up in this fantasy, and with my appetite for new experience again whetted, I packed up those books I thought would be useful and most of my wardrobe (leaving some clothing for my usual holiday visits to Buffalo), and in 2000, once again, I drove across the country as I had the previous five years, this time looking forward to training for a new profession. *Allons.*

Transferences and Transformations

On my return to Berkeley, I immediately began the process of becoming an analyst by applying for training at the San Francisco Psychoanalytic Institute. With a strong letter of recommendation from my feminist colleague Nancy Chodorow, one of their star graduates, and the encouragement of Bob Wallerstein, the director—who, when I confessed that my primary interest was intellectual rather than a desire to heal, assured me that Freud also was more interested in theory than in patients—I was quickly accepted. But before I could actually begin to train, I myself was required to enter a full psychoanalysis, four days a week, in order to better understand my own neuroses before treating others. A requirement! Something I always had wanted but could never before afford: a four-day-a-week focus on my psyche, now required! And offered at a discount. It could finally—hopefully—help me come to terms with my troubled relations with men. Perhaps even with my father, dead these many years yet still pricking my consciousness.

Since the analyst was a parental figure for the patient, I was determined to find a male training-analyst who could readily stand in for my father. When an avuncular analyst agreed to take me on, I considered myself lucky. Dr. M's office lay in a charming terracotta building located in Laurel

Heights, a pleasing, well-to-do San Francisco neighborhood. Entering the small foyer, I immediately came face-to-face with a door that had his name on it. It opened into a small waiting room, empty now. A bit nervous, I sat down. A few moments later, an inner door opened, and there he was: a rather short, elderly man, with gray hair, glasses, and a warm smile. He ushered me into his inner sanctum: a leather chair near a couch with a napkin on a pillow at one end, a desk near a shaded window at the far side of the room, and bookcases lining the walls. He pointed to the couch, and as directed, I lay down, head on the napkin, feet facing away from the window. He sat on the chair behind me. After a few minutes of silence, I began to speak. He occasionally commented, asked a question, but mainly it was me talking for fifty minutes, telling him why I wanted to be an analyst, what I knew about Freudian theory, a bit of my recent marital history. I talked mostly about my present situation; there would be other sessions to visit the distant past. And then it was time to leave. I thanked him for accepting me as a patient and walked out the door onto the tree-lined street. Passing a small boutique, I stopped to look in the shop window, saw my reflection in the glass, and felt a surge of elation. Suddenly I became aware that I was humming a familiar old song. What was it? The first line came to me: "I'd like to get you on a slow boat to China." Wow! Transference—the analyst, as a romanticized father figure—already appearing unconsciously after my first session! This analysis would be a productive encounter, I was sure.

Productive it was, though not in the way I had anticipated. After just a few weeks, my analyst and I became embroiled in heated arguments over the meaning of certain incidents: keys misplaced that had made me late for a session, the content of a previous hour forgotten, my inability to easily free-associate to dreams. The sessions became increasingly tense, the silences between us longer and more unbearable. (Shades of my marriage!) After only a few months, he shocked me by dismissing me as his patient.

"We can't continue this analysis." (Rejection and exile!)

"You don't listen to me," he complained, when I asked why. "You don't want analysis. And certainly not with me."

"But I *need* to be in analysis in order to train."

"You should find a woman analyst. That's your only hope."

I was taken aback. Was he right? Was my relation to men beyond rec-lamation? Psychoanalysis tells us that we always see the other through a fog of early childhood associations, and here he was again: my father, my antagonist. "Resistance," Dr. M. called it. But shouldn't an analyst have used my "resistance," if that's what it was, as part of the analysis rather than dismiss me as uncooperative?

Swallowing the hurt as I had so often swallowed my anger, but not really digesting it, I took his advice: I quickly found a woman who was a training-analyst. Moreover, her office was advantageously on my side of the bay—*on my side*, I duly noted, turning it into a metaphor of support. But I went to my first appointment feeling as though I had already failed an exam.

A small, slim woman of about my age, with a smile that broadened to include her eyes crinkling, Dr. S. welcomed me amiably, telling me, as I entered the room, that she had read my autobiographical essay—part of my application for the institute—and admired my writing. Although it pleased me to hear that, I immediately thought less of her—as if her admiration was a misrecognition, a lack of judgment—as if she were too soft. But I liked her taste in decor; the warm interior colors of her office—salmon and gold and mauve—seemed restful, and the corner windows looked out onto the street, where the green leaves of trees filtered the light coming in. She watched me as I looked around: there was the couch on one side of the room, the familiar napkin on one end of it telling me where to place my head, a comfortable-looking leather chair behind it, a desk on the other side of the room near the door, and oriental rugs on the floor. A pleasing space. I lay down facing the door; she sat down behind me.

And so, once again, I settled into a relationship with a woman analyst. Yet the warning of the male analyst—"You don't want analysis. And certainly not with me"—still echoed in my mind, and I wondered: would I discover anything here that I didn't already know?

The next step in the training program was to become educated in clinical practice. Assigned as a therapist to a neighboring institute's low-cost clinic, I found myself one day not in the comfortable room with a fire blazing in the hearth that I had once imagined, but in a cold, barely furnished institutional space with a desk, two chairs, a box of tissues, and a clock.

"But I won't know what to do," I had complained to the director of the clinic who had assigned me my first patient—an older woman who wanted to see someone her own age. "I don't even have a supervisor yet!"

"You'll be fine," he answered. "Just use your common sense."

He should have known: there is no common sense in the psychoanalytic space.

She came in talking, a woman not unlike myself in height and build, her thick black hair disheveled, a red scarf falling around her shoulders, a large, slightly worn, brown leather shoulder bag swinging awkwardly against the front of her body. I'd prepared for this encounter: my very first experience as a therapist with a live client. I'd set out two chairs, face-to-face, but subtly suggested a difference between them: I had placed the box of tissues on a table next to one chair, and my briefcase on the floor next to the other, making my statement of position quietly. My first surprise: she looked around quickly and sat down in my chair! For a moment I was totally disoriented, and found myself saying, "Oh, you want to sit there? Then I'll sit here." But even as I sat down in what was meant to be her chair, I knew it was the wrong move; she had already defined our roles for the hour; she was in control. And she continued in that position while I squirmed for fifty minutes under her manipulations, following her lead. She knew what she was doing. I didn't.

After that botched initial session, my anxiety level rose to an over-whelming question: what the hell was I doing in this field? I couldn't even maintain the line between therapist and patient. Meanwhile, as a patient myself, I grappled with my own analyst's style. Dr. S. didn't just listen; she also talked, at times even challenging my interpretations with her own.

Me: "That's my dream, not yours."

Dr. S.: "You brought it here to share with me, so it's not just your dream anymore. It's ours."

She also challenged my moral compass. Having borrowed a copy of *House Beautiful* in the waiting room one day, I mentioned the fact the next day in her office and drew a judgmental response.

"Why do you think you have the right to take that magazine?" she asked.

"Well, there's a piece in there that I want to read before I buy a new couch," I replied somewhat testily. "I didn't think it was a big deal. There are other magazines in the waiting room."

"But you took that one, and so others can't read it. I put it there for my patients. Please bring it back before our next session."

Humiliated, I copied the article I wanted and brought the magazine back the next day, all the while recalling my San Francisco analyst's accusation years ago when I parked in her driveway: "*You want special privileges at the expense of others!*" I hadn't accepted that characterization then. Was it true? Thrashing about in my mind like an infant seeking some comfortable position, suspicious of this kind of interactive psychoanalysis, I took my psychic temperature: was a change occurring, or was I only repeating my old patterns? I wasn't even sure of my goals anymore. Why had I just recently started correspondence with Barney, who had been homesteading on a farm in northern Canada with his wife and four sons for several decades? Why was I so inordinately pleased when his letter arrived saying he was excited to have received mine? Did I really need to recapture the thrill of that first romance? To cancel time passing?

Certainly, time was not canceled when I looked at Barney's photograph on the CDs he sent me a week later; I hardly recognized this bearded old man who now collected and recorded folk songs of rural northern Canada. Still, his voice was the same, and as I listened to the CDs, my nostalgia ballooned and then sank deflated in the muddied waters of unfulfilled wishes.

"Late Life Love"

For several months, I had been dating a lawyer I had met through the internet, both of us enjoying each other's company for dinners, intelligent conversation, and satisfying sex. Neither of us expected more. When he broke off our relationship because he had resumed an affair with an old flame, I felt some mild regret—he had been a good companion and had made me feel sexually alive. But I also welcomed the clearing of the space in my life he had occupied—space now open for any new relationship that might offer more.

The phone rang only a week later, and a voice at the other end with a Scottish brogue introduced itself as belonging to Robin Buik, the husband of a former college classmate. She had recently died, and he was on a kind of pilgrimage, mourning his loss by traveling across the country to revisit the places he and his wife had lived. He was in Berkeley for the weekend; a mutual friend had given him my number.

"Would you like to meet for coffee?" he asked.

"Yes," I answered, smiling to myself at the pleasing lilt in his voice.

I met him for coffee, this curly-haired and rather boyish man with a tousled look and an infectious sense of humor; the meeting turned into a long and easy conversation about Berkeley in the sixties. The conversation continued at dinner the next evening, and then he was gone—back to his life as a professor of political science in Wisconsin. But not before we had exchanged email addresses and I had calculatedly thrown out a lure: I might be touring Scotland the following summer after a conference in Britain. Perhaps he could show me around if he were there.

The lure did its work. What had begun in the early autumn as an exchange of emails about Scotland turned into an epistolary relationship that deepened as the months went by. Each evening, I looked forward to reading Robin's long and beautifully written emails, and I answered with long enthusiastic emails of my own. But it was only when my friend Marilyn tried to arrange a dinner date for me with an eligible bachelor—a well-known, attractive San Francisco analyst—and I discovered I couldn't accept, that I realized how committed I had become to my epistolary companion. "Nothing unites two people so completely, especially if . . . all they have is words," Kafka had written in his *Letters to Felice*. Robin and I had virtually only words between us; none of our letters were romantic; yet somehow, a romance had developed. "In all conscience," I told Marilyn, "I'm otherwise involved."

The following spring, I invited Robin to visit for his semester break—I had a guest room, I said, leaving that door open. He accepted my invitation; I offered to pick him up at the airport, my nerves jangling with anxious anticipation; he arrived, a big smile on his face, and I was besotted anew. By the end of that week's visit, not only had we marched together in a San Francisco anti-war demonstration, holding hands—a gesture he initiated that sent an electric current through me as if I were a teenager—but afterward, as the two of us were standing in my kitchen, I fell into his open arms, we bonded as a couple, and he assured me that summer he would take me on a personal tour of Scotland, *his* Scotland. And he did.

So yes, once more, yes again to a romance, so unlikely at my age, now sixty-eight. If I seemed too prone to enter sexual liaisons, this one was different, I told my analyst, hoping that was true. This was neither a passing sexual fling nor a romantic illusion; this felt real despite the equally real distance between Wisconsin and California. That I was still married didn't enter my mind as an impediment to our intimacy, nor had I mentioned that small fact to Robin. But when, during our tour of Scotland that summer, he playfully suggested we elope to Gretna Green, a Scottish Reno known for quick marriages—a fanciful notion that I allowed myself the pleasure of considering for a moment—I had to clarify in Scotland what I should have made clear in California: that I was still legally married and had an arrangement with my husband that I didn't want to disturb. As I spoke the words "I'm still married," a tremor passed across Robin's face and I winced, realizing that I had misled him by omission. I also realized that I had no intention of marrying again even if I were free. Although I had fallen in love with Robin, I had come to value my independence too much to risk losing it again. Or so I thought.

But of course, how naïve. Love intrudes on independence; it compels us to care. And love later in life contains an additional subversive element: intimations of mortality that, willy-nilly, can weaken even the desire for independence. But also, of course, there were delightful compensations. From the very beginning, Robin's boyish looks, his whimsical humor, his political astuteness, his sensitivity to others, and not least, the Scottish lilt of his voice had charmed me. I would, I swore to myself, make this relationship work. Living some two thousand miles apart, during the next few years, we continued to write long emails and to call each other regularly. But wanting more than words, one weekend of every month, we took turns traveling across half the country—by plane, bus, and automobile—no mean feat for a weekend. The relationship deepened, each of us exploring the unknown territories of the other. Even my erotic life took on a new dimension as we two, growing bolder and more inventive than I had anticipated, in the midst of some quotidian activity, would break into a sexual playfulness that seemed to belong to a younger me. To Kitty.

Yet the fact of our advanced age was inescapable, and to some, apparently comical in a romance. One summer evening, while vacationing in Provence, we were strolling hand-in-hand through the little French village near our farmhouse when a villager standing with a group of his friends laughingly pointed to us and shouted out, "*Les américains amoureux*" (the in-love Americans). So yes, there we were, publicly exhibiting the visible—and risible—features of young love, in late life. And what, we laughingly asked each other, would our children think of our behavior?

My son, Robin's daughter—would they accuse us of not acting our age? More seriously, would they resent our new attachment to each other?

Whatever they might think, there was no question about this relationship: I had given myself over to love—and indeed "give" was the new operative word, pointing to a new flexibility in me that my friend Marilyn attributed to my psychoanalysis. Perhaps. But I knew that there was another reason for the change. Not only was I in love; I was fast approaching seventy; this would likely be my last hurrah, if I didn't mess it up. Time would tell.

Carpe Diem

In other ways as well, time became a formidable antagonist as I considered the place of psychoanalytic training in my own more-complicated future now that I was no longer "doing alright by myself." Although those words were ironic in O'Connor's story, "A Good Man Is Hard to Find," a good man *was* hard to find. I had found one, but he had a rival for my time: psychoanalytic training. The next step in my training was to take on three full-time psychoanalytic cases for two or three years, each four times a week, each under hourly supervision. But Robin was already talking about the two of us going to London for his upcoming sabbatical semester, and to Edinburgh the following year. What if I didn't have the time for him? Time had been flying by. Time would bring me down to earth.

With my analyst's consent to a plan for continuing by phone, Robin and I spent his first sabbatical semester in London, filling our days with theater, street markets, and museums, enjoying the urban life of Islington where we had rented a flat. At the same time, I had arranged to take classes at the London Institute to make up for my suspended classes in San Francisco. As for continuing my own analysis by telephone, four nights a week, at eleven fifteen in the evening, I promptly lay down on the couch in London and called my Berkeley analyst. By now fully trusting her to listen and understand—she was on my side, after all—I spoke freely to her about my daily experiences for forty-five minutes. Once again, it seemed as though I could have it all.

Yet on my return to Dr. S. in Berkeley, it was with some trepidation that I brought up the subject of another leave of absence. As I lay there in her office, aware of the late afternoon daylight passing through the wooden blinds behind her desk, I talked about continuing the analysis by phone again the following year, when I would be with Robin in Edinburgh for the second part of his sabbatical. Out of thin air, her voice broke into my verbal reverie with the question I had not yet allowed myself consciously to ask: "I think we need to terminate, don't you?"

Terminate. An ugly word for a humanistic profession. I caught my breath as the word pierced my resistance with its full meaning, and I recognized that everything I had been saying had led to this conclusion: if I wanted more time with Robin, I had to drop out of the training program. That also meant ending this analysis since I couldn't afford her actual fee. I couldn't have it all, after all. If love and work were the ideal duo for achieving happiness, each equal in importance as I had claimed in teaching, love, I discovered, was now taking precedence. Anguishing over that realization for several weeks, I finally fixed a date for the last session. Of course, I was still a scholar and could continue to write critical articles and personal essays, yet the sense of having given up on my desire to become an analyst rankled. But I had made the decision, and so I plunged, or rather fell, into the process of termination.

During the next several months, a strange temporality took over. Time expanded—between each session, within each hour—as Dr. S. and I began to articulate a story that had been unwinding itself slowly over the last few years. And as it took shape, I began to see it as a female variant of the classic picaresque narrative: the story of a lower-class rogue who has a series of adventures that exercise his wit and inflate his ego. Melville's *The Confidence-Man*, Mann's *Confessions of Felix Krull*, Kerouac's *On the Road*, even my once-beloved "Puss in Boots"—male heroes, tricksters all, all male. In my version, I was a "picara" who, feeling undervalued as a girl, sought out exploits that gave me a heightened sense of mastery. My automobility was a way out of my limited circumstances and into a larger world of romantic adventure. I had thought my days on the road had ended in Buffalo when, in a triad of transformations, I became professor, wife, mother. Closure. Yet prompted by marital disappointments and ever-conscious of wanting more, when the time was ripe—overripe, some might say—I had ended both career and marriage, and fashioned yet another life—most likely my last.

At least for the present, this story, created through the analytic interchange between me and my analyst, made something coherent of my experiences. Yet both she and I knew that it was provisional. Real life is not coherent, not so readily linear, let alone singular in its theme during the course of a lifetime. Where might this story go now? On my way to my final session with Dr. S., I was already asking that question, as well as anticipating a gap in my life that she had filled. I had come to understand that autonomy is not the full story of the mature self, that who I am is in great part composed of my relations with others. Losing a relationship changes the self, and now I was losing her.

With that recognition, I entered her office, lay down on her couch and, before I could speak, began to weep—slowly at first, and then I could not stop. The hour went by timelessly in a river of tears that continued to rise up from an unfathomable source. Intermittently, I heard her voice asking questions or making remarks. Intermittently, I responded, immersed in the multiple arteries of loss. And then it was over; it was time to stop and say goodbye.

Afterward, walking toward my car, drained of all emotion, it occurred to me that severing my relations with my analyst had implications also for my relationship with Robin, which had run along a parallel timeline. I had shared an uncanny intimacy with both, a sense of the interpenetration of minds, of a convergence of streams of consciousness that was remarkable. It might have been expected in analysis, less so with one's partner. So often in conversation, I had discovered Robin and I were thinking the same thoughts or about to say the same thing, even using the same words. Such a twinning had been at times comical, at times comforting. Would I now place on him alone the entire burden of mirroring me to myself that he and Dr. S. had shared? Risky for any relationship. I would have to remember it was also Robin's *difference* that I valued—and to remember it without an external reminder. Sameness and difference: both were necessary for a flourishing relationship. Such a simple truth. So hard to come by. Opening the car door, I slid behind the wheel and started the engine, prepared to go forward.

Regeneration

While Robin and I had been forging the bonds of love, my son Jake had forged his own: he had become deeply involved with an attractive young woman who, much to my delight, was a feminist with an academic degree in psychoanalytic criticism! They had met at a party while studying film at Columbia University, and when my name came up in their conversation—"My mother teaches feminism and psychoanalysis," Jake had bragged—Terry had responded: "Claire Kahane? Your mother is Claire Kahane?" In a network of coincidence, Terry had been part of a graduate student group that had invited me to speak at her university several years earlier. And how remarkable were other parallel threads linking Terry's history and my own. Both of us had struggled psychologically to separate ourselves from our parents' influences; both of us had floundered for a number of years, unsure of our aims; both had come late to our career choices. And perhaps most uncannily, when Terry and Jake married, Terry—like me a generation earlier—was hugely pregnant as she walked down the aisle.

Jake and Terry's "shotgun wedding"

Fortunately, there was a real difference: their wedding was a joyous occasion, with Robin and me and Rainer and Madeline—no longer "the other woman"—all in friendly, if wary, familial attendance at the celebration of their union. A few months later, my daughter-in-law gave birth to a beautiful girl. My disordered domestic past had borne sweet fruit.

Memento Mori/Memento Vivere

It would be satisfying to end on that happy note, all the knotty relations somehow ironed out into a harmonious pattern, celebrating the next generation. But another event soon afterward reminded me, as if I needed reminding, that the life force has its limits, that death necessarily waits around in the shadows to dispel any fairy-tale ending. Rainer, who already was suffering from congestive heart failure, had developed kidney disease. Although the presence of Madeline, his partner and now also his caretaker, freed me from the obligation to help actively in his daily welfare, I still worried about him. I flew out to visit more frequently, noting with each

266

visit how frail he was becoming, his face revealing more and more of its skeletal structure, his sunken cheeks now darkly shadowed. Jake also came up from New York more often and was recording a video interview with Rainer about his life, even as Rainer himself was fading away.

Rainer's memorial photo

Rainer died in 2011, two years after Jake's marriage. I flew to Buffalo without Robin for the final ceremony of my quasi-married life, as did Rainer's daughter Alexa. We, his closest intimates—Jake, Madeline, Alexa, and I—had shared in his life; now we shared in the making of his funeral. I had chosen a favorite composition of Rainer's, Albinoni's *Adagio in G Minor*, to be played as a meditational piece as people arrived, and let myself imagine that he and I were listening to it as we often had in our best moments. When it was time for me to speak, I tried to emphasize what had been most positive in our marriage—our love for Jake foremost, but also our mutual love of travel, literature, and music, of those aspects of life which had connected us even unto death.

And then it was his children's turn. To celebrate Rainer as a father even though he had been absent for much of her childhood, Alexa quietly recalled a scene when she was reading her picture book while Rainer lay beside her: "I remember the feeling of having your complete attention and encouragement. I learned to read this way, at your side, reading the same books over and over." I had not known of this intimacy between them; I envied her memory.

When it was Jake's turn, he began his eulogy with these words:

I have a few stories I'd like to share about my Dad . . . such as the one when as a teenager he was declared, being German, an enemy alien in Napa, California, and so couldn't tell his parents about scoring three touchdowns at his high school football game, because he wasn't legally allowed to travel to the game, which had been in another town. . . . He had so many stories—he really did live so many lives, from Stuttgart to Evanston to Buffalo—and it is a deep regret of mine that I don't know more of them. I always thought there would be more time for that.

Listening to Jake's words—"*he had so many stories, he really did live so many lives*"—I realized how Rainer's "many stories" and "many lives" were themselves the product of a profound alienation that had pushed him to move from one place to another, from one marriage to another, from one life to another. No place was truly home. I, too, knew that feeling.

As I continued to listen to Jake talk admiringly about his father—about Rainer's fierce independence of thought, his strong sense of social justice, his distrust of authority, his contempt for small-mindedness—I found my own regard for him being heightened. Seeing Rainer through the eyes of his son—my son—I was compelled to recognize how admirable Rainer had been, in ways I hadn't fully acknowledged. Then the lights dimmed, and the video Jake had spent the last year making appeared projected onto a large screen behind him, and there was Rainer, larger than life, a living presence at his funeral, telling his stories to us all.

Sitting in that large room with all the others who had known him listening to the on-screen Rainer recount his émigré experiences, I found myself grieving, not just for Rainer's death, but for all the endings, both wanted and unwanted, that I had instigated and suffered, all the losses to which I had closed my heart before I had understood their full worth. How many of my intimates had died before I realized or could tell them how much they had meant to me? My parents, who had died without my ever telling them I loved them. The men in my life: Barney, enshrined as a first love—he'd had a fatal heart attack up there in northern Canada shortly after our correspondence began, and I had never answered his last letter. John, my mentor in adventure, who taught me to be brave—he had settled with his last partner in the Sacramento Delta, and I rarely saw him before he died of the complications of a long life. Malcolm, killed in a car accident at the height of his success as a writer—I never told him how much my becoming a graduate student of literature was due to his impassioned encouragement. Charlie, beloved co-editor, colleague and friend—pancreatic cancer got him while I went off to teach in Israel, assuring him I would see him when I returned, another lie told to a dying person. And my women friends: Roberta, the first of my CCNY quartet to die, a skeletal figure lying in her bed when I last saw her in 1985, being eaten away by cancer, dispensing her fashionable clothes to Valerie and me. I had taken her hand-knit sweaters but never said, "I love you. I'll miss you." And Joan, dear old buddy become bag lady, wandering around in the Village in her last years, dead while my head was turned in another direction. I didn't know death would undo so many, so soon. As Rainer's funeral made clear to me that day, we are composed as selves through our relations to others. Yes, and we shrink a little when they die.

Turning to look at Jake standing beside the projector, intently looking and listening to what he, the filmmaker, already knew, I detected a visible measure of pride inscribed in his grief. Pride in his father, pride in their relationship, pride in his own video. He concluded his eulogy by saying, "Of course, I loved my dad, but throughout my life, I found myself delighted by how much I really *liked* him." And I couldn't help but wonder: would he say that at my funeral? Was I *liked*? Envy poking out its ugly head again. So, in confronting the death of those we know and love, it seems we also confront and judge our own lives. I was now judging mine.

Turning back again to Terry and my two-year-old granddaughter sitting beside me, both of them absorbed in looking and listening to Rainer on screen telling the story of his life to Jake, and then aware of the whole room absorbed in the same act of looking and listening, all of us forming one giant circle of empathy through loss, I took a deep breath, for the moment, clarified. In the midst of death, there was life. *We are constituted by our relations to others.*

I would be returning to Berkeley, and to Robin, with a full and ready heart. Pie in the Sky?

"Pie in the sky" in Scotland

Lucky nine.

Permissions

About the Author

Claire Kahane is a retired Professor of English at the University at Buffalo and a visiting scholar in the English Department at the UC Berkeley. A feminist-psychoanalytic critic, she has published books and essays on hysteria in British fiction, the Gothic as a genre, and Holocaust trauma in literature. She lives with her partner in Berkeley and still travels the globe, from New York to Scotland to Tanzania. But she no longer hitchhikes.

www.ingramcontent.com/pod-product-compliance
Lightning Source LLC
Chambersburg PA
CBHW032040090426
42744CB00004B/70